CW00839264

Sins *of the* Father

Sins
of the
Father

The untold story behind
Schapelle Corby's ill-fated drug run

EAMONN DUFF

ALLEN&UNWIN
SYDNEY·MELBOURNE·AUCKLAND·LONDON

The author can be contacted at eamonnduff@ymail.com

First published in Australia in 2011

Copyright © Eamonn Duff 2011

'The Gambler' by Kenny Rogers reproduced on page 25 courtesy of the Sony Corporation.

All rights reserved. No part of this book may be reproduced or transmitted in any form or by any means, electronic or mechanical, including photocopying, recording or by any information storage and retrieval system, without prior permission in writing from the publisher. The Australian *Copyright Act 1968* (the Act) allows a maximum of one chapter or 10 per cent of this book, whichever is the greater, to be photocopied by any educational institution for its educational purposes provided that the educational institution (or body that administers it) has given a remuneration notice to Copyright Agency Limited (CAL) under the Act.

Allen & Unwin
83 Alexander Street
Crows Nest NSW 2065
Australia
Phone: (61 2) 8425 0100
Fax: (61 2) 9906 2218
Email: info@allenandunwin.com
Web: www.allenandunwin.com

Cataloguing-in-Publication details are available from the National Library of Australia
www.trove.nla.gov.au

ISBN 978 1 74237 817 6

Typeset in 11.5/15.5pt Sabon by Midland Typesetters, Maryborough, Australia
Printed and bound in Australia by Griffin Press

10 9 8 7 6 5 4 3

MIX
Paper from responsible sources
FSC
www.fsc.org   FSC® C009448

The paper in this book is FSC certified. FSC promotes environmentally responsible, socially beneficial and economically viable management of the world's forests.

'Oh! what a tangled web we weave
When first we practise to deceive!'

Sir Walter Scott

Contents

Prologue

Malcolm McCauley is one of those tobacco-stained blokes who looks like he's somehow lived two lives in one. On some days, perhaps even three. He is always a ghostly shade of pale, his face tired and gaunt. The lines across his forehead and nose are so deep it is hard to tell whether they are wrinkles or battle scars from one bar brawl too many.

When police quizzed one of his drug couriers, he provided this thumb-nail description of McCauley: 'Short, scruffy, skinny and old; grey hair and a moustache.' When asked if there was anything odd about his build or manner that might help identify him, the courier added: 'Just his glassy eyes, they look like they can't see properly.'

It's true that, while McCauley often dresses well and regularly even dons a collared shirt, this fails to disguise the fact that alcohol has always been his best friend.

Another former drug courier says: 'Malcolm is a true alcoholic. The first thing he does as soon as he gets out of bed is go to the toilet and then have a beer.' It's a common joke amongst McCauley's inner circle that nobody has ever seen him eat. Yet those who know him also agree that, when he's not drunk, he's a loveable rogue who possesses great knowledge and a sound vocabulary with a razor-sharp wit to match.

In December 2005 the wily Adelaide drug dealer needed

all the guile and cunning Mother Nature had bestowed upon him when he was spectacularly hurled into the national spotlight. A photograph of McCauley posing with Australia's most infamous drug smuggler, Schapelle Corby, was splashed across the front pages of the Indonesian and Australian press. That photograph of the seemingly unlikely duo had been taken in Bali's Kerobokan Prison on 13 May 2005.

Five months after that picture was taken, McCauley was busted by South Australian police for his key role in a multi-million dollar cannabis trafficking syndicate operating between Queensland and South Australia. McCauley's 'holiday snap' with Schapelle was discovered by police during the bust and leaked to the media. Immediately the press was asking: 'Why is a drug dealer visiting Schapelle?'; 'How well do they know each other?'; 'What is the link?'

There are two opposing accounts of how those photographs came to be taken. Malcolm McCauley now says he had a history of dealing with Schapelle's father, Mick Corby, which led him to fly to Bali twice and speak with Schapelle in the lead up to her verdict trial. He also claims he became a member of her mother Rosleigh Rose's inner circle during the trial, regularly drinking with them in their favourite Balinese bar. The Corby family—especially Rosleigh—maintain that he was a random Aussie holidaymaker in Bali who approached them with offers of sympathy for Schapelle and free drinks at the bar. Whatever the truth may be, for a long time McCauley stuck faithfully to Rosleigh's version of the story—that he and Schapelle were casual acquaintances with no links whatsoever, and that he was just one of many other tourists who visited Schapelle to wish her luck during her court case. But he now says that was all a desperate disguise born from a pact he made with

Mick—to save everyone's skin, not least his own. He adds that for that reason he loyally toed the party line, even conducting media interviews saying it was a chance meeting with Schapelle in the jail and a sheer coincidence that they had marijuana in common.

The Australian media accepted the story he was touting and moved on. McCauley's supposedly unrelated court case then slipped under the radar and quietly, without fanfare, he kept his silence and went to jail for 14 months after being convicted of trafficking cannabis from South Australia to Queensland.

But life behind bars wasn't kind to McCauley. He suffered the horrors of being forced to go off the grog 'cold turkey'. He nearly lost his marriage, his family and everything he owned. As time slowly passed in jail, the sober silence was deafening. Every week he waited to receive word from the Corby clan—specifically Schapelle's father, Mick. There was nothing, not even a Christmas card. Since his imprisonment, it was clear he had been dropped, even though he had stuck to an agreed code of silence.

As stated, that pact had been made with Schapelle's father, who I originally met and interviewed for my newspaper seven months after her arrest. As I stood drinking beers with Mick at his home in Queensland in March 2005, he looked me straight in the eye and insisted his daughter had been framed. 'This family has no links to marijuana in any way, shape or form so none of this makes any sense,' he said. 'We don't know anyone who moves in those sorts of circles. I'm still trying to work out how this possibly could have happened.'

Little did I know that three years of my life would later be spent researching that claim. With hindsight, I wish I had been armed with the knowledge I now possess because the fact remains that even if you remove Malcolm McCauley's claims from the equation, Mick Corby lied to me that day.

Meanwhile, seven years on from her arrest, Schapelle has grown to become a mass media commodity. The Corbys have amassed what is estimated to be more than two million dollars in earnings when you add their media and book deals to their hefty defamation case payouts. Furthermore, the exclusive deals with women's magazines show no sign of stopping. However, although they received much assistance from the Australian government and the media with legal costs, flights and accommodation, a prolonged trial and two appeals plus the need to offer practical support to Schapelle must have swallowed up a part of that income.

But the industry of innocence that has flourished around Schapelle's captivity has now boxed a vulnerable young woman into a corner. All the promises from the media and her family—that she would soon be set free if she continued to do more interviews, more exclusives, pose for more photographs and keep telling the world that she is innocent—appear to have come to nothing. Relentless chequebook journalism and authorised books condemning the Indonesian judges and prison system have severely damaged Schapelle's chances of an early release.

'I'm just sick of all the bullshit. Too many people have been hurt by all the lies,' says Malcolm McCauley. So, when he finally emerged a free man from Townsville prison in 2008, he was in the mood to set the record straight. Filled with self-loathing, he had plummeted to rock bottom; the only way out of the abyss was an avowal of guilt.

Over the course of the past two years, McCauley has since released his inner demons in a series of revealing interviews for this book. His startling allegations, and the story that emerges of Schapelle Corby's high-risk drug run to Bali, has been scrutinised during an extensive investigation that includes new revelations and insights from politicians, police, government insiders, drug dealers and former Corby confidants.

In 2005 and 2006, noted film-maker Janine Hosking and her team conducted extensive interviews with the main participants in the Corby drama for her highly acclaimed two-part documentary series screened by the Nine Network in Australia as *Schapelle Corby: The Hidden Truth*, and as *Ganja Queen* on HBO in the USA in mid-2008. Access was made available to significant and, in some cases, never-televised footage filmed during the making of that documentary. Unless otherwise stated, all direct dialogue from members of the Corby family, pot grower Tony Lewis, Schapelle's travelling companions, members of her former defence team and Indonesian customs officials were recorded on videotape during the filming of the documentary.

As the journey of the pot from South Australia to the Gold Coast and across international waters to Bali is charted, the hidden narrative of Australia's most intriguing drug case unravels from behind the headlines of blatant media spin partly orchestrated by the Corbys.

This is the story of a reckless father with a dark past, an old Adelaide drug trafficker who knew too much, and of the Gold Coast beauty school dropout who kept her mouth shut and took the fall for the syndicate.

PART ONE

Mick Corby
and
Friends

CHAPTER 1

Meet the Corbys

'I've never been involved with drugs. I don't like drugs. It's not my drugs, I wouldn't even know where to get the drugs from.'
—Schapelle Corby

Obscured by shady trees, the wide wraparound wooden verandah encircling Tony Lewis's farmhouse at Iveragh, near Gladstone in Queensland, has always been his favourite place for sharing a joint with friends.

On a chilly winter's morning, the verandah was the place to seek comfort, particularly when there was the warmth on offer that only a home-grown reefer can provide. On summer evenings, meanwhile, it became Party Central—the open-air fridge brimmed with home-brew rum and the air was pungent with the smoke of a generously shared bong. Late at night the cosy setting induced one to become philosophical, deep and searching, vowing to change one's life, the vibe thick with the intense ramblings of truly dedicated stoners. But as the morning light returned, so did a mellow resistance to change.

Tony Lewis could pour a rum, roll a joint in one hand and spin a good yarn all at the same time. His soul mate

(second only to pot) was a former coal miner named Mick
Corby. They had coexisted in parallel worlds, throughout
Central Queensland, for almost thirty years. Tony felt closer
to Mick than to any woman he'd ever met. In May 2006,
interviewed by Janine Hosking's documentary film crew as
he wandered around amongst his vegetable gardens behind
the farmhouse, he said of his best friend: 'If you ask him
what the stars are, you've got a three-hour conversation.
You know, things like that—that is just how Mick is, and
he's got that much knowledge on things like that.'

Mick Corby and Tony Lewis were like two straight,
platonic, less-pretty versions of the gay cowboys in the
Hollywood feature film *Brokeback Mountain*. They were
a couple of loners who liked sex with women but preferred
each other's company. In Mick, Lewis had found his perfect
partner. They shared common interests in real estate, sustain-
able living and irrigation methods. Tony explained it like
this: 'Me and Mick were both into um . . . self-sufficiency.
We read all the *Grass Roots* magazines. We would sit and
drink a carton of beer and talk over 'em, and that's why
we both wanted a property 'cos that's the way we were—
we're into all the grassroots and self-sufficiency stuff. This
was the dream.' The two neighbours made home-brew beer
and distilled liquors and debated the perfect technique for
growing sweet potatoes. And, if you listened to the rumours
circulating around town, they also grew 'kick-arse' hydro
together.

Mick and Tony had spent so much time with each other
that the two 50-year-olds had morphed into twins. Both had
hard and round beer guts, grey hair, bushy beards and a
certain dangerous allure that only men with a past can have
for a certain kind of woman. Mick's most outstanding asset

4

was his flashing blue eyes. Soft and seductive when he turned on the charm, the same eyes could be murderously intense when he was provoked. Those rebellious, look-deep-into-your-soul eyes and that fiery temper had been passed down to his youngest daughter, Schapelle. Long before she was making the front cover of women's magazines, Mick was captivated by and proud of Schapelle's striking looks. 'She's got the sort of face you never forget,' he said. Mick was right. Those memorable photogenic features she had inherited from him would one day become both her gift and her curse.

It was on Tony Lewis's verandah, in broad daylight, that a police informer would later allege she saw Lewis sharing joints with Mick Corby. But Lewis insists Schapelle 'was a drinker—I never ever saw her smoke a joint. Never. None of the kids, not one.' Reluctantly, Lewis acknowledges that he often used to sit down with Schapelle to drink beer as she confided in him about her father's health: 'She was worried about her father's drinking problems. She thought he was going to drink himself to death and he wouldn't be around to see her get married and have kids.'

Despite living in each other's pockets, Lewis claims Mick Corby was never aware he was a pot smoker. And naturally, as he gets on a roll with this particular tale, Lewis smiles wryly and claims he never saw Mick Corby smoke a joint.

Michael James Corby was born on 27 September 1949. He grew up at 44 Ellington Street, between the suburbs of Ekibin and Tarragindi, about seven kilometres south of Brisbane city. In the 1960s, cheap weatherboard and fibro homes dotted the dirt roads that were still being cleared of scrub in the area.

Graham Woolley lived a couple of streets away from Mick and also went to school with him. Throughout their early twenties, they socialised in the same tight-knit group. Graham says, 'Mick was two years younger than me. He lived in Ellington Street at Wellers Hill, which is now called Tarragindi. Like myself, he went to Junction Park State School and after that he went to Brisbane High School.' Graham remembers Mick being top of the class at school and having a brilliant mind. He says: 'He never studied but he had a photographic memory. He could have done anything. The teachers wanted him to go a long way. At Brisbane High, they pushed and pushed him; but he objected to that. He rebelled against them and the school.'

One of Mick's closest friends growing up was Noel Vinall, who lived barely a hundred metres from Mick's house. Noel has fond memories of a young Mick Corby getting a job as a telegram delivery boy. He also recalls Mick having a strongly rebellious streak. He says: 'His telegram job was with the PMG. Its nickname was the "Public Money Grabbers" but it actually stood for the Post Master General's Department. Mick used to ride his pushbike around town and in the inner city areas, delivering telegrams all day. I can still picture him now in this smart little uniform and with a bike which, from memory, was bright red.' Noel says that, while it was a hard job with low pay, many youngsters used it as a foot in the door. 'They then climbed through the bureaucracy and went far in the organisation. It was a starting point; but it quickly became a finishing point for Mick. He got the sack.'

Mick Corby's first cousin, Alan Trembath, grew up around Mick as a child and recalls visiting the family home in the 1950s. Mick's mother Pearl was Alan's aunty. Alan remembers Mick joining the navy: 'Michael's father was ex-navy and that was how Michael got in. Michael was in the electronics side of it.' Mick's service card shows that he enlisted in the Royal Australian Navy in June 1968 at the age of nineteen. He signed up for nine years and also undertook some electrical training while serving.

On 3 June 1969, the Royal Australian Navy aircraft carrier HMAS *Melbourne* was taking part in naval exercises in the South China Sea, 650 miles southwest of Manila. Mick Corby was on board the *Melbourne* at this time and below decks with most of the crew when at 4.12 am the ship's siren suddenly blew. Next the sailors heard a loud noise and felt a huge thud in the early morning darkness. The 20,000 ton aircraft carrier shuddered as it rammed into the US destroyer USS *Frank. E Evans*, slicing it in half. Seventy-four American sailors were trapped inside the bow section of the destroyer, which sank straight to the bottom of the ocean. Some of the crew from HMAS *Melbourne* had to dive into the water to rescue surviving American sailors who were covered in oil and screaming out for help in the dark. More than 200 servicemen were eventually dragged to safety. Incredibly, there were no casualties aboard the HMAS *Melbourne*.

Years later, however, Mick was still plagued with nightmares about the collision and, according to Tony Lewis, he often had trouble sleeping. Sometimes Mick was so stressed from having these recurring nightmares he would go over to Tony's house to avoid sleeping on his own.

It appears that Mick had a problem obeying orders in the navy. The young sailor had a habit of taking off without permission and the records show he went absent without leave on 5 August 1970. Two weeks later, on 22 August, he wound up in deep trouble and was subsequently marched out. The young seaman had only lasted two years serving in the RAN.

A Canberra naval archivist who examined Mick's service card took one look at it and commented: 'The navy didn't muck around, and they got rid of him pretty fast.' Noel Vinall too remembers young Michael Corby getting kicked out of the navy and elaborated further: 'He was off the ship and he got into some real bother. He was arrested by the cops for stealing, shall we say, some goods; but it's not for me to be going into details, because he wouldn't have wanted me to. But, needless to say, if you had a criminal conviction you couldn't serve in any government job, and Mick ended up with a criminal conviction. And so he came home.'

Some years later, Mick's eldest daughter Mercedes would describe her father as a 'hero' of the navy but, curiously, Mick preferred not to talk about his naval experiences to anyone. He often complained, however, about the fact that he'd never received a military service pension; but getting kicked out of the navy may have blown his chances on that score.

After leaving the navy in 1970 Mick Corby returned home to Ekibin in Brisbane. Alan Trembath says that Mick's father was furious about the dishonourable discharge: 'We sort of raised eyebrows and thought he must have done something pretty severe to get booted out of the navy, because I can remember his parents having a big blue over it.' Mick's old school friend, Graham Woolley, recalls that Mick had changed when he returned from his stint serving in the navy: 'Mick came back a totally different bloke. He was drunk a lot and he was into the drugs big time.' It's possible that, after the traumatic experience of the HMAS *Melbourne* incident, Mick was suffering from post traumatic stress disorder, and he turned to beer and pot to cope.

While there was no denying that Mick was highly intelligent, Graham thought there was always something wrong, something driving him to rebel against the world. He says: 'Clearly, there was an issue with authority and discipline from a very early age. It happened at school, it happened in the navy. Evidently, it happened all throughout his life.' With so many problems adjusting back to city life in Brisbane, Mick soon moved to the outlying suburb of Salisbury.

Noel Vinall, Graham Woolley and Mick were part of a close group of local lads who passed the hours back in those early days by hanging out together in Salisbury. The young men were all into bikes, cars and beer, Graham says: 'Back then, we all used to drink at Noel's workshop. It was a car repair business and at one stage, Mick had half the shed. He used to lease it.'

These days, Graham and Noel have both moved on from their old stomping ground. Noel now lives in northern New South Wales; Graham's job as a construction company foreman sees him constantly on the move across rural Queensland. In August 2009, he was based in Kingaroy.

Graham fondly remembers Mick as a carefree young bloke who liked to hoon around town on a Triumph motorbike, complete with an old timber side-car built with his own bare hands. 'There was nothing flashy about the side-car,' he says. 'There was no roof or anything—it was just wooden floorboards with sides on it. It looked like a heap of shit, but it was quite novel at the time. Certainly Mick was the only person driving around with one, so you could see him coming a mile off.'

Noel explains that Mick was doing a bit of work as an auto-electrician when he returned home from the navy. An old mechanic who was about to retire had offered Mick his business 'on a plate', but Noel recalls Mick wasn't interested: 'He was young, he just wanted to party.' Mick later began using some space at Noel's car repair garage: 'We just let him come there and do some of his things. Generally, he used to just buy old bombs and do them up.'

Mick was good with engines and tinkered away on cars and bikes, but Graham remembers his other main passion—growing and smoking pot. He says: 'I remember very clearly that he was always drunk or doped up out of his head. I saw him smoke it there in the shed, and he used to say, "There's big money to be made out of growing this stuff." I'm aware he had dope plants growing there in the garage.'

Noel confirms that Mick was growing marijuana, but acknowledges that so too were many other people in the early 1970s, particularly if they were on the dole: 'Back in those days, a labourer would earn probably $60 a week tops. On the dole, they could get $30 a week or close to it. Some were taking the dole and growing marijuana to make up the numbers. Mick was one of those blokes back then who was just trying to grow it. I can't speak for what happened in later years, because I wasn't around, but in the early days everyone was trying to grow it because, if you could, you could make a buck. But we're not talking commercial quantities. We're not talking Griffith or anything.'

Growing grass in the back of a mate's repair shop was one thing, growing it outside a pub was another. Graham remembers how surprised he was when Mick started nurturing plants in the flower gardens outside one of their regular drinking haunts: 'It was the Chardon's Corner Hotel in Ipswich Road. You know how you have flower gardens out the front of pubs? Well, he had a couple of plants growing in there. It was nothing serious, but I mean it was just bullshit to do it somewhere like that. It was yet another indicator of how carefree he'd become and how the dope had taken over his life.'

Graham believes that, as time passed, Mick became more involved with the Rebel bikie gang: 'There were two pubs on opposite sides of the road at Waterford. You had the River Wild on one side of the road and the Club Hotel on the other. The Club Hotel used to be where the Rebels all met, but something went down and they all got tossed out and so they moved across to the River Wild. My last recollection of Mick is in the River Wild. I was sitting with him and the Rebels. There were joints being passed about everywhere.'

In 2008, Alan Trembath broke family ranks to speak out about Mick's long association with drugs. He also remembers a strong bikie connection. 'He used to hang around with a bikie group on the Gold Coast [in his early twenties]. I can remember him and my Aunty Pearl, his mother, having arguments and fights over it when I was staying at their house in Ekibin.' In 1973, three years after leaving the navy, Mick got busted twice by the Queensland Police for possessing marijuana. Alan says: 'Michael used to be in and out of trouble with dope and things over the years. I can remember some hell of a big blue with his parents. As far as I know, Michael had two altercations with the police over drugs, but I haven't seen a police report to state that.'

Alan's memory is correct—those two court appearances are still held in the Queensland Police Service archives. In 2009, a Queensland detective went back through the police records and confirmed that Michael Corby was twice arrested in 1973 for possessing and using cannabis. In one court appearance his place of residence was recorded as Tannum Sands, near Gladstone on the Queensland central coast. It was only a few kilometres from a farm he would later buy for his retirement more than two decades later. In his second court appearance that year, 24-year-old Michael James Corby was registered as a resident of Middlemount, a mining town in Central Queensland.

Noel Vinall remembers very clearly Mick getting busted by the cops for possessing pot in the early 1970s. He says: 'There's quite a funny story behind one of those early marijuana convictions. Mick was on his motorbike, high as a kite, when he smashed straight into the back of a parked car. He was lying there on the ground. His leg was messed up and broken and he couldn't move. He was going nowhere. Mick was on his back and as he stared upwards, he could see someone standing over the top of him looking down. His vision was all over the place, but he could see there was someone standing there. So he shoves his hand in his pocket and pulls out a bag of grass. He then holds it up to this fella peering over him and says, "Quick, mate, hide this before the coppers come." The bloke standing over him took the grass and said: "Thanks, mate—I am the police and you are under arrest."'

Fast forward three decades on from this bizarre arrest. When Graham Woolley saw Schapelle Corby on the television news in 2005, surrounded by Indonesian police in Bali, he didn't realise that she was the daughter of his old mate. It was only six months later, when Graham saw Mick on television, that it all fell into place. Says Graham now: 'The first thing I thought when I saw Mick in the news was that the marijuana had come from him. It was an automatic thought—that he had to be tied up in it. It was in keeping with the man I knew, albeit in those early years.'

CHAPTER 2

Enter the Leg Model

'I brought my kids up to be strong. And I do take thanks for that, that's why they are so strong.'

—Rosleigh Rose

For a man who has spent a lot of his life stoned, Tony Lewis recalls with astounding clarity the days when Mick Corby began courting the wildly blousy Rosleigh Hatton, as she was known then. 'What a woman!' he remembers affectionately. 'She was a stunner—just like Schapelle when she was the same age.'

In the early 1970s, not long after being kicked out of the navy, Mick Corby met the former self-described 'leg model' Ros. Apparently Ros would sit perched on the back of Mick's bike, all legs and attitude. Ros was the love of Mick's life. She had been the love of many men's lives. Tony recalls seeing her on the back of another bikie's machine: 'Yeah, I shouldn't be telling you about this,' Tony once confided to a television producer, 'but Rossie used to go out with a Hell's Angel biker—Rocky-something his name was.'

To say that Rosleigh Hatton had a difficult childhood is an understatement. She grew up in the town of Dubbo in central western New South Wales. Her mother, Esma Hatton, had at least nine children to several different men. Sadly, the local newspapers, the *Western Age* and *Dubbo Despatch*, carried no birth notices to announce baby Rosleigh's arrival.

It appears Esma landed in Dubbo in the late 1940s after leaving her first husband, a farmer named Jack Hatton. Esma Hatton shows up briefly on the electoral roll for the Dubbo district in 1953. Records show Esma and Jack were married in a small country town called Baradine, 200 kilometres north of Dubbo, on 5 July 1939. Esma had five children with Jack before the marriage broke down. It was difficult to get divorced back in those days, so it took some time before the marriage was eventually dissolved on 16 April 1953.

In 2010, Jack Hatton's brother Keith, who was then 87 years old, went on record for this book. Keith had never been interviewed about Ros before. He said that after Esma split with his brother Jack, she moved to a small town near Tamworth and later to Dubbo. Rosleigh was among Esma's second bunch of kids, Jack says: 'I don't know where Esma brought them up—she just moved in with whatever joker she hooked up with.'

Jack Hatton recalls that later in life Esma's kids got in touch with him: 'Some of Esma's kids contacted me to try and find out who their fathers were, but I didn't know. It was a bit of a mixed-up business.'

After Esma arrived in Dubbo, she had another four children, including Rosleigh. Ros was given the surname 'Hatton' even though she had a different father. One of Jack Hatton's other relatives, Dulcie Hatton, says that Esma worked as a live-in housekeeper and had the four children to the different men she lived with over the years. She confesses: 'I guess we did look down on her in a way because there were so many different fathers to the children.'

Dulcie also says that Esma had a temper and often belted the living daylights out of her daughter, Caroline. Dulcie remembers: 'Esma used to hit her so hard, she turned blue. The brothers put her [Caroline] on the train and sent her away from Dubbo, back to Baradine so she could get away from her mother.'

In 2007, Mercedes Corby told the *Daily Telegraph*: 'Mum worked hard to give us everything she'd missed out on in her own childhood. She'd done it tough, spending her early years in and out of orphanages.' Ros once joked that it was a miracle that her baby brother Shun had survived, because the other kids in the family used to steal his milk.

Although Mick and Rosleigh never married, they had three children in quick succession—Mercedes, Michael Junior and Schapelle. Their youngest daughter was born in a Brisbane hospital in 1977 and Ros invented a French-sounding name for her. But Mick Corby wasn't sound husband material. In 1979, when Schapelle was two years old, Mick and Ros split up. Mick later admitted he was lazy and unreliable: 'I'd go out for the paper and come back several weeks later. I don't blame her for giving up on me.'

Ros was the sort of high-octane firebrand who needed constant male attention and, on the rebound from her failed relationship with Mick, she soon married a man named Michael Rose and together they had a son, Clinton. The close-knit Corby kids had a new stepfather and stepbrother in their lives. The couple moved from Queensland to Tasmania with the kids for a while, but it wasn't long before the marriage broke up. The kids don't like to speak his name.

'Mum doesn't like us to talk about him,' says Michael Jnr. During these troubled years it fell upon the shoulders of the eldest child, blonde-haired Mercedes, to look after her little brother and sister.

Never long without a man in her life, Ros's next live-in lover was to be a Tongan man named James Kisina. The couple had two children, James Jnr and Melenae. The stormy relationship with James Kisina Senior later ended badly. All up, Ros had six children to three partners.

As Schapelle's young half-sister Mele was to tell journalist Paul Toohey from the *Bulletin*: 'We're the Brady Bunch, three girls and three boys. Or maybe we're the Corby-Kisina-Rose Bunch.' Ros then quipped to Mele in front of Paul Toohey, 'It doesn't matter. At least you all know who your fathers are.'

After they separated, Mick Corby remained close to Ros and the kids and he let her keep the family home at Loganlea on the outskirts south of Brisbane, where she lives to this day. Loganlea is a low socioeconomic suburb dotted with cheap, besser-block houses, some decorated with tiny, plastic Australian flags tacked to the front fence. Like most people who reside in Loganlea, Ros lives without pretension. Her modest home, purchased by Mick, is clean and cramped, but has a generous backyard and a recently added swimming pool, which is often the centre of drinking sessions and boisterous family barbecues. Ros and her various partners have lived in the house with their kids for over twenty years. By the time Schapelle was arrested in Bali in 2004, Ros had settled down with a new partner, a shy stutterer named Greg Martin who, like Mick, simply adored her.

Over the years, Greg, Ros and Mick would regularly drink and socialise together. Although she often complained about her ex-partner Mick, Ros blossomed when she was at the centre of male attention and Greg didn't seem to mind him lurking around. It took the heat off when Ros was nagging Mick to clean up and look after himself.

Like her mother, Ros ended up bearing several children to several different men but, unlike Esma Hatton, Ros is extremely close to her kids. The fathers may have come and gone over the years, but the Corby-Rose-Kisina clan is a tight-knit unit and Ros has always been the central figure.

Despite all of Mick's failings, Noel Vinall says there is no doubt that he loved his children and he continued to stay close to them as they grew older. He says, 'I know a lot of people don't have a good impression of him, but I really respected the love he had for his kids. Some blokes piss off out of their kids' lives after a separation, but he always provided for them. He was always there at Christmas and during the holidays, and that's why the kids adored him. Rossie ended up having another couple of kids to other blokes, but they even got on great with Mick too. He was that sort of bloke.'

After splitting with Ros, Mick left Brisbane on his motorbike and rode north towards the coastal town of Mackay, but he didn't quite make it. It was classic Mick—stuffing up before he'd even arrived. He crashed his bike just south of Mackay, coming around a bend on the highway near a small seaside town called Sarina, and spent about a week in the local hospital with a broken foot.

When Mick was discharged, he had no transport and no job, so he moved into a share house with Alan Trembath's brothers and borrowed Alan's car to get around town. One of the brothers offered Mick some work, Alan recalls: 'My brother turned around to him and said, "I've got a heap of lead and some sinker moulds. Take the lead and make some fishing sinkers," and so on. Michael took the lead all right, but he didn't make any sinkers out of it—he went and sold it to a scrap merchant in Mackay. He then went and bought a bag of dope.'

Alan remembers one episode where Mick had so many marijuana seeds in his trouser pockets that, after doing the washing and hanging out his clothes, some plants started to sprout under the clothesline. It was funny and it got a few laughs from his cousins, but Mick's relatives soon grew tired of him.

After living in Mackay for a couple of months, Mick started selling marijuana around town and Alan's brothers became worried they were going to get into trouble with the cops. Alan says: 'One day he was supposed to come and pick us up at Hay Point, about three o'clock in the afternoon, but he didn't turn up until after seven, stoned out of his brain. And then he tried to sell the dope to me brother's work mates in the Hay Point Hotel. He had a sandwich bag of marijuana. I watched him walk around the bar and start asking if anyone wanted to buy.' Soon after this incident in the Hay Point Hotel, Mick's cousins booted him out of their flat.

Before Mick left Mackay, he met Alan at the local Kooyong Hotel and made him an offer he never forgot. Alan remembers: 'Michael approached me and we went and sat down and he said to me basically straight-out, "Do you want to earn eighty grand?" And I said, "Eighty grand? What do I have to do—go and kill somebody?" And he said, "No, no. I'll get you to take a boat up to Cedar Bay, pick up a load of marijuana and bring it back down to Mackay, and you'll get eighty grand for it." At the time I thought—well, eighty grand, I could do with it. But if I got caught, ten years in jail at eight grand a year, when you've got three little kids, just didn't sum up. So I refused. But I would say that Michael still would have wound up getting his dope—he would have got someone to do it.'

Alan knew the eighty grand was bullshit. It might have been closer to five hundred bucks but, whatever the amount, he wasn't prepared to take the risk. Maybe Mick was just big-noting himself, but Alan thought that Mick was serious and had wanted to get into the marijuana business in a bigger way.

In July 2008, Alan told Mackay's *Daily Mercury* that he believed Mick had been using his car to sell grass around the town all those years ago. He said, 'The car would just go missing for days, he never asked my permission to take it and I can say, I was definitely not happy about it.'

Mercedes Corby later tried to discredit Alan, saying he was 'crazy and a drunk'. Ros also hit back at Alan in the local paper and said that Mick 'wasn't interested in drugs like that, he was just a worker who would go to the pub and have a drink. He was too busy sitting on the sofa to go out and smuggle drugs.' Alan responded by telling the *Daily Mercury*: 'Schapelle's mum said her husband was too lazy to smuggle drugs, yeah that's true, he tried to get me to do the dirty work.'

After Mick had disappeared further up north, the next time Alan heard of him he'd landed a job as a kitchen hand at a coal-mine in the Central Queensland town of Middle-mount. The two cousins caught up in Brisbane in mid-1985, as Alan recalls: 'I said, "How did a bastard like you get a job in the mines? You got to be pretty good to get in there." And he said, "Oh, I got a mate to write out a bodgy reference." And I thought to myself: yeah, typical Michael!'

Mick's navy training in electronics paid off—he soon graduated from the kitchen to a higher paid job in the machine workshop at the German Creek mine. Knowing his way around auto-electronics and engines, he worked on the mine's big coal-mining machines.

It was around this period that Alan lost contact with Mick: 'I stopped having anything to do with Michael in 1985. Honestly, the amount of drugs that he was smoking and dealing, there's no way Michael would have stopped when he went to Middlemount. I would say it would have increased, because he would have had more money.'

Middlemount is a small coal-mining town about three hours drive inland from Rockhampton. It has a small population of about 2000 people. The Queensland electoral roll shows that Mick first arrived there in the early 1980s and lived in the 'Single Person's Living Quarters'. He later moved to 14 Gunsynd Street, a comfortable brick home not far from the German Creek mine. Living next door, at number 16, was Tony Lewis.

Tony Lewis spent his days changing tyres on the big mining machines and his nights punching back bongs. He had first tried cannabis at the age of 35, after his marriage broke up. He was feeling depressed at the time and he noticed that one bloke went from being sad and depressed to 'very happy', so he asked him what his trick was. The fellow worker suggested 'Get high!', so he did; and he'd been happy ever since. Lewis admitted to Rockhampton Court in May 2006 that he had become addicted to pot during his days in Middlemount.

Tony Lewis and Mick Corby quickly became best mates. Even back then, they had a lot in common. Tony later said: 'I knew Mick in the early days, mainly 'cos of Mick's involvement with auto-electricians. I was racing speedway cars and I often got Mick to help me fix parts, that's how I first knew him. He's a pretty fantastic bloke, a very knowledgeable person. A lot of people put shit on him, but I think he's just Mick. Yeah, he's good.' Another miner who'd worked with Mick Corby and didn't want to be named said of him: 'Yeah, I worked with him—he was a fucking idiot.'

Michael Stothard, a local miner who once lived across the road from Mick and Tony, remembered that 'Tony and Mick associated with each other all the time. They lived next door to each other and worked at the open cut together, so, yes, they were pretty friendly.' On weekends Mick and Tony would often drive down to Sarina on the coast to escape the heat and dust for a couple of days.

Despite living in Middlemount for many years, Mick always kept in touch with Ros and his three children and occasionally they all headed up there for a visit. When Schapelle was in her mid-teens, Ros apparently started having problems with her and, not knowing how to handle the situation, she packed her off to live with Mick.

While the miners were reasonably well paid, life for their families was mind-numbing. In Schapelle's autobiography, *My Story,* she writes: 'Wow it was boring, even for me who rarely feels bored. There's nothing in Middlemount but mines.' Tony Lewis remembers Schapelle living next door and says: 'She, yeah, seemed quite bright—just always on-the-go sort of a girl. Yeah, she was good.' Schapelle attended the local Middlemount School for a while, which would at least have given her something to do on weekdays.

On 1 January 2006 the ABC's *7.30 Report* broadcast a story about Mick Corby living next door to Tony Lewis, a man who had been busted with a hydroponic marijuana crop. This was the first time that the town of Middlemount had been mentioned in relation to Mick Corby by the media. A former teacher from Middlemount had been watching the program that night and wrote a letter to the ABC, which has never previously been published. It read, in part:

> I have chosen to write to you, simply to support the assertions in this week's *7.30 Report* item on Michael Corby. I was a school teacher in the Central Queensland Town of Middlemount in the mid to late 1980s. Drug use and hydroponic cultivation of drugs was rife in the community then. There was only one police officer in the town . . .
>
> When the shift changeover occurred at the German Creek mine around 3 pm, you could set your clock by the cavalcade of miners' vehicles heading back into town. They drove their vehicles into their driveways and headed straight to their garages to check their crops and have a smoke. By 3.30 pm you could smell the stench of dope along the back fence line of the homes. You wouldn't put your washing on the Hills hoist to dry in the afternoons, because it would pick up the odour!
>
> Drug use in the town was frightening. People were so bored with little to do other than drink excessively or play sport at the Cap Coal built facilities. So many wives were addicted to the illicit and prescription drugs that were readily available. Many teenage children were addicted to it too. Truancy rates were high, with distinct patterns. Many of the senior students would not turn up to classes in the afternoons—they couldn't, they were as high as kites. Those who did turn up were either in uncommunicative trance-like states or giggling like little girls.

Any parents with any sense put their kids into boarding school at Rockhampton, or got out of town altogether. I felt sorry for the children of the new families to the town—the culture shock was so great. I counselled many of them—I knew the signs. If they refused the drug taking and associated vices of under-age alcohol and sex parties, they were ostracised. I organised after-hours social activities for children to provide a safe haven for them.

Quite a number of teachers were on drugs. Staff turnover was excessively high. Teachers' parties were to be avoided if you wanted to avoid the pressure to participate in the drug taking. They were often gate-crashed by drunken and stoned teenage girls looking for sex. It was a competition to see how many of the male teachers they could bed . . .

Many of the miners and contractors were in Central Queensland motorcycle clubs, which assisted the trafficking of drugs. There were a lot of Vietnam vets in the community and mental health was a major concern. There was a mass exodus of people to Mackay, Rocky, Airlie Beach or Blackwater on the weekends. Many peddled their home-made drugs there.

In 1996, Tony Lewis bought a farm in a tiny place called Iveragh, located about thirty minutes drive south of Gladstone on the Queensland central coast. He paid $117,000 for the property at Rodd's Bay Road. But he didn't leave Middlemount straight away and continued to work at the mine for a while longer. Two years after Tony bought his farm, Mick followed suit and in 1998 bought the property next door to Tony for $100,000. On Mick's farm most of the scrub was uncleared, and the thick bush was hard to see through. The land could be used to graze cattle, but not much else. Mick had a traditional weatherboard Queenslander-style house on stilts, which kept the place cool in summer.

Iveragh has an official population of about 80 people, but you'd be lucky to find 20 folk in the area on any given day. Most tourists heading along the Bruce Highway on the scenic South Pacific Ocean would miss the signpost to Iveragh, which insignificantly points down a dirt road into the scrub. The properties along Rodd's Bay Road are mostly hobby farms, with ample rain water supplying private dams, making it suitable to keep horses or a few head of cattle. Iveragh is perfect for those who wish to escape the city life but still want to be near the coast and experience the country lifestyle.

It is also a perfect place to grow pot. The town is small, without too many nosy neighbours, and yet close enough to the coast to be near the beachside marijuana market. In 2006, a local Queensland police officer said: 'If we raided every home in Iveragh, we'd find small amounts of marijuana in almost every house, it's all over the area.'

Victor Ferris is a local farmer who used to own the property next door to Lewis. He later sold it, but he still owns another big farm a few kilometres up the road in Iveragh. He was about 70 years old when he was interviewed in 2005 for the *7.30 Report* and had by then been a resident of the town for fifty years. He said that Lewis's farm was too small to support a large herd of animals, so Lewis had run 25 of his head of cattle on Mick's neighbouring property. Mick and Lewis hadn't bothered to build a fence between their properties, and the cattle roamed freely back and forth between their two farms. When Ferris once asked his new neighbours what their plans were, Lewis told him that he and Mick were going to 'breed pigs'. Ferris tells this story with a thoughtful smile—he knew when to mind his own business.

Back in the years before his youngest daughter became Australia's most celebrated and debated drug smuggler, Mick Corby led an uncomplicated, reclusive life. With no Ros to pester him, dirty plates often piled up on the kitchen sink and faded newspapers rose from the floor, obscuring any sunlight coming through the windows. Outside, the property was a junk yard with rusted car bodies strewn everywhere. Mick always said he'd fix the wrecks and on-sell them, but he rarely mustered up the energy.

When the mood took him, he would sing country music songs to himself. Only the cows could hear him, and they didn't seem to mind. One of his favourite memories was of driving along the highway with Schapelle by his side. Both were fans of the country music singer Kenny Rogers and they knew the lyrics to his hit song 'The Gambler' off by heart.

Strong, loud and perfectly in sync, father and daughter would sing the lyrics out loud:

Ev'ry gambler knows that the secret to survivin'
Is knowin' what to throw away and knowing what to keep.
'Cause ev'ry hand's a winner and ev'ry hand's a loser,
And the best that you can hope for is to die in your sleep.

You got to know when to hold 'em, know when to fold 'em,
Know when to walk away and know when to run.
You never count your money when you're sittin' at the table.
There'll be time enough for countin' when the dealin's done.

CHAPTER 3

Beyond the Sausage Factory

'The way Malcolm fell into marijuana was sort of like fate. Only it was bad fate. From that point on, there was no stopping him.'
—Kathleen McCauley

Malcolm McCauley didn't know the girl, had never met her. Her death had nothing to do with him or anyone he knew. And yet indirectly, through one of those strange twists of fate, her passing altered the course of his life forever. Had this catastrophic event never happened, he would almost certainly never have become a drug trafficker. In turn, he and Schapelle Corby would never have crossed paths.

During the early nineties, McCauley's wife Kathleen worked in an Adelaide sausage-skinning factory. It was messy, mundane work with a lousy wage to match. Sometime before that, McCauley suffered a serious accident while working as a foreman for an earth-moving company. Amongst his many injuries, he sustained a crushed vertebra. His pain was later eased by a $100,000-plus compensation payout: 'It was a lot of money in those days and so I bought myself a boat,' he recalls. It was a custom-built fisheries pursuit boat, resembling a typical American coastguard vessel. He christened his new toy *The Wanderer* and began chartering it out to fishing clubs and groups of hotel guests from the north side of Adelaide. He charged $100 a head per day and, in no time, the boat began to rake in a regular flow of pocket money.

But while McCauley was spending his days out on *The Wanderer*, Kathleen was continuing to sweat and struggle in the sausage-skinning factory. It wasn't so much the work she hated as the pittance she was earning: 'And so we decided it was time to break away and set up a similar business ourselves,' recalls McCauley. Reluctantly, he sold his beloved boat. He and Kathleen then went in search of the perfect premises, which they eventually found at Gawler River. It was an exciting time for the couple. He was 48 and she was 43. They had been together for thirty years, but had always struggled to make ends meet.

Kathleen, or Leen as she is known to her friends, was born in 1950 and was only 13 when she fell hopelessly in love with McCauley. She was small and petite, with tight brown curls and a pretty face. The other boys in the neighbourhood were already showing plenty of interest, but her heart had long been taken. Over the next two years a teenage crush developed, and by age 15 she was slipping quietly out of her house and then running a kilometre or so to McCauley's place. Once she arrived she would sneak in slowly through the back door, tiptoe up a flight of stairs and then finally snuggle up in bed beside him.

McCauley lived with his parents and seven other brothers at the time. While the love-struck sweethearts always did their best to hide the fact that Leen had crept in, his late brother Rodney often realised, whispering, 'Goodnight, Malcolm! Goodnight, Kathleen!' as he drifted past their door on the way to bed. It's hard to imagine, but somehow Kathleen kept Malcolm waiting before she finally succumbed to his advances. On reflection, she did well. Two years later, in May 1967, not only were they married but she had given birth to the first of three daughters, Leanne. Later, she became a grandmother at the grand old age of thirty-four.

Kathleen and McCauley raised their family in Salisbury North. The suburb sits 25 kilometres north of the Adelaide CBD and was originally designed to provide housing for employees of a long-range weapons research facility in nearby Penfield, after World War II. In the years since, it had descended into one of the low-employment, high-crime housing commission communities that can be found on the outskirts of most major cities. The couple had remained anchored there for so long because it was all they could afford. But better times appeared to be just around the corner—they were about to work together for the first time. They shared a common goal and it felt terrific.

They named their sausage-skinning business Allied Casing but, like any new venture, it encountered teething troubles. Kathleen recalls: 'In order to start up, we needed to acquire a specific machine to process the sheep intestines. We searched around—there were some units available locally, but nobody wanted to sell to us because of the additional competition. Finding a machine became a bit of a problem but, as with all things, Malcolm eventually fixed it. He turned around one day and said, "That's it. If they won't sell us one, we'll make our own." And so he did. He actually made the machine.' McCauley elaborates: 'I made this bloody great machine out of a bed frame, some old printing rollers and . . . what was

it again? Oh yeah, a telegraph pole. It worked beautifully.'
He adds: 'I know what you're thinking—that it don't sound
too hot in the hygiene stakes. But let me tell you—it was a
strict industry, or at least it was supposed to be. When the
inspectors turned up to approve its use, it got the green light.
No troubles at all.'

For the next two years McCauley, Kathleen and a small
team of experienced staff worked twelve-hour shifts, six
days a week. 'We built that baby up from scratch and we
were starting to do real well,' said McCauley. 'We were even
looking to expand. But it was round about then that that
poor little girl died.'

On Saturday 21 January 1995, four-year-old Nikki
Robinson nibbled away on a garlic metwurst which was
riddled with *E. coli* bacteria. The food snack was manufactured by an Adelaide-based company called Garibaldi
Smallgoods and was part of a contaminated batch that struck
down 190 people. Within two days, a severe food poisoning
epidemic had hit South Australia and 24 critically ill children
were hospitalised with horrifying symptoms.

As a result of the outbreak one seven-year-old victim,
Kelly Owen, spent several months in and out of hospital
emergency wards, suffering two strokes along the way. She
endured abdominal surgery and temporary blindness before
eventually pulling through. Nikki was not so lucky—she died
as a result of a brain haemorrhage brought about by the food
poisoning incident.

A subsequent inquiry uncovered incompetence, negligence
and complete disregard of health and hygiene standards
by the owners of Garibaldi, who had ignored a string of
previous warnings all relating to hygiene. 'Not surprisingly, it destroyed the industry,' says Kathleen. 'Everybody

stopped buying processed meat. Sheep were no longer being slaughtered. On top of all that, we were ordered to upgrade our facilities. It ruined our business almost overnight.' With each passing day, the McCauleys lurched closer towards bankruptcy.

But then, an intriguing offer suddenly fell the McCauleys' way. 'Our factory had this big chiller inside it,' explains Kathleen. 'One day, an acquaintance of Malcolm's approached him and said it would be perfect for growing a crop of marijuana.' McCauley says: 'His exact words were, "Let me grow hooter in there and I'll pay you good returns." Up until then, I'd never been involved with marijuana in any shape or form. But we had hit difficult times and it was too good an offer to refuse, so I said yes.'

McCauley watched closely as his friend set up a sophisticated indoor hydroponic system. There were 52 plants in all. As the weeks passed, the retired sausage-skin maker sat and monitored the crop as it began to grow. Then, without warning, the factory was hit by a second wave of bad luck: 'The cops came snooping around, looking for some bloke with an amphetamines lab, and I panicked. I rang my mate and said: "What do I do?" and he said: "I'm out of here. I suggest you do the same. Run!"'

McCauley describes his desperation as he frantically uprooted the plants from their pots: 'The hooter wasn't even ready for cutting, but I chopped it all up and shoved it into two barrels. I was pretty naïve back then. I had no idea how to get rid of it. In the end, I dumped some of it by the side of the road and practically gave the rest away.'

Although McCauley's brief foray into the drug world had ended badly, he realised there was potential to make more money than ever before. He did some research. Had he been growing it outdoors, as everyone once used to do, he would have been resigned to one reasonable crop of natural bush weed each year. But indoors, hydroponically, he was guaranteed three—perhaps even four—yields per year. And this wasn't just any old marijuana—it was top quality skunk weed. It was stronger and worth far more on the streets.

McCauley then did his sums. One good plant was worth $5000—so fifteen plants could raise $75,000 every three to four months. That was more than enough dough to put food on the table, petrol in the car and fill the outdoor fridge with West End stubbies for years to come: 'You can fit fifteen plants in your bloody bathroom. To me, it seemed like a no-brainer.'

And so in August 1995, at the ripe old age of 50, Malcolm McCauley entered the drug game. He started out by converting a spare bedroom in the family home so it could accommodate an indoor set-up. His first crop was very much trial and error, but a reasonable success nonetheless. Then, in another bizarre twist, he almost came unstuck on his second batch: 'I was in the kitchen one day when my worst night-mare appeared from nowhere. A copper suddenly stormed in through the back of the house and he was carrying a bloody gun. He pointed it straight at me and asked: "Who are you? Who are you?"'

McCauley said he threw his hands in the air and immediately identified himself. 'It's ok. I'm Malcolm, Malcolm McCauley . . . I live here, mate . . . I live here!'

While the officer's eyes darted around the kitchen and adjacent rooms, he whispered: 'Where are they?'

'What do you mean?'

But the guy just responded in a hushed tone: 'Come on, come on—where are they?'

'Who?'

'Your wife! Where's your wife?'

McCauley was confused. 'She's at bingo,' he said, adding: 'What about my wife? And why you whispering?'

The copper appeared to be mapping out the house in his head, checking the rooms that were open and unoccupied, while moving cautiously around those that were closed.

McCauley then had a brainwave. He headed back into the kitchen, grabbed a scrap of paper that was sitting on the workbench and handed it to the officer. It read: '*Malcolm, I've gone to bingo. Feed the cat.*'

Now it was the officer who appeared confused. Pointing to a closed door and still speaking in a lowered tone, he asked: 'What's in here?'

'It's . . . it's the spare bedroom.'

That wasn't strictly true, thought McCauley nervously. It used to be a spare room; but on the other side of that door now sat eighteen adult marijuana plants that he had lovingly nurtured from scratch.

'Is there anyone in there?' asked the officer.

'Err . . . um . . . no.'

'Open it!'

At that point, McCauley knew the game was up. It was plain and simple—he would have to open the door. Reluctantly, he grabbed the handle. Then, with a gentle turn, he slowly edged the door open to reveal a fluorescent-lit room crammed full with cannabis plants.

The officer stuck his head inside and was confronted by a sea of green. There was a long pause and the silence between the two men was broken only by a strange bubbling sound being generated from the hydroponic equipment in full flow. When the copper turned back towards McCauley, he was wearing a look of utter astonishment.

'His face said it all,' recalls McCauley. 'Of all the things that could have been on the other side of the door, he definitely wasn't expecting that.'

But then, never in a million years would McCauley have anticipated the officer's next response. He simply said: 'Mate, get rid of that now!'

In the time it took for those words to filter through, the detective had dashed out of the door. As McCauley followed him out, he was confronted with the sight of a fully armed tactical response team and a crowd of stickybeak neighbours out the front. There was even an ambulance parked in waiting, several doors down.

McCauley says: 'He told one of the other cops, "It's the wrong address." And I heard his colleague say, "Yeah, we know—it's just come through [on the radio]."' Kathleen explains: 'It turned out there was a hostage situation somewhere close by. Some bloke was holding a woman at knifepoint. Her husband was apparently also in the house. God knows how they arrived at our address.'

The drama that day was enough to convince McCauley that growing dope at home was not a good idea. He took the copper's advice on board and cleared the room. But there was no chance he was going to quit growing, not now. He was enjoying the buzz—he was convinced he was on the verge of something big. He decided the safest way forward would be to set up and fund a series of satellite growers, otherwise known throughout the industry as 'gardeners'. He canvassed some people, visited their houses and sniffed out the most appropriate room for a system to be installed. Cellars, sheds, garages and concealed rooms were always the best option, but if none was available then a spare room, like his, would suffice.

'I set up six or seven people from scratch,' he recalls. 'I supplied all the equipment for an indoor set-up and guided them through the first crop, teaching them the tricks of the trade. I then guaranteed them a certain amount of money per pound on the first three crops, at the same time recouping my costs for the installation.'

At the end of those three crops, McCauley would turn around to his gardeners and say: 'Congratulations! It's all yours now—but on one condition. You sell the hooter to me at the current market value.' Which was $2200 per pound. 'I could always offload it for $3000,' he explains. 'It meant I was making 800 bucks on every bag. Not a bad return in anyone's book.'

One of McCauley's gardeners was a guy called Peter Dudley. If ever there was a man who knew how to rub people up the wrong way, it was him. 'I've got three words to describe Peter,' says McCauley, 'A-grade bullshit artist.'

Dudley claims he was born in England in 1954. He then migrated to Australia with his parents when he was a teenager. He drifted through his early years working as both a truck driver and general labourer. He then became an accredited rigger and joined the army, working with petrol, oil and lubricants. That much is true. The rest, thereafter, depends on who's telling the story.

Dudley relates an action-packed tale full of mystery, courage and endeavour. He says: 'I was seconded by, selected and seconded to Special Operations for a short term where I worked in Ireland and the UK collecting intelligence for the British government.' Dudley certainly has the physique of a real-life action hero. There is not an inch of fat on his body—he looks lean and mean. Along the way he has acquired the nickname 'Scarface', due to deep facial scars that start on both sides of his mouth and run right the way up his cheeks towards his ears. He has often boasted that those injuries were the result of him having been attacked while serving in an Australian army special operations unit. There are others, however, who dismiss that as pure fiction.

One associate, who does not wish to be named, says: 'Dudley's an arrogant know-it-all and a liar. He's a loose cannon. He's always had a big mouth, and sooner or later that mouth was going to land him in the shit.' The alternative version of the origin of those scars is that Dudley was at Adelaide's annual German folk festival, the Schutzenfest, one year when he wound up in big trouble: 'He got on the piss, smoked too much dope and then got into a fight in a toilet,' says a former friend. 'It continued on at the bar. Some guy smashed a broken beer jug in his face. It cut the shit out of him. He had to be rushed to hospital, where they stitched him back up.'

McCauley and Dudley originally met during the early nineties at McCauley's favourite drinking hole, the Salisbury RSL. By that time Dudley had left the army, developed a chronic dope addiction and notched up numerous assault charges and marijuana convictions. In more recent times he had worked for the State Transit Authority, which later became TransAdelaide. He boasted, to anyone who'd listen, that he was a rail supervisor, but others who worked for the company say he manned the lost property office.

Reflecting on his early days as a drug grower for McCauley, Dudley says: 'The clones were all supplied in the first instance by Malcolm and it was usually skunk. As time went on, he selected different types of plant, obviously for a better crop, more weight, more gain.' Skunk has a very high tetrahydrocannabinol (THC) component, which gives it greater value as it gives you a better high that lasts longer. Dudley adds: 'Malcolm taught me how to grow hydroponic marijuana and helped set up the room that I grew the product in. I then supplied him part of that product. One guy might be growing four plants in his house or shed, another would be growing six. At the end of the day Malcolm took possession of it.'

To begin with, McCauley was selling marijuana within the boundaries of South Australia but, as his list of buyers and contacts began to bloom, so did opportunities further afield. By 1998, he was delivering interstate. McCauley says: 'It started off small. Someone, who shall remain nameless, had a contact in Darwin who needed the occasional supply. I put my hand up for the run and got it. We were only sending up fives [five pounds] at the start. But quickly it turned into sevens. It grew with each delivery. Darwin was the start of everything.'

McCauley says that initially he was blown away by the demand for South Australian hydro: 'Compared to the rest of the nation, South Australia had very relaxed laws regarding marijuana cultivation for personal [use]. We were producing more of the stuff than the whole country put together. I realised that every dealer from north to south was desperate to get their hands on a regular supply. I thought, "Malcolm, there are mega-bucks to be had here if you can get it to 'em."'

But there was more to the business than sourcing large amounts of marijuana and McCauley knew that reliable, trustworthy drivers would be the key. 'I couldn't just throw anyone in a car and send them packing, so I started to think of the people I had around me at that time.' He road-tested a handful of drivers on his early runs to the Top End.

By the time opportunities opened up in New South Wales, with regular runs to Sydney and Wagga, he'd found the perfect candidate. Ken Ray—not his real name, because he actually managed to escape getting caught for his role in the syndicate—had been a long-time friend of McCauley's, since 1973. When the offer of a nice little earner was thrown his way, he had no problem accepting: 'I did a good dozen journeys to Sydney. It would take me about fourteen hours to get there,' says Ray. He confirms there were two different delivery points on the run. 'One was the major one—Homebush—where I went about ten times and in 2000 they held the Olympics there. I used to drive there in a green EL Falcon 98. Malcolm went twice with me, because he had to show me first. I then taught Peter Dudley that particular run—I showed him where to go.'

Describing how the exchanges took place, Ray continues: 'We used to go to a hotel, and there was a chap called Triple B, I don't know his real name—all I know is his name was Triple B, because he was a bastard of a bloke. He used to fly over from Adelaide to Sydney, and then get a cab out from Sydney Airport to Homebush. I used to sit in the hotel and he used to take my car. He then used to come back an hour later and give me $30,000 in cash, for the ten pounds of marijuana. That was my work done. I either went straight back, or I slept overnight and came back the next day. There were also the runs to Wagga. I did about fifteen of those and that was done in a blue NC Fairlane. They were also ten-pound jobs at a time.'

McCauley explains that whenever he travelled and delivered the goods personally, buyers had no problem meeting him face to face. He was the main man after all. But when strangers such as Ray pitched up on his behalf, it was a different story altogether. He said his contacts would exercise far greater caution.

'They were called "cut-offs",' he explains. Ground rule number 1 was: 'Ninety-nine times out of 100, the buyer does not want any contact with a driver. The driver could be dodgy; the driver might have been followed by the cops. Anything could have gone down.' Ground rule number 2: 'The buyer will always want to conduct the exchange at a neutral venue. If I'm sending a courier who is unknown to them, then they'll send someone neutral as well. So, again, the driver has no knowledge of who they are or where they live. It's pretty simple really. These are not normal circumstances. We're not talking pandy-andy shit. We're talking big bucks and big repercussions if things don't work out the way they're supposed to.'

With New South Wales now in the capable hands of Ken Ray and Peter Dudley, McCauley's time was freed up to canvas his contacts for opportunities further afield. And there were plenty. An opportunity soon arose for a regular run to Alice Springs and, as his list of buyers grew, he began to meet all sorts of characters. 'A sheila who I knew from around the traps had heard that someone in Cairns wanted some hooter. I travelled up with a sample; but he wanted to go fishing bigger, which I couldn't do on that particular trip. On the way back, I called through to Charters Towers in outback Queensland to see an old friend. She introduced me to a bloke by the name of Wayne Williams.'

Wayne Leslie Williams was known rather menacingly in Queensland underworld circles as the Pig Shooter. For several years he had controlled North Queensland's marijuana supply. He ruled by fear, and if anyone ever dared to tread on his territory, it is safe to say there would be consequences. Williams loved the rush of killing and regularly disappeared into the bush for days on end to track wild boar. It was rumoured he could skin a pig so fast with his bare hands, he'd sometimes be finished before the beast had even stopped breathing. It was also said that if anyone ever got on his wrong side, they would receive an invitation to join him on his next hunt. Funnily enough, nobody ever accepted. Not to anyone's knowledge anyhow.

Williams's hard man reputation was cemented from an early age. At school and during his early twenties, he was one of the roughest, toughest rugby league players around. By the time he had reached his thirties, he had also developed into a very handy boxer. He was tall and fit, with a body built like a lorry. If his enormous frame didn't cause him to stand out in a crowd, then his trademark long blond ponytail certainly did. He had grown extremely rich through selling drugs, but few people had ever met him in that capacity. He was too smart to do the dirty work and always employed a small army of dealers to distribute the marijuana on his behalf. In turn, it made his illicit activities extremely hard to prove.

McCauley says: 'I had hooter left over from the Cairns trip. I showed it to Williams and he loved it. He said: "Let's put something together."' So McCauley brokered the same deal he offered to all his interstate clients—he would keep it flowing at the same fixed price of $3000 per pound and, if ever there was a rise in costs, he'd try and wear it.

Towards the end of 1999, a second regular Queensland drug run fell McCauley's way. This particular buyer was based on the Gold Coast, and his name was Mick Corby.

CHAPTER 4

Mick, Mal and the Gang

'I read anything from history, religion, the Seventh Day Adventist stuff that comes around . . . Gabriel Garcia Marquez, National Geographic, War and Peace . . . *well, that's a struggle, forget that one.'*
—Mick Corby

There was a time, not so long ago, when Australian domestic air travel was as carefree as catching a bus. Passengers simply rocked up to the airport, dumped their luggage at the check-in counter and then just collected it on arrival at the other end, regardless of what was inside. No sniffer dogs. No security. No scrutiny.

For several years Schapelle's father, Mick Corby, had successfully exploited that system to transport South Australian hydro back to Queensland. It was quick and easy, not to mention cheap. 'Mick was using domestic flights between Adelaide and Brisbane for years,' confirms Malcolm McCauley. 'There were no x-rays or anything. It was dead easy, seemingly foolproof. But all good things must come to an end—it got too dangerous.'

In the late nineties, a series of high-profile incidents had alerted authorities to the fact that Adelaide Airport was essentially doubling up as a drug parcel depot. In October 1998, 32-year-old Paul Dignan was caught with nine kilos of Adelaide's finest just prior to boarding his flight. A court heard he had travelled to South Australia from Darwin to purchase the grass. He then intended to return north and sell it for a tidy profit.

Six months later, in March 1999, the same airport would make national news headlines. Adelaide police had received an anonymous tip-off about two men planning to smuggle more than 3.5 kilos of cannabis from Adelaide to Canberra on an early evening Qantas flight. Plain-clothes detectives drifted unnoticed at Adelaide Airport and later spotted the suspects checking in a soft-looking green bag. At the same time federal Labor MPs Martyn Evans and David Cox, who were returning to Canberra, had checked in a soft green Samsonite suit-bag similar to the one being carried by the two suspected drug couriers.

It was a case of mistaken identity waiting to happen. The Australian Federal Police in Canberra were warned that the two suspects 'may be travelling under the names of Cox and Evans'. In a Keystone Cops bungle of major proportions—later dubbed the 'Cheech and Chong Affair'—both politicians were marched off the aircraft the moment it landed in the Australian capital, even though their appearances were not even remotely similar to the suspects that had been under surveillance at Adelaide Airport. By the time they had been searched and interrogated by the AFP, the real couriers had recovered their bag of marijuana and long left the airport.

In the wash-up, not surprisingly, Adelaide Airport went on to receive a major security overhaul and the days of express delivery were finally over. Mick Corby now needed an alternative trusted solution to get the Adelaide hydro back to Queensland. Enter Mr Troubleshooter, aka Malcolm McCauley: 'I met Mick around 2000 through a mutual friend and grower who had been heavily involved in the previous operation. He told me what had gone down and that the flights had become too hot. So I said, "Please, mate, can you put me in touch with this person you're selling to?"'

A meet and greet was swiftly arranged: 'I met with Mick for the first time, and over a few beers I put my cards on the table and offered him a solution to his problem.' McCauley told Mick about the business he had built up from scratch. He told him of the established runs to Sydney, Wagga, Darwin and, more recently, Queensland. 'It'd be no trouble to pass by and see you on the way through,' he added.

Mick, in turn, outlined his requirements. 'He wanted top quality hydro at a good price and he wanted continuity. He also made it clear that, if we were to do business, there could be no funny shit—it had to arrive when he needed it to arrive.' McCauley later added: 'Over time, I found him to be a top bloke. He was down to earth, rough as guts, your typical Aussie. He was a straight shooter and, while others might have bagged him, I never had any problems. I came to know him as a client. No more, no less.'

After a few trips, the system was running like clockwork and a natural trust developed between them: 'Mick and I had a good business rapport, which stood the test of time. It was the same with Wayne Williams, but there was always extra emphasis on punctuality where Mick was concerned, and in time I discovered why. Mick needed the hooter to land at a specific time because there were occasions when it needed to be prepared and repackaged for a second run. And when I mean a run, I mean a run to Bali. In the early days, I understand there was a system which included shipping it there by boat. Later on it was going by plane and, when I was sending, there were flights booked, arrangements in place. He couldn't afford to leave anything to chance.'

Back in 2000, Mick Corby had made a shrewd real estate investment, purchasing a large two-storey house in the Gold Coast beachside suburb of Tugun. Tugun is about an hour's drive south of Brisbane, located at the southern end of the Gold Coast. A far cry from ritzy Surfers Paradise, it's not the prettiest place in the area and two major highways join together on the edge of town.

The two-level yellow-brick townhouse situated on Coolangatta Road was big, but badly in need of renovation. Over the next two years, the Corby clan would transform it into a house that could accommodate at least six people. In turn, various members of the family—Schapelle, Michael Jnr and his then girlfriend Hamita, Mercedes, her husband Wayan and their two children—all periodically lived there. The house was only a short stroll away from Tugun beach, so it suited the young ones down to the ground. Mick, in turn, also began treating the house as his second base. It allowed him to spend more time around his beloved kids, and geographically it was also far more convenient for doing business than the remote farm at Iveragh.

Whereas Wayne Williams liked to use the same truck-stop service station for most of his drug exchanges, Mick Corby's favoured location was the biggest single slab of concrete on the Gold Coast—the car park at Jupiter's Casino. The distance between Jupiter's and Mick's house at Tugun was exactly 15 kilometres—less than twenty minutes by car. McCauley explains the logic for using such a busy location:

'If you have a pedestrian walking down the middle of Pacific Highway, he's gonna stand out like dog's balls. But if you plonk that same pedestrian in a shopping mall, he blends in to the point where you don't even see him. Similarly, a busy car park was always a great place to do a hooter exchange. And, for Mick, Jupiter's was perfect. It was convenient to where he was. Secondly, there might be cameras about, but they're not really focused on you, because you're not doing anything untoward. You're just taking two suitcases out of your boot because, as far as anyone else is concerned, you're staying at the hotel. And the guys greeting you for the exchange? Well, they're just buddies, aren't they? All normal behaviour.'

At this time Ken Ray was the most reliable courier by a mile, so McCauley handed him the initial drug runs to Mick and also accompanied him in the beginning. According to Ken: 'I'd just stop outside the casino, and Malcolm used to take my car and he'd be back within three-quarters of an hour. I used to stay at the coffee place just on the outside there— just walk about and have a smoke and things like that, and then he'd be back.' When asked what Malcolm was doing when he took the car, Ken replied: 'I knew what he was doing—he was emptying the suitcase. He used to take it to Corby's place.'

Once Ken Ray knew the route and was over any initial teething troubles, he began making the journey without his boss, meeting go-betweens in the casino carpark. He dates his trips to Jupiter's as being between late 2000 and April 2003. Malcolm would just suddenly say to him: 'I've got another run for you to do.' Explains Ray: 'Sometimes it could be two and a half weeks; sometimes it could be five. He [Malcolm] would then make arrangements and say, right,

I'll be there at such and such a time.' Ray also confirmed a strict condition attached to the Gold Coast runs was that he always had to arrive on time.

'I was always on the spot,' he says. 'I used to leave [Adelaide] about 8 o'clock in the morning and lob over there round about 7 or 8 o'clock the next day so I could always meet them at 10 o'clock. And if I said I was going to be there at 10 o'clock, I was always there at 10 o'clock, no matter what happened.'

Ray says that, once he arrived at Jupiter's, he would be met by sometimes up to four different men outside the main hotel: 'I'd give them the suitcase, we'd exchange money and that was it. I'd find some place to sleep because it was 22 hours, sometimes 24 hours coming through from Adelaide. Sometimes I used to sleep in the back of my car, sleep on the back seat with a pillow and a blanket.' Ray says he was always aware of the reasons why the exchange had to take place at the casino—he knew it was somewhere on the Gold Coast that Corby lived: 'That's one thing they wouldn't allow—me or my car to be seen on their property.'

Ray was doing a solid job for McCauley who, in turn, was developing a reputation as a sound operator up and down Australia's east coast. But if there was one drawback, it was that McCauley's days had now become increasingly consumed by cross-town road trips around Adelaide. There were always places to go and gardeners to visit; there was cash to either collect or deliver. And there was one small problem with all that—McCauley didn't actually possess a driver's licence. 'I forgot to renew it and it expired,' he explains. 'I continued driving; but then one day I got caught and, because I'd let it lapse for ten years, I had to go back to the beginning and get my learner's permit, which in all honesty I couldn't be bothered to do. That's the laziness in me. Eventually, it became easier for me to sit on my arse and do the looking around while someone else did the driving. That was when I met Suzy. Boy, did I land on my feet there.'

Suzy said her association with McCauley started in the late nineties, when she gave him occasional lifts to places. Over time, she slotted in to become his chauffeur, adviser and protector all rolled into one. 'Malcolm was one of the good guys,' she says, adding: 'He'd always go out of his way to help people. That said, you certainly wouldn't want to cross him. Step on his shoes and he was the sort of bloke who'd break your neck.'

Suzy brought with her contacts in both the Australian Federal Police and Customs Service. Explaining how that all came about, she says: 'It started out as "You scratch my back, I scratch yours." I've assisted them in a variety of different cases through the years. Not necessarily drugs—there's been abalone, opals, gems, everything. I suppose I'm an informant of sorts. They [the authorities] come and seek advice on where stuff might have ended up, that sort of thing, because eventually, I tend to find out.'

In return, her police contacts would provide 'little snippets of information every now and then' which, in turn, would get passed along to friends, including McCauley. That information sometimes included intelligence about drug surveillance operations happening around South Australia. It meant Suzy was often able to provide McCauley with a clear run all the way to the state border: 'Whichever way his drivers might be heading, I was usually able to help out. There's never been consistent surveillance along those routes. Coppers get bored—sometimes they sit around for two weeks, then they drop off completely. The moment we heard about that, Malcolm would be away.'

Suzy, however, acknowledged her information was only beneficial up to a point. 'Once he was out of South Australia, I was no good to him. He had to find his own contacts and his own way there.' She summed up their association this way: 'I was the little devil on one shoulder, but also the angel on the other. I'd tell him what to do and what not to do so that he could keep his nose clean. When he listened, he did well. When he didn't, he got himself into trouble.'

Malcolm McCauley had certainly come a long way from being the naïve man in an apron who used to skin sausages for a living. And aside from Suzy's contacts within the AFP, it is fair to say he'd been doing some police networking of his own. Since the early nineties, he had been boozing periodically with an Adelaide-based Australian Federal Police officer by the name of Roger Rathjen. By 2001, they had become good mates. It was a friendship that in the coming years would raise more than a few eyebrows, and for obvious reasons. One was the head of a major interstate drug syndicate; the other was a senior AFP officer with more than thirty years service under his belt, including a long stint in drug surveillance.

Rathjen is a short, plump, balding man who, like many cops, loves to talk shop. In 1980, he was drafted in to work on the controversial Costigan Inquiry, which was a royal commission established by the Australian government to investigate organised criminal activities within the militant Painters and Dockers Union. Almost a decade later, he was to work alongside an ambitious young rookie cop by the name of Mick Keelty on the infamous National Crime Authority investigation into Barry Moyes, the now disgraced former head of South Australia's drug squad.

Keelty discovered a large dope syndicate had been thriving under Moyes's protection. Rathjen, in turn, headed the subsequent surveillance operation, which proved Keelty's intelligence correct. Moyes had been stashing drugs that should have been destroyed from past police raids and he was distributing these drugs to alleged mafia associates. Moyes was arrested in 1991 and later jailed. While Keelty took all the plaudits and eventually scooped the country's number 1 policing job, Rathjen had to return to the daily grind of domestic drug monitoring. He later drifted between general surveillance duties and VIP protective services for the AFP, eventually retiring at the end of 2002.

Long before McCauley became a significant drug figure, he had befriended Rathjen. As the two old friends sat together in the backyard of McCauley's Adelaide home in January 2010, reminiscing about their past, Rathjen recalled: 'We met after I joined the Salisbury RSL in 1989. Certainly I knew Malcolm when he ran the sausage-skinning factory in the mid-nineties. In fact I spent one weekend up there welding for him. He promised me a big stick of metwurst and I'm still waiting for it today. He was really good at making and fixing things. He could have been a first class engineer had he chosen that path. Anyway, I started having a beer with him on a regular basis. He's an old has-been now, but I still enjoy his company.'

The two men would regularly hang out at the Salisbury RSL; in the coming years, they would head off crabbing together and even embark on the occasional weekend camping trip with mates to remote places like Swan Reach in South Australia. Rathjen says: 'My wife refers to Malcolm as a likeable rogue. Back in the old days, he could certainly work a crowd. He was a ladies' man. Even though he was married, he had the girls eating out of his hand. He also knew how to take care of himself in a fight. He didn't mess about. Take Lloyd Montgomery, for example.'

McCauley takes up the story: 'There was this big bloke, Lloyd Montgomery was his name. One night he started causing a bit of bother down the RSL and then invited me into the toilet for a blue. I duly obliged. It was probably my best individual touch-up ever. He was struggling badly in the corner beside the sink. But my fear was he was strong enough to come back at me, so every time he tried to get back up, I put him back down. On reflection, I went a bit too far.'

Rathjen agrees: 'Malcolm nearly killed him.'

After knocking Montgomery unconscious, McCauley staggered out in front of a packed pub, covered in blood. The room fell silent and all eyes were staring his way. Casually, he pulled himself together, collected his glasses from a table and then 'got the fuck out before the cops came'. McCauley continues: 'I got charged with GBH by the locals [state police], but Roger had been in the pub during the fight and went out of his way to speak with Montgomery after he'd left hospital the following day. I don't know what was said, but it later turned out that Montgomery had had a change of heart over the incident. He said, on reflection, he probably deserved what he got and even signed a stat dec to that effect. A couple of the other guys in the pub also provided witness statements, saying I'd acted in self-defence and eventually the matter was dismissed in court.'

As the years passed, Rathjen practically became an extended member of the McCauley family household. The federal cop would sometimes swing by McCauley's place in his police car and, if the grandkids were playing out in the front yard, he'd occasionally even switch on his flashing blue light as he rolled up the driveway, just for fun. 'It always used to freak the poor little buggers out,' giggles McCauley.

By 2000, however, the friendship had been well and truly compromised. McCauley had grown to become the head of a thriving drug syndicate. Technically, he and Rathjen were now on opposite sides. They were Adelaide's own version of the Fox and the Hound.

Ken Ray recalls the bizarreness of McCauley's friendship with 'a police officer from the Federal Police who was high up in the Narcotics Division. His name was Roger—we used to call him Roger Ramjet, but I think his name was Rafferty. He knew what Malcolm knew and why he didn't intervene in this particular area has got me tossed, absolutely tossed.' According to McCauley, Rathjen had laid down some early ground rules. 'Rog warned me that if I ever strayed onto the bigger stuff, like powder, he would haul me in no question. And that suited me fine, because there was no way that was ever gonna happen.'

Once there was a clear understanding, McCauley said he slowly became privy to the inner workings of AFP surveillance operations. 'Rog had been a team leader in the narcotics division and of course, this was an area I was particularly interested in. I loved listening to his many anecdotes about surveillance, how it worked, who they targeted, and all that.'

Over time, McCauley said he never held anything back from Rathjen either. 'Rog knew about the runs to Sydney and Wagga. He knew all about Charters Towers and the Gold Coast. He knew the whole fucking lot, because we would drink all afternoon. I had a big mouth and I'd tell him.'

Rathjen explains it this way: 'Did I know Malcolm was a drug dealer? I knew he engaged in the odd minor street deal; but if you were to bust everyone in Salisbury for minor marijuana issues, there'd be virtually nobody left.' He added: 'To be honest, it was only after I'd retired, in November 2002, that I discovered how serious the situation was and what he'd got himself into. Did I ever dob him in? No.'

But in August of that year, clearly someone did.

CHAPTER 5

4.2 Kilos

'Everything was running smoothly. And then bang! Wagga happened.'

—Malcolm McCauley

It was 11 August 2002, two years before Schapelle's arrest, and Malcom McCauley gazed out of the window as his car crossed an endless procession of grain fields, having just passed through the tiny rural South Australian outposts of Sherlock and Lameroo. He was swigging on cold beer and humming along to a medley of songs on the radio as he travelled east along the Mallee Highway in a world of his own. It was one of those delightful days when nothing seemed to matter. The sun was shining and the road was clear. More importantly, he was bang on time as planned.

McCauley had left Adelaide two hours before on an interstate business trip to Wagga Wagga in New South Wales. The eleven-hour road trip would be completed in style, courtesy of a chauffeur-driven limousine. Well, technically it would. McCauley was slumped barefoot in the passenger seat of his trusty old, battered white Ford Falcon. His 'chauffeur' meanwhile was a dependable acquaintance called Pete, recruited several nights earlier down at the local pub for $250 cash. McCauley had told Pete as much as he needed to know about the trip. There was a contact to meet, a parcel to deliver and some cash to collect. It was a routine procedure that had gone like clockwork on countless occasions before. But on this particular day, McCauley would never make the rendezvous.

As the two men approached Pinnaroo, a small town several kilometres shy of the Victorian state border, a marked police patrol car suddenly appeared in their rear-view mirror. They were being pulled over. Reluctantly, McCauley advised Pete to park some 200 yards short of the town's main drag. A police officer approached the driver's side window and McCauley quickly leaned across Pete's lap to greet him. 'Top of the morning to you,' he said. 'Lovely day to be alive, ain't it?'

The officer nodded, but then gazed at him with a frosty expression. Clearly, he was in no mood for McCauley's special brand of friendly chitchat.

After the cop had established, verbally, that it was McCauley's car, he asked him to step out of the vehicle. A series of routine questions then followed thick and fast about who he was, where he was from, and where he was headed.

'Would you mind me taking a quick look around the vehicle?' asked the officer.

'Be my guest,' replied McCauley.

The officer rummaged through a large overnight bag positioned across the rear bench seat. McCauley was then asked to open the boot. Then he was asked to open the bonnet. 'There's nothing of significance in there, officer,' said McCauley. 'Except, of course, the engine.' The officer, ignoring McCauley's banter, crouched down onto his knees and inspected the undercarriage of the car. Again, he found nothing.

SINS OF THE FATHER

Just when McCauley thought the ordeal was all over, two plain-clothes cops suddenly arrived at the scene and began assisting with the search. McCauley glanced nervously towards Pete, and also at his watch—twenty minutes had now passed and he was growing restless. He had every right to. The car's rear seat was actually no longer a rear seat at all. McCauley had stripped all the foam from inside and had had it specially fibre-glassed to create an air-tight case. Inside that mould was the very parcel McCauley was due to deliver to Wagga: 4.2 kilograms of vacuum-sealed hydroponic marijuana—the exact same amount Schapelle Corby would later get caught with at Denpasar Airport.

When the police finally finished their roadside inspection, McCauley sighed with relief. He presumed he'd outsmarted them and he had, but only for the time being. 'We're going to escort you down to the station,' said the officer who had originally pulled him over. 'There's just another couple of things we'd like to check out if that's okay.'

McCauley had gone to tremendous lengths to hide the consignment but, as he slowly tailed the police patrol car through Pinnaroo, he realised there was one small problem working against him. Never in its history had the Ford Motor Company manufactured a rear seat as uncomfortable as his. And when the hunt resumed back at the cop shop, it wasn't long before a detective climbed in through the side and realised it. It was game over.

Several hours later, back in Adelaide, South Australian police executed a search warrant at McCauley's home in Salisbury North and uncovered a further 3.3 kg of the same high-strength cannabis. While all that was happening, McCauley was banged up in a police holding cell, replaying the day's events in his head and wondering how the hell things had unravelled so quickly.

Initially, he was convinced his capture had been a chance event. The Mallee Highway was a well-worn route for South Australian cannabis couriers delivering interstate and he was well aware that police often uncovered drug syndicates by conducting on-the-spot, random inspections. Many of those successful police arrests involved drivers with legitimate jobs in the trucking industry and commercial transport sector. The bulk of seizures, however, flowed from buses, camper-vans and nondescript motor vehicles like the one McCauley was travelling in that day.

It still didn't add up though, thought McCauley—if the search was random, if normal circumstances applied, why didn't the cops simply give up after fifteen minutes, apologise for the inconvenience and allow him to continue on with his journey? And why hadn't they so much as questioned Pete? He was driving the car, after all. 'Jesus!' he cursed out loud in his cell. 'They knew the hooter was in the bloody car.'

It later emerged that someone had indeed grassed on McCauley. In his own mind, he narrowed it down to three people. He hated not knowing which was the snitch, but the harsh reality was that it mattered little now—he'd been caught with a collective seven and a half kilos and according to the letter of the law he was holding a one-way ticket to jail.

McCauley later pleaded guilty to all charges in court and was granted conditional bail. When sentencing day finally arrived on 31 January the following year, 2003, he arrived at the steps of the Central District Court in Adelaide and took one last look around. He'd had several months to contemplate the grim prospect of life behind bars and it had been torture. As he walked inside and drew a deep breath, he was convinced it was his final taste of freedom for some time to come. But then, when it was his turn to take the stand, something completely unexpected occurred. That dreaded feeling of despair, parked in his stomach all those months, suddenly gave way to hope.

As McCauley eyeballed Judge Peter Allan across the courtroom floor, he was spurred on by the hope that maybe, just maybe, this might be his lucky day. Now let's make one thing clear—McCauley was no mind reader. But when it came to decoding another man's expression, he had long prided himself on being up there with the best. It was a gift that had served him well in some difficult situations over the years and Judge Allan's face, as far as McCauley could tell, was consumed by pity: 'You got yourself involved in this activity because you were short of money at the time,' noted Judge Allan while skimming through his case notes. 'An acquaintance of yours offered you the money and in an exercise of bad judgement, you decided to do it.'

During the earlier part of McCauley's trial, the court had been told he was acting as a courier on someone else's behalf. He was to be paid $1000 for making the trip to Wagga. He had allegedly received $800 before he left, with the balance to be settled once the deal had been completed. That was his claim anyhow. Judge Allan continued: 'You are now aged fifty-seven. There is no suggestion that the trip to Wagga was anything other than your first trip.' He acknowledged, however, that McCauley did appear to have some previous minor marijuana convictions against his name.

In April 1998, McCauley had been convicted in the Elizabeth Magistrates Court, Adelaide, of producing cannabis and possessing cannabis for sale. McCauley had confessed back then that he had supplied it to friends 'from time to time'. The magistrate who was dealing with him then had ruled the matter was 'at the low end of the scale', and consequently McCauley received only a $250 fine. Judge Allan sided with his predecessor, adding he too was of the opinion that McCauley's past form was 'not relevant'.

He noted McCauley's health these days was 'poor', his 'wife was ill', and that due to a previous serious injury at work he had not landed a proper job for several years, forcing him on to the pension. But the tone of Judge Allan's voice then lowered as he went on to speak, rather sternly, about the evils of drug mules and the unforgivable role they play in destroying other people's lives: 'The courts have said many times that couriers are an important part of the drug industry and that people detected acting as such can expect to receive terms of imprisonment.' McCauley gulped nervously as the judge concluded: 'People must be deterred from behaving in the way you did. Accordingly I propose to impose a sentence of imprisonment . . .'

McCauley heard the word *imprisonment* and his body jolted with fear.

'. . . But the real question,' continued Judge Allan, 'is whether you should be required to serve any of that sentence at all.' He went on to describe it as 'a pity' that the old man had found himself in court at this time of his life; he felt there was the 'likelihood' that he would never again mix in criminal circles. He stared down at McCauley and, as he did so, he delivered a final verdict: 'I think that you will not offend in this or any other way again.'

Following that shock ruling, Judge Allan imposed a suspended sentence of two years and six months on the condition that McCauley submit an $850 two-year good behaviour bond.

'Certainly,' said McCauley, flabbergasted by his good fortune.

From there a few loose legal ends were tied up and, at 9.36 am, McCauley strolled back out of court a free man. His wife Kathleen was waiting for him outside and, when he made it down the steps, he planted an enormous kiss on her cheek.

'How on earth did you get away with that?' she asked with a smile.

'I tell you what, love . . . I have no idea,' he replied.

McCauley danced down the footpath, performing something that only slightly resembled an Irish jig. As he did so, two thoughts flooded his mind. According to his own rulebook, it was well past 'beer o'clock' and he was aching for a cold one. But, once he'd quenched his thirst, his second job was to conduct a quick ring-around and deliver news of his good fortune. In no time at all, he discovered there was more than enough marijuana knocking about town for a decent road run to Queensland the following weekend. Malcolm McCauley was back in business, although, if we are to be precise, he'd never actually shut up shop. 'I never stopped, not even after I was arrested on the way to Wagga,' he confesses. 'It wasn't the money so much—I just loved the buzz and the thrill. It looked like I was going down anyway. Safest time to work, in my book.'

Judge Allan must have presumed that morning that McCauley would crawl back to Adelaide a grateful man, then see out his remaining days on the sofa sipping tea and watching daytime television. He certainly never expected to see McCauley's face or hear his name again.

He could not have been more wrong. Two years later the name Malcolm McCauley would be inextricably linked to Australia's most famous international drug runner, Schapelle Corby.

CHAPTER 6

The Poet and the Stripper

'I was setting them up for the drugs, because there were innocent children, kids out there, high school kids, and these drugs would kill . . . So, I got more information and I handed it to the police and it was up to them from then on . . .'

—Kim Moore, police informer

Mick Corby's best friend, Tony Lewis, was a foul-mouthed raconteur with a deep voice honed to perfection by his 15-plus joints a day habit. Living in the bush brought out Tony's creative side—he wrote and recited his own poetry and, by his own admission, was blessed with a handy turn of phrase and a sly sense of humour. Lewis's favourite self-penned poem was a romantic verse about a girlfriend who'd dumped him. Whenever he performed it before an audience, he'd get so swept up by his own words that he'd bring himself to tears.

It was this sensitive side of Tony Lewis that captured the heart of Beth Lavender, though she wasn't the girlfriend in the poem. Beth was a nervous spinster who lived alone next door to Tony's mother in the northern Queensland town of Gladstone, not far from Tony's and Mick Corby's properties.

Somehow, against his better judgement and because of a lack of control over his own charm, Lewis had hooked up with the nervy, claustrophobic Beth. His wire-thin unofficial girlfriend wrote poetry too, but she wasn't brave enough to recite it out loud. Like her deepest desires, Beth's words were held captive and strangled within herself, waiting for the right man to prise them out of her.

Beth Lavender was typical of many middle-aged, anonymous, unmarried women in country towns, with no confidence in herself and no other options on the horizon apart from Lewis, who somehow had noticed her shrunken frame over the back fence of his elderly mother's house. They had struck up a friendship via a chat about computers. Tony had confessed he was having trouble understanding how to transfer his farm logs onto his computer and Beth, surprising herself with her own boldness, had volunteered to visit Tony's farm to teach him how to use his new-fangled machine.

How the seduction proceeded from there no one is saying, but slowly Beth ingratiated herself and weekend stay-overs at the Lewis farm eventuated. When he was in the mood, Tony would take Beth out on dates to the pub. Usually there were three in the group—Beth, Tony and Mick Corby. Beth came in handy when Mick and Tony had had too much to drink, as she was always happy to drive the two blokes home to their farms. The giddy apex of her liaison with Lewis occurred after he'd been busted for drink driving and lost his licence. Suddenly he needed her more than ever before, but she tried not to read too much into the timing.

At various times between 1998 and 2003 the Corby kids stayed at Mick's farm. Schapelle, Michael Junior and James Kisina came. So too did Mercedes, her Balinese husband Wayan and their two children—'Their kids loved playing with all the animals,' Michael Jnr later told Janine Hosking's documentary team.

It didn't take long for Beth to meet Tony's circle of friends, including Mick Corby's kids, whenever they made the eight-hour drive up from the Gold Coast. There were plenty of parties and barbecues at the Lewis place. Even the indomitable Rosleigh Rose made the occasional trip up from Brisbane to sample Tony's home brew, and Beth had Ros's telephone numbers in her mobile phone, confirming to Beth that she was now part of Tony's crowd.

Enter Kim Moore. A 46-year-old former stripper and heroin addict, Kim had attracted plenty of trouble through-out her life and was now in the mood to shake up the status quo. She had grown up in the small country town of Yass in the Southern Tablelands of New South Wales, where her father had worked as a station hand and farm manager on properties around the area. Like most young girls living in the country, she grew up with a love of horses. At the age of nine her parents had moved the family to Queensland, where her father got higher paid work as a station manager.

Kim left school at the young age of thirteen and got work as a stable hand grooming horses. She soon moved out of home and drifted towards the city life in Brisbane. By age fifteen she had her first child and began hanging out with some teenagers who were experimenting with drugs. Two years later, she was hopelessly addicted to heroin. As a young woman, she was a striking blonde; to support her drug habit, she became a prostitute and worked in 'The Valley', Brisbane's red-light district. She says, 'I spent up to 1500 dollars a day on heroin. When you can't find the money, you go out and sell yourself to get it.'

Over the next ten years, she ended up with five children. Her youngest son, Jack, was intellectually disabled. In her late twenties she went into rehab, got off heroin and went straight: 'It took me eleven months to get off it. I got off drugs because I had a very strong friend—if I didn't have that friend I would have been dead because I was shooting up all the time.' After breaking the heroin habit, Kim supported her young family by working as a kitchen hand in truck stops around Central Queensland. By 2002 her face showed the strain of the hard life she had led. Jack was now in his twenties and still living at home with his mother, who called him her 'baby'.

Kim and Jack had been living on the Queensland Central Coast at a place called Boyne Island near Gladstone. Their home was about twenty kilometres from Tony Lewis and Mick Corby's Iveragh farms. She and Jack had been staying with a man who was a violent drunk; after a series of beatings, she took her son and moved into a homeless women's shelter in Gladstone.

Gladstone had a Salvation Army store and Kim liked to do volunteer work there to keep busy and meet new friends. It was here that Kim befriended Beth Lavender. In amongst the musty-smelling second-hand clothes and cheap paperbacks, Kim and Beth discovered they shared a mutual love of poetry. Beth was impressed with Kim's claim that she was an author, with works published under a nom de plume. According to Kim, she and Beth 'clicked' and became good friends because they'd both survived relationships with violent men.

One day while the two women were sorting through donated goods in the Salvo store, Beth told Kim that she had a boyfriend called Tony Lewis, who lived on a farm nearby. She said that Tony smoked a lot of grass and had his own marijuana crop. Kim believes that Tony used to beat Beth when he was drunk: 'Beth had been with Tony for years. Many times she used to come into the Salvo's all bruised. Many times. And I've always been on to her—Leave! Leave! Leave! But she never would leave him.'

It wasn't long before Kim met Tony—at the country show at Mount Larcom, near Gladstone, in 2003. When Tony Lewis was interviewed in 2006 he admitted that he'd met Kim Moore, but he added: 'I had met her once for about twenty minutes.' After meeting him at the show, Beth invited Kim around to the farm. At the rear of the property she saw a shed full of marijuana plants. Kim recalls: 'There were a few hundred plants— some were ready to be picked, some had already been picked. The cannabis plants were watered via an irrigation system, comprised of black poly pipe. I recall, after Beth and I went and looked at the cannabis plants, seeing Tony in the drying shed. Tony asked me what I thought of the plants—if I thought they looked healthy. I think I told him they looked good.'

On another visit to the farm, Kim alleges that Beth took her down to a shed behind Tony's house. This shed, containing two motor vehicles and an assortment of tools, served as a drying area for cannabis: 'I saw cut cannabis drying in this shed on this occasion. The shed was a three bay shed. There was another shed on the property, but I never went inside that shed. I attended Tony's property up to six or seven times during the period I knew him and Beth.'

It was during one of these farm visits that Kim recalls first meeting Mick Corby: 'Beth had told me about him before, and she seemed intent on trying to set me up with him. I remember his beautiful blue eyes. We had a couple of drinks with him; but the marijuana smoke just got too much, so I was out of there.'

She alleges that Mick was at Tony's place on at least three occasions when she was there: 'I witnessed him smoke cannabis with Tony in the form of joints. I also saw Mick around the drying shed and looking at the cannabis plants. Interestingly, Tony's cannabis plants were irrigated with water from Mick's dam. Mick's house was about 500 yards from Tony's, maybe a little bit more. You could see Mick's roof from Tony's.'

Kim also alleges that Tony and Mick both had links to the Rebels outlaw motorcycle gang: 'I know this because I heard them make reference to the Rebels sometimes during conversations. I have also seen a Rebels jacket that Tony owned. Tony and Mick also discussed moving cannabis between Iveragh, Sarina, Charters Towers and Ravens-bourne,' she claims.

While Kim Moore says she never met Schapelle Corby at the Lewis property, she alleges she met other members of the Corby clan there enjoying Lewis's hospitality.

After living in Gladstone for about six months, Kim applied for a government-subsidised home and took the first one that came up, in a small country town called Miriam Vale on the Bruce Highway, about 30 minutes drive south of Gladstone. Kim's new rental house was just 30 kilometres from Tony Lewis and Mick Corby's farms.

One night Beth invited Kim to the Bororen Hotel, which was about halfway between Miriam Vale and Iveragh.

It was a nice pub and Beth said that a few friends were going to meet and enjoy dinner and a few beers together. Tony's neighbour, Mick, was going to be there too.

Says Kim: 'The second occasion I saw Mick Corby was at the Bororen Hotel. I went to the hotel with a friend, Neville Collett. Neville and I were just friends, not sexual partners. I had been doing some house cleaning for Neville and we had developed a friendship. Neville and I had gone to the bar prior to dinner to have a drink. Tony and Beth turned up at the hotel. They joined us at the bar. Shortly after a man I recognised, and now know to be Mick Corby, arrived at the hotel. Mick came to the bar and greeted Tony and Beth. After a short while we then moved to a dining table. Mick joined the group. I recall we waited a long time for our meals because they mixed up Beth's order.'

After dinner and a few beers at the pub, the conversation turned to grass. Kim said that Tony was talking about 'what price he could get up the north coast and the price of pot in Brisbane'. She alleges the two men told her they had taken 32 kg of cannabis to Sarina, and that Tony had 7.5 kg left over to offload.

Beth had told Tony Lewis that Kim had been a heroin addict and had spent years hanging around 'The Valley' in Brisbane. Kim alleges that Tony Lewis then asked her if she would get in touch with some of her old Brisbane contacts and sell a few kilos of pot for him. She recalls: 'They asked me if I could take the marijuana off their hands at a better price than what they were getting. Tony seemed to feel that I would be able to get more money for the cannabis than he could. Tony wanted me to sell 7.5 kilograms of his cannabis.' Even though Kim knew that Tony had a stack of grass growing on his farm, she says that she was still shocked when he asked her to get in touch with her old drug contacts—'I felt like a leaf going down the gutter.'

Tony Lewis didn't know it back then, but his 'home grown' cannabis lifestyle was drawing to a dramatic close that would inevitably have consequences for Schapelle and Mick Corby.

CHAPTER 7

The Law of Averages

*'Malcolm was always capable of fixing things in times of trouble.
Problem was, there was always times of trouble.'*
—Kathleen McCauley

Kathleen McCauley's patience had been severely tested since her husband had risen to become a drug kingpin. His criminal activities were taking over her life and pushing her closer towards breaking point. And yet an ember of the love she had felt for him as an innocent schoolgirl was still burning somewhere deep in her heart. After he escaped doing jail time for the Wagga run in 2002, she pleaded with him, one last time, to scale down the operation.

But instead, production multiplied and Malcolm found a business partner, Jeff Jellese, to share the increasing workload. Jellese and his parents had emigrated from Holland to Australia in 1966. He was aged 13 at the time. Now 50, he had owned his own garbage removal business for thirty years, clearing industrial waste from places such as prisons, factories, surgeries and shops. In stark contrast to

Peter Dudley, Jellese was a polite, all-round likeable guy. He was fairly tall and well built, with dark hair and a thick but well-groomed moustache and beard.

'Jeff was a grower who already had a small send down to the Greeks in Victoria, so he knew the game,' explains McCauley. 'More importantly, though, he was a money man. He had the disposable cash to buy big loads of hooter as and when we needed it.' McCauley adds that, once Jellese had taken over the financial side of things, the business began operating like a well-oiled machine: 'I was never good with money. But, once Jeff was on board, I was able to concentrate on what I did best, which was sourcing hooter, getting it to clients and making sure we had enough drivers to fulfil the demand.' Jellese recalls that, from the start, it was his understanding there was a business arrangement with Schapelle's father: 'He [Malcolm] used to call her old man. He used to do a lot of business with Dad.'

Every rock star has a golden era and, if McCauley is any indication, then so do drug dealers. Around this time, he was cashed up and carefree. If customers were occasionally unable to pay, he was never the sort to be chopping off fingers and thumbs. He simply took whatever his clients could give him.

Jellese recalls the very first moment he met the man who a short time later would become his partner in crime: 'I got to know Malcolm through my mate Peter Dudley. We normally had a drink on Saturday at Peter's place. A few blokes came around and he says: "Oh, I want you to meet one of my mates, Malcolm McCauley." And he drove up in his Porsche, and I said: "That's a nice car." It was about eight or nine years old, but it was in very good condition. And Peter said: "Yeah, he got that through doing business.

THE LAW OF AVERAGES

Transports marijuana . . . and he grows marijuana and he sends it to Brisbane." '

McCauley was living a crazy existence and on the outside, at least, it must have appeared as though he had it all. For his neighbours in Salisbury North, doing it tough, it would have been hard not to feel some jealousy when he pulled up outside his place in a $50,000 Porsche convertible. But he was also treading a fine line. If it weren't for his guardian angel, Suzy, constantly watching his back, his fate might have been very different.

In early 2003, McCauley had been busy preparing for another road run to Queensland. This particular load was heading to Mick Corby and, like clockwork, it was due to be dropped at Jupiter's. But, at the very last minute, Suzy caught wind of some alarming intelligence. She says: 'I received some information that the cops were sniffing around Mal. He couldn't pull out of the deal with Mick, so we found some-one else to finish the job. He gave the marijuana to that someone else. That person then delivered it to a driver and he was supposed to courier it through.'

Suzy explains that, as per usual, the driver made it safely out of South Australia but later, when he arrived in New South Wales, he was pulled over by highway police. She continues: 'When they nabbed him, he sang like a canary. He told them where the exchange was to take place. He spilled everything. The cops ordered the courier to continue on with the journey, so the deal could still take place. They also warned him that if he tried to make contact with anyone beforehand, they would know about it.'

She says the courier 'never made a single call' and yet, somehow, someone at the other end still found out about the arrest. 'The courier got intercepted by some heavies along the highway. They were bikies and they bashed him to within an inch of his life. The drugs, predictably, got stolen, meaning the exchange could no longer take place on the Gold Coast.' She quips: 'The AFP would have had a team in place at the other end but, I tell you what, they would have been waiting a long time.' Of the ill-fated trip, she adds: 'What can you say when something like that goes down? We concluded that after those officers radioed the incident through to the local cops on the ground in Queensland, the details found their way out. Clearly, there was a warning from someone that prompted that attack. Mick Corby must have had connections on the inside. How else was the driver suddenly cut off in that way?'

McCauley was stunned when the news emerged. Nobody ever owned up to the bashing but, as far as he was concerned, they didn't need to. He'd just lost 30 grand's worth of marijuana but this was one of those situations where there would be no witchhunt. It was further proof that he was in way over his head. Around this period of time there was a sense that anything could go down, at any moment. Others were starting to feel the heat too.

The following year, in late 2003, Ken Ray began to feel uneasy about the size of the loads he was being asked to deliver to Wayne Williams in North Queensland. Recalling that time, he says: 'Bloody hell, that was big, big—that was their undoing. That went for three-odd years—every fortnight to three weeks. They were taking up to 26 pounds. That's when I walked away from it. I said, "No, I've had enough of it. You're getting too heavy. I want out." '

Sadly, another person to throw in the towel at that time was Kathleen. The drug syndicate had grown so large, she had no choice but to pack her bags and escape: 'He thought he was untouchable, and I couldn't see a time when it would ever end. The family house no longer felt like a home, so we put it on the market, eventually sold it and split the proceeds. He stayed on and rented it off the people who bought it. I went and got my own place. I still saw him and everything, but I started my life again.'

Alarm bells should have been ringing loudly in McCauley's ears the day Kathleen packed her bags and left. Instead, he continued to roll with the punches. He wasn't the only one.

There are no guarantees when it comes to drug smuggling but it is safe to say that, if you cut corners or add additional risks to the equation, something is bound to go wrong sooner or later. 'There were often occasions when I couldn't fulfil an order,' said McCauley. 'Sometimes I couldn't get a driver but, more often than not, I simply couldn't source the hooter in time. There was this one particular occasion when I had to turn Mick away because he needed to go fishing too quick. He ended up getting what he needed off another mutual contact in Adelaide and then to save on the travel time, they decided to revert back to the old arrangement—you know, fast-track it on a domestic flight to Brisbane.' According to McCauley, the risk backfired: 'The courier boarded the flight in Adelaide, having checked in a suitcase full of hooter. But, when he landed in Queensland, the suitcase turned up on the carousel empty. From there, the courier returned on the first available flight back to Adelaide. He then kicked up a major fuss and started threatening staff at the airport. Everyone's feathers were up after that, not least Mick's. The courier had a meltdown; the cops got involved. Oh Jesus, some major shit went down, I can tell you.'

South Australian Police sources have confirmed the bizarre incident indeed took place. Sturt Criminal Investigation

Branch Detective Chief Inspector Sid Thomas said he himself launched an investigation after an interstate drug courier threatened to kill two Virgin Blue airline staff on 26 May 2004—five months prior to Schapelle Corby's arrest in Bali. As Inspector Thomas recollects: 'We became involved after complaints that a drug courier was harassing Virgin airline staff. It seems the courier arrived back at Adelaide Airport from Brisbane—which is where the drugs were supposed to be delivered. He then made some major ripples, claiming someone from the airline had knocked off the dope from his suitcase.'

According to the official police intelligence report, the 'so-called victim' initially tried the softly-softly approach. He explained to staff that the package contained $70,000 worth of dope. After accusing one employee of taking it, he then offered him $30,000 to find out who did take it. Bemused staff then watched the man leave the airport in a hurry. They later described him to police as being Caucasian, large, masculine and clean-shaven, with short brown hair. He was wearing a tracksuit and apparently left in a Nissan Sedan.

Inspector Thomas says: 'In a last-ditch attempt to recover the cargo, several death threats were later made by the unknown male over the phone. During subsequent interviews of airline staff, it was alleged that two particular staff had told others that they found the dope and knocked it off.'

Inspector Thomas notes that, because police never recovered the drugs, nothing eventuated: 'We were never able to identify who the courier was. As for the two employees supposedly involved in the theft, well, they denied it. During police searches, one of the employees was charged with possession of marijuana, but certainly not the commercial quantity at the centre of the drama. To my knowledge, they ended up leaving the airline by mutual consent. It was one of those unusual cases I would have loved to have got to the bottom of—but didn't.'

Mick Corby had known for years that Adelaide Airport was problematic. Despite that, he'd still gone ahead with this arrangement. Not for the first time, he'd weathered the storm and sailed through unscathed. Next time, he mightn't be so lucky. According to the law of averages, his time was drawing near. The same applied to McCauley—but relentlessly he continued running his syndicate and increasingly spent his time troubleshooting.

With Ken Ray's sudden departure, Malcolm now had transport problems. Hence a new courier was assigned to the Mick Corby run. Her name was Brenda Joyce Eastwood. Drug runners come in all shapes and sizes, but this particular mule was unusual to say the least. She was a 51-year-old grandmother of three, born in Port Augusta in 1953 and raised single-handedly by her mother after her father was jailed when she was just two.

Granny Eastwood dropped out of school in Year 10 and gained work as a sewing machinist, then as a shop assistant in a South Australian department store. She married at the age of 18 and, less than a year later, gave birth to the first of four children. In public, Eastwood tried to maintain the impression that she lived a happy existence, but behind closed doors it was a different story. Her husband was a chronic alcoholic who abused her both physically and mentally. Like many women, she endured years of domestic torture and punishment for the sake of her kids. Then finally, in 1985, she could face no more and broke free.

Eastwood remarried ten years later, after a chance meeting in a pub. His name was Richard and he dressed like a country singer. They shared a passion for jive dancing and he swept her off her feet. But, as time progressed, he suffered health problems and she was forced to become the sole breadwinner in the household. Her cause wasn't helped by the fact that she had also developed a chronic addiction to the pokies. By 2002, she was deep in debt from her gambling habit.

McCauley met Eastwood through a neighbour. For some time, he quietly monitored her ongoing money worries. 'Once Ken had left, I was on the lookout for a decent courier and Brenda was an attractive proposition in that regard,' he says. 'She didn't fit your usual mould—she didn't smoke the hooter; she was tall, with short blonde curly hair and a reasonably good figure. How many of them do you find transporting car loads of hooter? Not many, I can tell ya.'

The temptation of a fast buck was too much for Eastwood to resist, and by the end of 2003 McCauley had already accompanied her on her first two runs to Queensland. In the coming months, she would make the Gold Coast and Charters Towers runs her own: 'Apart from jive dancing and the pokies, Brenda's true passion in life was driving,' said McCauley. 'She loved it. Once she was on that highway, she was like a bird set free.'

McCauley says that, over time, he and Eastwood developed a love/hate relationship: 'Brenda was a great courier but she was also a fairly intelligent creature and, when it comes to drugs, the first rule is that you can't trust anyone. She was certainly no exception. If I was sending hooter up to Mick [Corby], it was always a drop-off to a bunch of unknowns. It was a straight-out transaction, plain and simple, and then the driver was out of there—regardless of whether it was

Ken, Brenda or whoever. But with Wayne Williams, he came to know Brenda reasonably well, because she was making the trip so bloody often. Anyway, I don't know what her motive was, but she and Williams's wife ended up going out a couple of times socially—and I had to put my foot down on that. I said, "Listen here, love, that ain't right." '

McCauley says the reason he had acted so swiftly was because it was exactly the sort of thing he would have done to 'get in and eventually take over supply. So why wouldn't she?' That was the first time McCauley had grown suspicious. The second occasion erupted into something far bigger. 'She tried to do me over big time,' he says.

In early 2004, Williams suddenly needed a ten-pound half-load and Eastwood agreed to take the trip at short notice. McCauley remembers: 'I charged Williams an extra $3000 because it was a fast turnaround. Brenda drove up there, completed the exchange and picked up the dough. But then she rang and told me she'd been robbed in a caravan park in Townsville. The story didn't gel. I quizzed her for details and she told me that, aside from the loot, they had taken her watch. I thought to myself, "Why would they want your bloody watch when they've just landed $33,000 cool smackeroos?"'

McCauley says his outrage was fuelled by visions of Eastwood 'loading up the pokies at an RSL somewhere in Queensland'. He wanted to throttle her, but he didn't let her know that. 'Don't worry, love, there's nowt we can do now . . . just as long as you're okay. Make your way home,' he told her down the phone.

McCauley had already been scheming. He had concocted a cunning plan to catch Eastwood out. 'I decided I was going to intercept her—lie in wait like a fox along the highway— and then stop her before she got home. Then I'd strip the vehicle, because my guess was that she was heading straight home to hide the cash.'

When McCauley had last spoken with Eastwood she divulged her exact whereabouts, giving him time to fine-tune his plan. He convinced Kathleen to drive him out to the Main North Road at Roseworthy, some 30 kilometres north of Adelaide. He then waited patiently for his prey to pass by. He says: 'I was gonna pounce on her. But silly me, I didn't think it out properly. There was a pub by the side of the road—the Roseworthy Hotel is its name. I thought to myself, "Why sit in a car for hours when I could be in there?" So we parked our arses behind a window at the front of the pub and watched, and we waited. Later on, we took the beers out into the car park and finished them while we sat in the vehicle.'

In a scene reminiscent of a Road Runner cartoon, McCauley describes the moment when Eastwood suddenly came into view: 'It was after lunch. There she goes! I dropped my beer and off we went. The only problem was, the car was situated on the wrong side of the bloody road. We watched her drive straight through and we couldn't turn around quick enough to catch her. By the time we'd got across, she'd turned onto the freeway and was long gone.'

Kathleen adds: 'She drove past with a massive smile on her face. We went to chase her, but we got caught in traffic. It was a complete stuff-up.'

About ten minutes later, McCauley realised there was one more tiny issue working against him: 'I knew roughly where she lived, but I didn't actually know the address. By the time I bloody well found it, she'd unloaded the car and hidden the cash. I fucked up real bad.'

Eastwood had just climbed out of the shower when Kathleen and Malcolm arrived at the front door. 'Brenda maintained the money was all gone. She was putting on a real show—the crocodile tears were coming thick and fast. Her husband, Richard, was there. I laid it on him too, but he also played dumb.'

McCauley says that, following that standoff, different tactics were deployed. He tried to reason with Eastwood that, if she owned up, they could strike a deal which might see both of them walk away happy: 'Jeff was obviously in on the run to Queensland. In fact it was him who stood to lose most out of this whole sorry saga. I said, "Brenda, love, if you come clean with me, we can go halves and then we both win. You stick to the story with Jeff that you were robbed; I'll back you 100 per cent and nobody will be any the wiser."'

Under intense pressure, Eastwood finally cracked: 'She was out of her depth and, through some general persuasion, she eventually caved in. We had one final chat. I reassured her there would be no repercussions if she owned up. At the same time, I warned her there would be some serious shit if she didn't. I said, "It's obvious to me what has happened here. Are we going to keep working together or not?"'

Eastwood repaid the money, minus a small chunk. Kathleen's theory is that, after completing the drug deal with Williams, she had dipped into the money to have a gamble. After an afternoon's losing streak on the pokies, she then panicked and came up with an excuse. Either way, she was digging herself into a hole.

At this point, Eastwood's instincts should have told her to get the hell out. Instead, over the next eighteen months she completed numerous additional journeys to both the Gold Coast and Charters Towers. According to McCauley two of those runs, in particular, would end up playing a pivotal role in everyone's downfall, including Schapelle Corby's.

CHAPTER 8

Angel of Bali

'She [Mercedes] *is the anchor in the most turbulent of storms.'*
—Tony Wilson, reporter *Gold Coast Bulletin*

Of Mick Corby's children, Mercedes is the one most like him. While the striking Schapelle captured everyone's hearts, it was Mercedes who was the street smart, lateral thinker who always had an amazing ability to think on her feet. 'Mercedes should be running Australia,' declared proud Ros. 'It would be a far better place.'

During the aftermath of the second Bali bombings in October 2005, Mercedes was hailed a heroine. She was on her way out to dinner and passing through Kuta when a bomb explosion erupted from inside the popular Raja's Restaurant in Kuta Square. With little regard for her own safety, Mercedes fearlessly ran against the crowd that was fleeing the scene and into the destruction zone to help save lives. With her surf life-saving skills to the fore, she quickly rescued a young Indonesian woman who was lying on the ground haemorrhaging blood badly, with her skull blasted open and half her face missing. Without any qualms, Mercedes immediately whipped off her t-shirt and wrapped it tightly around the woman's head; now dressed only in a bikini top and shorts, she compressed the woman's wounds as the two of them were lifted onto the back of a ute and taken to the nearby hospital.

Two days later, Merc's good friend, the newspaper journalist Tony Wilson, back in Brisbane, hailed her the 'Angel of Bali'. Amid all the death and mayhem, Mercedes had been lucky enough to score herself some positive press after enduring weeks of negative media backlash about her and the family.

In the years before her sister's ill-fated drug run, there was a time when Merc Corby didn't have to worry about her image. She was just another free-spirited surfer girl looking for adventure. Mercedes is the most entrepreneurial and forward-thinking of the Corby clan and her ambition always went further than spending life at home on the Gold Coast. So she was not yet out of her teens when she headed to Japan for work and play. Former best friend Jodie Power would join her there, too. In years to come Jodie would become Mercedes's nemesis, but during their carefree single days the two girls were soul mates.

In Japan, Jodie and Mercedes were among the thousands of young western women who, as well as backpacking and teaching English, made good money working as hostesses in nightclubs and bars. Back then, hostessing by foreigners used to exist on the relatively 'innocent' fringes of the Japanese sex industry.

Little is known of Mercedes's life in Japan. In 1993 and 1994 she was there on a working holiday and was living in Toyama, a city located on the coastline of the Sea of Japan, some 300 kilometres northwest of Tokyo. While in Japan, Mercedes sent letters to Jodie Power back in Australia detailing her experimentation with drugs. In one letter Mercedes wrote: 'Japan has the best mull. I only need two or three puffs of a joint and I am wasted.' In another letter, she refers to putting on weight, then writes: 'I think when I get home I might go on a speed diet.' She also writes in other letters: 'I'm getting stoned and enjoying myself' and 'Tell my brother Michael I said, "hi" and say sorry I could not send the "e's".' These letters were later tendered as evidence in a defamation case, where it was alleged that 'the e's' referred to the drug ecstasy. Mercedes denied that she had sold or trafficked drugs, and told the court that she'd only used a small amount of marijuana and ecstasy.

Mercedes was always a leader and, wherever she went, her younger brother Michael and baby sister Schapelle usually followed. But at age 17, Schapelle was living in Middlemount with her father and near his best mate, the dope-smoking Tony Lewis. Ros and Schapelle had been clashing at home, so Mum packed Schapelle off to live with Mick in the 'teen hell' that was outback western Queensland. While Mercedes was living in Japan, she was encouraging Schapelle to get the hell out of Middlemount and try living overseas for a while. Mercedes offered her sister a place to stay and even paid for her flight to Japan.

After spending a couple of months in Japan, Schapelle returned to Brisbane and moved to the Gold Coast so she could be close to all the beach and nightclub action. By chance she met there a young Japanese surfer, Kimi Maekawa, while he was working in Coles supermarket at Pacific Fair on the Gold Coast. After having just returned from her adventures in Japan with Merc, she plucked up the courage to introduce herself to this cool-looking Japanese guy. They exchanged telephone numbers and she invited him to her 18th birthday party a few weeks later. Schapelle and Kimi started hanging out together, but it took quite a few months before they were seriously dating. It didn't take long before the pair fell in love.

Kimi was in Australia on a working holiday visa, so eventually he had to return to Japan when his visa expired. Not wanting to be apart, Schapelle and Kimi decided to move to Japan together. However, visa extensions in Japan were a continual problem for Schapelle, so the lovebirds travelled back and forth between the Gold Coast and Japan so they could keep renewing her Japanese holiday visa in Australia.

With it getting harder for Schapelle to get an entry visa to Japan, finally the young couple decided that getting married would be a solution to their problem. So in 1998 Schapelle travelled back to Japan where Kimi and she started living together in Omaezaki, where he worked as a surfboard shaper and seasonal tea farm worker. They were finally married in June 1998, with an unceremonious signing of names at the city prefecture office.

With strong waves from the Pacific Ocean crashing into the surrounding beaches, Omaezaki is a famous surfing and windsurfing destination that attracts surfers from around the world. A small isolated town on the east coast of Japan, it was once a drawcard for surfers competing in world surfing championships, but the downturn in the Japanese economy during this period swallowed up sponsors and it became a lonely place for Schapelle. Unfortunately for the pair, their marriage wasn't to last long in this 'surfers paradise'. Schapelle, disconsolate at the prospect of leading a frugal life in a tiny apartment near a windswept beach, soon upped and left for the bright lights and action of Japan's capital city, Tokyo.

After moving to Tokyo, she soon found work as a hostess in bars in an area close to the homes of the rich. In their quest to help tired businessmen reassert their masculinity after a hard day's work, hostesses can typically find their duties varying from serving drinks to singing songs at karaoke clubs for their clients' entertainment and escorting them to expensive restaurants. Some Japanese men pay just to have a drink with a western woman, who can barely speak Japanese; but sometimes they also proposition for sex.

This kind of hostessing is unique to Japan, evolving over the past forty years or so out of the 400-year-old geisha tradition as a concession to changing times. The biggest part of a hostessing job is to act as an enabler at a banquet or drinking party, assisting men in having fun. The hostess gets paid to drink and chat with men and ensure that they have a good time at outrageously priced entertainment clubs.

A hostess also gets paid to develop highly stylised relationships with customers—extensions of her work at the club. In most cases, she does not sell sex; she sells love or, rather, an embellished variety of it. Yet the hostess is always, in some form, selling the most alluring of sexual fantasies. She reminds her customers of sex and sensuality after they've spent the day in a work environment that treats them more like robots than men.

Schapelle and the Corbys have always denied that her hostess work in Tokyo ever involved being paid for sex with Japanese businessmen, and they declare that Schapelle was only ever serving drinks and lighting cigarettes while their karaoke song was being prepped. Schapelle's Uncle Shun was outraged about suggestions that she was working as a prostitute in Japan. He told the Brisbane *Courier Mail* in May 2005: 'It makes us so mad, because Schapelle was definitely not into prostitution or anything of the sort. She's a prude. It was a traditional Japanese gentleman's club, where the girls were fully clothed.'

Schapelle eventually returned to the Gold Coast from Japan in 2000. After her arrest, the Corbys were certainly not keen for any media to find Kimi in Japan, going to the extraordinary lengths of telling one newspaper journalist that the family could not remember his surname. Apparently, the last that Kimi heard from Schapelle was an unexpected phone call from Bali in October 2004, after she had been arrested, during which she told him that her father was very sick. Kimi, however, had remarried by then and was also a father, so he asked her not to call again.

While Schapelle's pace of life had been slowing down post divorce, her older sister was still right in the thick of the action and constantly on the move. By the age of 29, Mercedes had enjoyed a long association with Bali. She had first travelled there in the early nineties, when she was almost 18, after winning first prize in a competition riding a mechanical surfboard at a Gold Coast bar. That trip had lit a fire in her belly and given her the passion to want to travel and experience other countries and cultures.

In 1993 she met her husband-to-be, Wayan Widyartha, while he was competing in pro surf competitions throughout Asia. Apparently it was love at first sight for Wayan, but for Mercedes it was a bit more of a gradual thing. With their love of surf and sea in common, the couple looked like a good match—Wayan with his deep tan and cute boyish face; Mercedes the fit, sporty westerner just as keen on surfing as her Balinese boyfriend. Wayan was a local Balinese surfing

star who, through his competition success, had earned spon-
sorship deals with famous surf companies like Billabong and
Rip Curl. As a highly regarded semi-professional surfer, he
was idolised by Balinese teenagers wanting to follow in his
footsteps and break into the pro surfing ranks.

The young couple led a free-spirited surfie lifestyle and
travelled carefree between Australia, Bali and Japan. In Bali,
Wayan also worked as a tour guide, helping professional and
amateur surfers find the abundance of ideal locations around
the island—especially between April and November, when it
becomes a mecca for those keen to ride the huge waves.

Mercedes and Wayan both speak Japanese, which came
in handy when dealing with the lucrative Japanese tourist
market burgeoning in Bali. Wayan was a star attraction,
being promoted online and elsewhere. For example, 'Bali
Freak', an online tourist guide written in Japanese for the
HIS Japanese Travel Agency, gushed about Wayan in the
following terms:

> Totally cool Chuppa (nickname—pronounced chooppa)
> is a resident from the Gold Coast in Australia. He has an
> Australian wife and two children. Bet they are cute! In
> Australia he works at a fish factory. At the moment he is on
> vacation and has returned home to Bali. He has previously
> experienced coming 2nd in a Quiksilver Contest.

In this way Wayan was able to make himself known to
millions of Japanese tourists and young surfers with disposable incomes intending to travel to Bali. In the 'Land of
Waves', having a surf guide is a safe and hassle-free way to
get star treatment while chasing the waves and good times.
Surf guides do everything from ensuring visitors and their

boards are ushered through customs without fuss, booking accommodation and arranging transport as well as taking their clients out at night to restaurants, bars and making sure they have invitations to the best parties. Mercedes and Wayan often mixed with the surfing elite, the likes of Kelly Slater and many other top pro surfers.

After several years of surfing and travelling together, Mercedes realised that over time she had fallen in love with Wayan; they eventually married in 1999 in a traditional Hindu ceremony in Bali. The Gold Coast Corby clan joined the other guests at the wedding and the festivities went on for a month, in accordance with the Hindu tradition. Wedding photos show the Corbys had adapted to the Balinese customs well—Dad Corby even donned a sarong and traditional ceremonial dress for the occasion.

Living the surfing lifestyle in this beautiful paradise was fun, but it proved difficult after Mercedes gave birth to the couple's first child, Wayan Jnr. They were living on a relatively small income in a home that was nothing like the villas owned by the wealthy, well-dressed young expats who hung out in Bali's surf and party scene. Any pipedream Merc and Wayan had of owning a fancy villa needed to be put on hold while they returned to the Gold Coast to be closer to her family and better hospitals and schools.

Wayan got on well with the family—he was easygoing and Ros took a shine to him. She told the documentary makers: 'He'd never seen a lawn mower before, I don't think. Never used one, so it was like a new toy to him. I didn't have to mow the lawn any more.'

Michael Corby Jnr told the documentary crew that Mercedes and Wayan regularly stayed at Mick Corby's farm up in Gladstone. In 2003 they were on the guest list for

Tony Lewis's 55th birthday party to be held at his property. Michael recalled the family travelling from the Gold Coast up to Gladstone: 'We borrowed Mum's van. It was me, Mercedes, Wayan and James [Kisina], I think Schapelle was there—yeah, she was there.'

But after the long drive, the party turned out to be a fizzer because old Mick had suddenly become very ill. Tony recalls: 'He didn't even come to my party, no. Mick was laid up over in the caravan in the shed—he wouldn't even go in the house, 'cos he left the house empty for the kids to stay in.'

In the days that followed the anchor of the family, Mercedes, once again swung into swift action. Tony says: 'Mercedes stayed here and took Mick to hospitals and everything—got all the tests and that.' But the outcome of those tests was a dire diagnosis—inoperable prostate cancer. As it turned out, he had been suffering symptoms for a long time but he hadn't wanted to go to a doctor. 'I was a bloody idiot,' was Mick's later verdict. 'I tell every bloke I know now—go and get downstairs checked!'

After that, Mick Corby proved to be a difficult and irritable patient. Schapelle and Mercedes took turns staying at the farm to keep an eye on him. 'She [Schapelle] came up and helped me up north, because the medication I was on was knocking me around,' Mick told the documentary makers. When he proved hopeless at looking after himself, his family finally convinced him to move full-time to his second base on the Gold Coast, where they could keep a closer eye on him. They were mostly concerned about his dark depression. He took some convincing, but finally Mercedes laid down the law. For the first time in thirty years, Tony Lewis and Mick Corby were separated by hundreds of kilometres. The family claim the two men hardly ever kept in touch and that Mick rarely went to the farm again once he was living with the kids in Tugun.

After four years of enduring mundane, low-paid jobs, Mercedes and Wayan decided to return to Bali in July 2004 for an extended holiday. Wayan had been missing Bali but, in particular, earning money in Australia hadn't turned out to be easy. He had tried a variety of jobs—fruit picking and working in a welding shop, as well as in a fish factory. He struggled to speak English at work and recalls, 'I think people got angry with me too on a busy day, but I do not understand.' Meanwhile Mercedes supplemented the family income by doing casual jobs, including packing supermarket shelves and working in the family shop, Rox's Seafood Takeaway, in Southport.

Mercedes had given birth to their second child, a daughter named Nyeleigh, while they were eking out a life in Australia. Like most young couples Wayan and Mercedes were not without ambition, but their best chance of getting ahead was in the surf scene, which they lived and breathed. Records show that, prior to leaving Australia on their six-month holiday to Bali, Mercedes cancelled with the Australian Tax Office an ABN-registered business called Ocean Selancar (Ocean Surfing). This sole-trader business had been registered since March 2003, but there is no record of what business Ocean Surfing might have been trading in. Mick Corby later commented that his oldest daughter 'had many lofty business plans, but none of them ever came off'.

Later on, during the media's intense scrutiny of her past, Mercedes continually stressed that, back in 2004, she and Wayan had only planned to stay in Bali for six months, in order to give their children a taste of Balinese culture before their youngest son, Wayan, started school in Australia in

2005. However, it was in fact far easier for her husband to get work in his native country as his legendary status on the local surf scene had won him strong and loyal contacts within the surf industry. As a result he picked up regular surf guiding jobs and potentially lucrative contract work selling merchandise for the big international surf labels to local surf outlets on the island.

Bali was also a much cheaper place to live than the Gold Coast. With a thriving and lucrative tourism market, cheap living and lower taxes, it was the perfect situation for an aspiring young couple who wanted to make a go of it. Mercedes still hadn't given up her dream to purchase their own villa and there was talk of buying land at a popular surfing spot called Canggu.

Canggu is a small village on the beach about twenty minutes north of Seminyak and halfway to the famous Tanah Lot Temple. The surrounding beaches offer some renowned and challenging surfing. With a backdrop of quietly undulating terrain and rice paddies dotted everywhere in the landscape, at this time Canggu was quickly being transformed from a surfer's paradise into the next big place for tourists and well-heeled expatriates. Holiday villas and long-term rentals were springing up everywhere as the market moved away from hotel stays in central Kuta. Tourists preferred to rent a luxury villa in the rice fields and be close to the beach, rather than rent a cramped hotel room amidst the street noise and craziness of daily life in central Kuta.

Mercedes would often draw sketches of her favourite dream villas, with all the trimmings, but for now her dreams were out of reach as she and Wayan faced the reality of bringing up their family in a small crowded Balinese family compound in Kuta owned by Wayan's family.

During the months leading up to her big thirtieth birthday party in Bali, Mercedes planned her celebrations with precision. If she couldn't afford to buy her own villa, at least she was definitely going to hire a luxury villa for her party and make it the Night of All Nights, with an awesome guest list. With the invitations sent out, Mercedes' extended family and friends were expected to be flying in from all parts of Australia to join the celebrations.

Despite suffering from inoperable prostate cancer and his need to have Schapelle as his full-time carer, Mick Corby was clearly feeling well enough to travel solo to Bali a few weeks before returning to Australia at the end of September 2004. When he was later quizzed by the media about this, he claimed that he wasn't able to get tickets on the same flight as Schapelle to Bali, so he'd travelled to Bali a few weeks earlier to see Merc. But, for some inexplicable reason, he didn't stay on the island for the upcoming birthday celebrations on 8 October.

Malcolm McCauley believes he knows the reason why and that it had nothing to do with visiting Mercedes: 'Couldn't get tickets? Give me a break. History now shows that Mick got an order—that's why he went over a few weeks before. He needed to iron out the details. Dates, times, logistics . . . Visits to people who normally helped smooth the way. Then he had to return [to Australia] and start the ball rolling. That's how it worked. You don't just ring in an order and say give me ten pounds, and then tomorrow it lobs up on your doorstep. You've got to source the drugs, transport them, iron out the creases, then send them over the drink [the sea]. Things had to be worked out. Lots of things.'

But, while Mick was away in Bali on that trip, the shit hit the fan back home.

CHAPTER 9

A Woman Scorned

'What they found in Bali I believe was the sophisticated hydrophonic [sic] stuff, it was great big buds. You won't get as stoned on the stuff I grew as you do on that hydroponics . . . the hydrophonics, it's whack and bang.'

—Tony Lewis

There was major trouble looming in Tony Lewis's world. His girlfriend Beth Lavender's new best friend, Kim Moore, was still feeling bitter that she had been asked by Tony and Mick Corby to sell cannabis for them in Brisbane. Since kicking her heroin habit, Kim saw herself as an anti-drugs crusader, like the American environmental campaigner Erin Brockovich, whose life story was made into a Hollywood movie: 'I've been clean twenty years and I'm not going back, and I'll put anyone else in who tries to get me back on it. Drug dealers don't give a damn about human life, all they give a damn about is lining their pockets with greed, with money. That's all it is.'

After spending months stewing over Mick and Tony's business offer, Kim finally took action. She walked up to a local police officer she knew and trusted in Miriam Vale and told him that she had information about a man who was growing a big marijuana crop. She recalls: 'I pulled the local policeman up in the main street in Miriam Vale outside the post office and said that I had some information for him.' He told her to drop by the station and make a statement. Later that day Kim told the Miriam Vale police everything she knew about the marijuana operation on Tony Lewis's property. She says: 'I gave them directions to where they would find a lot of the things.'

Tony Lewis later claimed that Kim Moore was 'a woman scorned, I won't say no more—I think you understand'. Incredulous, Kim denies the insinuation: 'I knocked him back—he was the jilted one!'

Motivations aside, before the police could act on Kim's allegations they wanted to make sure that her story was true, so they asked her to obtain a sample of marijuana from Lewis's property. Kim then devised a story for Beth Lavender about how she needed a sample to show to her drug contacts in Brisbane.

One night in the car park at the back of the Salvation Army store in Gladstone, Beth gave Kim a small bag of grass marked 'hydro'. Kim claims: 'Beth said that she had something out the back for me, a special present, so I went out the back of the store and she gave me the grass in a sandwich bag.' Kim promptly handed the bag of dope over to the police and they tested the sample, and confirmed it was cannabis. Tony Lewis's days of cultivating crops of pot next door to Mick Corby were about to come to an abrupt end.

It was 9 September 2004, four weeks before Schapelle Corby's arrest in Bali, and Tony Lewis was about to have a very bad day. Mick Corby was in Bali and Tony was home on the farm by himself. It had been a relaxing morning, hanging about on the verandah, thinking about lighting up a joint. Then, at about 10 o'clock, Lewis heard the sound of a car gunning it down the driveway towards his house: 'I was sitting on the verandah, in me jocks actually, and I ran in to grab a pair of shorts to put on, and by the time I got back out the police were here.'

The police cars and quad bikes raced across the cattle grid at the front gate so fast they were temporarily airborne—their engines whined before their tyres bit back into the dirt road. Tony recalls: 'I was worried about 'em running over me dogs.'

Lewis knew he was gone. It was too late to hide the marijuana in the shed—all he could do was stand there in his underpants and wait for the cops to pull up outside his house. He says he was thinking: 'This is it, I'm busted.'

It didn't take the cops long to find the marijuana plants inside a shed at the back of the property. The shed's walls were lined with corrugated iron to hide the plants from view. 'The police say I had over a hundred. I reckon there would've been a hundred there, but probably only half of them would have lived. I probably would have had thirty or forty plants,' says Tony, trying to downplay the seriousness of the raid's haul.

For the record, there were a total of 197 plants. The police photographic evidence shows that some were three to four feet high, and thick with leaves and buds. The photos also bear witness to a man with such a profound proclivity for hoarding marijuana that, even in the privacy of his own home, he was balancing a fine line between drug user and drug supplier. Small plastic clip-seal bags containing green heads lay open on the bedside table; kief was scattered on the coffee table, sprinkled in the sink, even stored in the glove box of his car. As the cops ploughed through the property searching for more evidence, they hit their heads on small wooden boxes hanging from the washing line. These boxes were germinating marijuana seeds. It seemed that wherever Tony Lewis went, a trail of Mary J followed.

For a man whose housekeeping skills were somewhat haphazard, Lewis was meticulous when it came to labelling his stash. Adhesive labels on small plastic bags were initialled 'HD'. When Lewis was later asked what 'HD' meant he said, 'That doesn't mean hydro!' When he was asked about the label 'TB' he said, 'I can't remember what that meant.' Some of the sample bags were given more nostalgic labels like, 'Tony long time'.

In the deep-freezer, under a layer of cryovacced meat, was cryovacced marijuana looking forward to an early release, tightly straining against its plastic jail. Most showy of all were the 197 cannabis plants, at various stages of maturity, daringly blooming in the pig shed. Lewis had nurtured these plants from aspiring buds, but now he could almost feel his soul cracking as the police pried and pulled and exposed and condemned his meticulously executed handiwork.

Tony Lewis was quick to tell the cops that he only grew and stored the plants for his own personal use. He was at pains to stress that it was not a hydroponic set-up. His story was that the plants were grown in sunlight inside the shed, and not with lights. He elaborates: 'I had some pots growing in the chicken coop, and I mixed pig shit and a bit of chicken poo in it with a bit of dirt and that's how I grew it. There was no hydroponic set-up on this farm.' He wanted it to sound like a hokey amateur hobby, not a professional operation. 'You won't get as stoned on the stuff I grew as you do on that hydroponic,' says the pot connoisseur and cultivator. In fact, he claims to prefer his home-grown outdoor hooter. 'Hydro is whack and bang. Yeah, different sort of stuff apparently,' Lewis explains to anyone who will listen, trying not to appear too much of an expert.

However, Tony Lewis did admit to growing seedlings inside a small cabinet with fans and a light, which he proudly showed to *The Hidden Truth* documentary film crew: 'This is the little cupboard I had with the light in—just to start the seedlings for me veggies. And I did have some cuttings of marijuana in there, at the time, when the police came, yes.' The police also found that Lewis had illegally diverted electricity from the power lines running down Rodd's Bay Road into his farm. The illegal power cable stopped him running up big power bills, which is the most common way that marijuana growers are caught.

The power line could have been used to grow a large hydroponic marijuana crop, but Tony Lewis claimed: 'None of them were hydroponic. They were grown in pots and the lights were going there just to get 'em going a little bit earlier 'cos of the seasons.' As well, the police found jars of cash and coins, a mess of water pipes, electrical cables and plastic bags all around the farm. Although he would later claim he was just innocently stockpiling the pot for his own use, Lewis was relieved when police failed to uncover the seven rifles he had hidden away in the house.

But what the police did find was three and a half kilos of marijuana in a freezer, stored inside vacuum-sealed plastic bags. Marijuana suppliers usually seal cannabis inside vacuum-sealed plastic to reduce the size of the bags and lock in the smell. Tony Lewis claimed that the marijuana was not sealed inside plastic bags for trafficking, but only for storage. He said: 'I have my little machine. I put it all in the bag and I do me veggies and everything else like this, and me meat. And you just put it in this bag and it sucks all the air out and the bag halves in size and there's no air in it. And it just about lasts forever.' He also claimed he needed a vacuum sealing cryovac machine to reduce the size of the grass: 'Because we've got ultra lights flying over here all the time, someone's going to see something. So, if I can get a stockpile and put it in the fridge, no one's going to see nothing.'

After the successful bust, Queensland Police issued a media release. Tony Lewis wasn't named in the release, so his connection to Mick Corby would go undetected until well after Schapelle's trial in 2005. However, the police photographs of his much-loved hooter were splashed across the front page of the local paper under the headline '$600,000 bust'. Lewis was charged with producing a dangerous drug, possessing a dangerous drug, supplying a dangerous drug, possessing equipment used in connection with producing a dangerous drug, and stealing electricity. The hapless Beth Lavender was also charged with producing and supplying cannabis.

But police informer Kim Moore wasn't finished raining on Tony Lewis's parade just yet—she had one more shock in store. One week after the bust at Tony's place and just three weeks before Schapelle's arrest in Bali, Kim made another statement to Miriam Vale police. She told them that people close to Tony Lewis had been taking drugs to Bali. The police officer on duty typed her statement up under the heading, 'Queensland Police Crime Intelligence Report'.

Kim claimed amphetamines and cannabis—wrapped in heavy, waterproof tar paper to avoid detection by x-ray machines, and hidden inside a bag with a false bottom— were being taken to Bali on commercial passenger flights. These flights to Denpasar were purported to depart on Mondays. In her police statement, Kim claimed that two of the drug couriers were from the Gold Coast. She said the couriers sometimes used false passports to avoid attracting the attention of Customs and the Australian Federal Police. One of the men named in her statement cannot be identified for legal reasons, but the other involved in the operation was named 'Michael'. Years later, Kim elaborated on her allegations: 'I recall on at least one occasion whereby Tony, Mick, Beth and myself were at Tony's. Tony and Mick were discussing moving cannabis to Indonesia. Tony said he had a relative who was a baggage handler at Sydney airport. Tony and Mick discussed going to Bali on certain days so that Customs in Bali would let them go through. I also heard Tony and Mick discussing a prior event, whereby cannabis had been smuggled into Bali. They were talking about how lucky they had been because the guards in Bali had changed an hour before the cannabis arrived in Bali.'

Despite the explosive allegations contained in Kim's police statement, made several weeks before Schapelle was arrested in Bali for drug trafficking, and the indisputable fact that Kim Moore had proven herself to be a reliable informer by correctly tipping off police about Lewis's marijuana culti- vation, her allegations about drugs being couriered to Bali were supposedly never followed up.

For years, Kim's statement remained buried under paper- work at head office, along with thousands of other crime intelligence reports detailing the lives of dodgy and desperate

Queenslanders rolling the dice on commercial drug operations. But the time bomb was ticking.

Although no one knew it back then, the raid on Tony Lewis's farm would become an invisible but ever-tightening noose around Mick Corby's neck.

PART TWO

Come and Party

CHAPTER 10

The Invitation

'Mercedes is always clean. She is Miss Clean all the time.'
—Vasu Rasiah, Schapelle's former
defence co-ordinator

A bright yellow sun with a smiling face announced Mercedes Corby's 30th birthday bash in Bali. The exclusive invitation promised good times, plenty of sun and fun at the beach. 'Come and party, Mercedes 30th birthday: Bring bikini and boardies for swim and spa.' For a woman who'd spent much of her life on the beaches of the Gold Coast and Bali, the image of the sun god from a tarot card seemed the perfect choice, symbolising optimism, happiness and success. The sun god on Mercedes' birthday invitation also sported sunglasses and a moustache, a cheeky reminder not to take life too seriously.

Mercedes was looking forward to the future, but unfortunately things were not going so well for her younger sister. Prior to their father's diagnosis with prostate cancer, Schapelle had been enrolled in a nine-month beauty course at the Gold Coast Institute of TAFE's Ashmore campus. She was on her way to earning a beauty therapy diploma when she suddenly pulled out of the course after failing to attend classes. She later claimed, during her trial in Bali, that the pressure of looking after her 'dying father' was too much and left her no choice but to pull out from the rigours of beauty school.

A former friend of Schapelle's, who completed the beauty course and then worked at the Phoenician Spa Retreat at Broadbeach, recalled that: 'What most people wouldn't know is that for a long time she had been diagnosed with serious depression and she'd been taking medication to deal with the condition.' When Schapelle decided to try living without her medication 'she was feeling happy with her life—she had good friends around her and she was enjoying the beauty course, so she felt confident she could take the next step of coming off it'.

This fellow student said that Schapelle battled on for as long as she could, but without medication her bad days grew more common and she later suffered a serious breakdown: 'Her father's health was a big concern and she became more and more down. That's when she started missing classes and failed to finish the course.' She remembered Schapelle telling her that she didn't want to have to rely on medication but, after spiralling into a crisis, she realised it was the only option.

Schapelle's older brother Michael Corby told the *Sun-Herald* newspaper in Sydney that, while he had no personal knowledge of his sister's depression, it was 'unlikely' that she would have told him or her father: 'I think that, if she was going to tell anyone about that kind of stuff, it would have been her girlfriends.' The former TAFE girlfriend didn't want to be negative about Schapelle, or look like she was dumping on her: 'Schapelle is one of the loveliest, happiest, most genuine people you could ever hope to meet.' After dropping out of the beauty course, Schapelle began receiving a government subsidised carer allowance for looking after her father and apparently 'also started working part-time at Rox's Seafood Takeaway, her brother Michael's family business in Southport.

Young Michael's affectionate nickname is 'Splint' and he's a particularly popular guy, both with women and on the local Gold Coast surf scene. With his bleached blond hair and big smile, he adheres to the cool-surfie dress code of torn T-shirts and beanies; his wicked sense of humour has always made him a family favourite. Although he was once a surf life-saver at Tugun, Splint's work history is pretty patchy. He isn't embarrassed to tell anyone who asks that his main goal in life is to avoid being stressed so, instead of working, he prefers to chill out with surfer mates like the legendary surfboard shaper Skye Bourton and best mate Grant Ford.

So it was completely out of character when, in late 2003, after ten years of endless surfing and living a fun and happy-go-lucky life, the laid-back Michael bought himself a business. Splint's shop at 153 Scarborough Street, Southport, was a basic fish and chip shop selling Chiko rolls, crab sticks, fisherman's baskets and anything else you could possibly deep fry. By all accounts Schapelle hated working there, and one suspects that Michael did too. He was new to the small business scene and had owned the shop for only sixteen months before Schapelle's arrest.

One of his ex-girlfriends said he once had a job as a part-time life guard, and that he 'didn't own much'. When asked what else he had done between leaving high school and buying the shop nine years later, at age 27, she said she 'wasn't sure'. Somehow, without ever holding down a full-time job for any substantial length of time, he had managed to buy his own business. But in reality it was his mother Ros who did most of the hard work keeping the fridges stocked and the floors clean; there was never any doubt in Splint's mind that his mum ruled the roost.

Mother and son shared an easy joking banter behind the counter, interspersed with Ros goading him, in her shrill voice on high volume, to work harder. Splint took Ros's bossy antics in his stride because, quite simply, he idolised her. A large framed black-and-white photograph of Ros dominates one wall in her Tugun house. This airbrushed version of Ros is the product of a particularly flattering glamour photography session. It's an image of Ros as she sees herself—a magnificent lioness looking after her pride.

Michael's former girlfriend, Hamita, says that after Schapelle dropped out of TAFE the two young women spent most of their days watching daytime TV soaps like *The Bold and the Beautiful* at the Tugun house. 'We would just sit and stare out the window together, smoking cigarettes and drinking beer,' Hamita recalls. 'During what was to be her last month of freedom, Schapelle was broke, depressed and single. At this time things were hotting up on the Gold Coast, with the annual Indy 300 car race just weeks away and tourists starting to arrive in droves for the peak summer season. Schoolies Week was also coming up on the calendar— a time when high school leavers flock to Surfers Paradise for an end-of-year drinking binge. As tourists were pouring into the Gold Coast, Schapelle was keen to get out of town and head over to Bali for Mercedes's birthday party.'

Financially, things weren't going well. She claimed during

her trial that she needed a holiday before her father's cancer treatment got too onerous and that she had saved up $1300. But this still wasn't enough money to pay for the trip to Bali. Therefore, Ros gave her $500 and Mick gave her another $600 so she could travel to Bali for a beach holiday and the big birthday bash.

Schapelle had a very close relationship with her father and, according to her good friend and travelling companion Ally McComb, she was closest to him out of all the kids. Mick had previously bought her a second-hand car and Tony Lewis later said: 'Schapelle was always hitting her dad up for loans, but it didn't bother him because he had plenty of money. She was always biting him for some money. Schapelle wouldn't have had enough money to buy those drugs.'

The only fun Schapelle had on her horizon was Mercedes's upcoming party. She was determined to take some friends with her, to go nightclubbing and hang out at the beach and, despite her limited budget, she planned to stay in Bali for a few weeks and was booked to spend some of that time at the Grand Istana Rama beach resort in Kuta.

Although Mercedes never elaborated to the press just how big her party was intended to be, it's abundantly clear that it was far more than an intimate gathering of close family and friends. Sources in Bali say the party was to be held poolside at a rented luxurious villa, and would feature dance music from fashionable local disc jockey and bodyboarder DJ Suwenda, who had been booked to keep the party pumping. Son of the late legendary Balinese surfer I Wayan Suwenda, who was the licence-holder of Billabong Indonesia from 1990, DJ Daniel Suwenda is a regular fixture on the Bali nightclub and surf party scene. According to his Facebook page, 'DJ Suwenda takes pride in the fact that he only works the "big parties"' and, when contacted for this book, he confirmed he 'doesn't do cheap gigs'.

Eighteen-year-old Katrina Richards claims she didn't know Mercedes very well and in fact had only known Schapelle for a couple of years, but somehow she scored a place on the ever-expanding guest list. She was studying to become a kindergarten teacher and had met Schapelle while they were both working part-time at Rox's. Shy and softly spoken, Katrina had never travelled overseas. She told the documentary crew that Schapelle had urged her to go on the trip: 'She's like asking me and it's like I don't want to go to Bali, and she geed me up. I'm a little bit nervous—I had never been on a plane before.'

Katrina had a strained relationship with her parents but, while working at Rox's, she had grown close to Ros, who treated her like an unofficial member of the family. Ros encouraged Katrina to spread her wings and make Bali her first overseas adventure. Yet, while Katrina was comfortable around Ros and was a big fan of Splint, she was less sure of Schapelle. 'I found her to be lazy, and she was always hungover and didn't pull her weight in the shop,' she reluctantly admitted to the film-makers.

Schapelle also encouraged another friend to join the group on the Bali holiday. Twenty-five-year-old Alyth McComb had known Schapelle for about four years. In the beginning she had apparently been intimidated by Schapelle's beauty: 'Like, when I first met her, I was a bit—wow, she seems a bit stuck up, just because she's so good-looking and that sort of thing.' But they had subsequently shared an apartment together and become close friends. Confident and outgoing, Ally was an experienced backpacker and popular barmaid at the Mermaid Beach Tavern on the Gold Coast. She claims she first bonded with Schapelle over their mutual love of boogie boarding, saying: 'Oh, probably two or three times a week we'd go surfing and sunbaking.'

The airline tickets for the trip were booked at the Coolangatta Flight Centre. Ally remembers: 'We were always planning to go on the trip. Schapelle sort of organised it, though, when I was down south. So when I got back from that, I basically just picked up the tickets and then left.' She claims not to have known any details about Mercedes's party until two weeks before leaving, adding that her main priority for wanting to go to Bali was simply for a surfing holiday. Schapelle later claimed that there were continual delays in booking these airline tickets. She said she'd been unable to book a direct flight from Brisbane to Bali because so many Australians were heading there for the second anniversary of the devastating bombings outside the Sari nightclub and Paddy's Bar in Kuta in October 2002. According to Schapelle the direct flights from Brisbane were jam-packed, so the group had to fly via Sydney.

The three young women were also joined on the trip by Schapelle's seventeen-year-old half-brother James Kisina, who was still attending high school and living at the Loganlea family home with his younger sister Mele, Ros and her partner, Greg.

Apparently James, who had inherited his father's powerful, dark Pacific Islander looks, had always been quite a handful as a child. From the age of three he often 'rocked his cot back and forth' every night, inwardly distressed by something his mother could never identify. Ros was proud of the fact that James had once been a high school captain, but these days his main priority was to mould his big powerful body by lifting weights. Like many kids his age he was obsessed with rap and hip-hop, and had dreams of writing his own music; but Ros was worried that he was 'too quiet and wouldn't open up'. James mostly kept to himself downstairs at the Loganlea family home, in the undercroft space that had been partly converted into a bedroom.

Loganlea was James's uninspiring playground. It's a seedy area with a high crime rate; within its public housing areas there are high levels of family breakdown, unemployment, drug addiction and welfare dependency. While it's pretty common for Loganlea kids to get into trouble, James apparently wasn't on the police radar back then, but that would soon change after Schapelle's arrest. James was close to his half-sisters and brothers and had an easygoing relationship with Mick Corby. He often spent school holidays at Mick's farm in Iveragh or at the Tugun retreat, from which all of Ros's children would come and go.

James had been to Bali once before—in 1999, for Mercedes and Wayan's wedding celebrations—but the sullen teenager hadn't expected to be attending Mercedes's 30th birthday until his mother suddenly paid for his ticket just three days before the group were due to depart Brisbane. Ros told the film crew: 'He wasn't even going—it was like a surprise for him. Because I couldn't afford it, but then Qantas had a student, cheap fare.' The lateness of his booking resulted in him being scheduled to travel on a different domestic flight from Brisbane to Sydney than Schapelle and the girls. His flight was scheduled to depart one hour later and this meant that he would have to meet up with the rest of the group at Sydney Airport before they boarded the Australian Airlines flight to Bali.

Meanwhile, young Michael was leaving the fish and chip shop in Ros's capable hands. He was also heading to Bali for the upcoming celebrations but, unlike the others, he was travelling there the long way round—via Perth. Due to arrive in Bali two hours ahead of Schapelle's group, Michael said he went to Perth to visit his then girlfriend, Hamita's, parents before travelling to Bali.

While the Corbys were fine-tuning plans for their respective trips to Bali, back in Adelaide, Malcolm McCauley was working against the clock to meet Mick Corby's strict deadline for a shipment. Five days prior to Schapelle's ill-fated flight to Bali, McCauley was in preparation mode for what should have been another routine drug run to Queensland.

CHAPTER 11

The Boogie Board
Came Late

*'Never touched that bag! Never seen it! Never had nothin' to do
with the bloody bag!'*
> —Mick Corby

In Bali, rumours were buzzing in certain circles within the
close-knit expat community that a shipment of 'high grade
skunk' was shortly about to arrive on board a commercial
flight from Australia. Those in the know were looking forward
to the arrival of the 'Aussie Gold', as it was code-named by
those who had previously enjoyed its lofty pleasures.

Meanwhile back in Adelaide, despite having some
growing reservations, Malcolm McCauley had no choice but
to engage the unpredictable Granny Eastwood as courier for
the valuable hydro's road trip from Adelaide to the Gold
Coast. Her vehicle had received the once-over and the marijuana had been sourced well ahead of schedule, but there
remained one outstanding issue—McCauley was all out of
suitcases.

'In the beginning, I was buying brand-new suitcases,' he recalls. 'But it soon became clear that was a complete waste of time and money. They were an important part of the job, essential for deliveries. Trouble was, you never got the bloody things back. I mean, seriously, can you imagine asking for the case back at a drop? "Do us a favour, mate—empty the hooter into your boot, will ya, because the suitcase happens to belong to me."' He laughs, then adds: 'I don't think so.'

McCauley later came to the realisation that old suitcases never actually die. According to him, they are laid to rest in a variety of different places, where they hope and wait for someone to offer them one last journey somewhere: 'After I decided I wasn't going to buy new ones any more, I went rummaging around the local tip. They were there all right, but that was bleeding messy and I figured there had to be better places to pick 'em up. Second-hand shops and garage sales were always good. Loads there. But the best place by far is the side of the road, especially around clean-up time. Have a look next time—there are always hundreds of them in various shapes and sizes. Most of them battered and bruised, but that never mattered. In my line of work, the last thing on anyone's mind was a tatty suitcase.'

McCauley headed into town and, sure enough, he found two matching vintage numbers in a second-hand store. Once that chore was over, he returned home to prepare everything for Eastwood's departure. It was a painstaking process, but he'd done it so many times he could finish the job with his eyes closed: 'I always started in the kitchen. The hooter would be spread across the table. I'd grab a bag and throw in what I thought was a pound or thereabouts. I then weighed it on the scales. A few buds in, a few buds out, until I'd got it exactly spot on. I then tied the bag off and slipped it into a heat seal that would suck all the air out. Occasionally, you'd find a sharp stem or twig had punctured through one of the bags. If that happened, I'd have to push the stem back down, then place that bag into another bag and seal it again.'

At that point, one might have expected McCauley's job to be finished, but he wasn't even halfway there. Next, it was down the corridor and into the bathroom for stage two: 'I'd throw all the sealed bags into the bath. Then I sprayed them with household air freshener—whatever might be lying around in the cupboard at the time. They were then wiped down individually, so any lingering smell on the outside of the bag was well and truly removed. Fingerprints too. At that point, I'd place them in the suitcase. It was always ten pounds to a case. By the time I'd finished, it looked the part. And that was my work done. Away you go! The next person to touch the bags was always the recipient. Hopefully never the cops.'

On this particular occasion Brenda Eastwood had agreed to do a double run, involving drop-offs to both Mick Corby on the Gold Coast and Wayne Williams at Charters Towers in Northern Queensland. From a financial perspective, it made perfect sense for McCauley to complete two deals within the one journey. He might have to throw the driver an extra $500 but, in turn, he could halve his fuel costs and all other general travel expenses, including accommodation. The problem with that was that he'd never met a courier with the bottle, stamina or desire to complete such mammoth runs—until Granny Eastwood came along. 'I don't know how she would do it,' he says. 'She could do the Gold Coast, Charters Towers and back to Adelaide, and exist on the occasional half-hour's sleep by the side of the road. Her fee always included money for a motel but, if she'd had a bad week on the pokies, I'm sure she probably pocketed it.'

Once leaving Adelaide, Granny Eastwood generally liked to take the Barrier Highway, which would take her through outback towns like Broken Hill, Wilcannia and Cobar in New South Wales, then across into Queensland and onto the Warrego Highway, a fully sealed stretch of highway taking her through to Charleville and across to Roma. She could then easily continue east, if she was heading to the Gold Coast, or north if she had to complete the extra kilometres up to Charters Towers. Either way, it was a gruelling drive. She had hit a kangaroo on one journey and blown a tyre on another. Anything can happen on an outback country road that you share with animals and trucks and black bitumen that stretches forever, but that mattered little to Eastwood. 'Nothing seemed to faze her,' says McCauley.

On this particular journey, Granny Eastwood would be taking two suitcases—one for Mick Corby and one for Wayne Williams. Both contained ten pounds of marijuana. She would be expected to return with $60,000 for the pair of suitcases and there was no reason to believe she wouldn't. So, shortly before lunchtime on 6 October 2004, McCauley directed Eastwood out of his driveway, wished her well and then waved her goodbye. He watched her head down the road, indicate right and then disappear out of view. 'That's taken care of,' thought McCauley as he headed back indoors and straight to the fridge. 'She's as good as there.'

Eastwood's brief had been to head straight to the Gold Coast and drop Mick's marijuana off by early afternoon the following day. She was then expected to call McCauley and let him know the first leg of the journey had passed without incident. McCauley did receive a phone call the following day—but not from her. It was from Mick Corby, and he was beside himself. McCauley remembers: 'He rings up and he's screaming: "What the fuck is going on? Where's your fucking taxi driver?! I've got to fucking do this, and this is now fucked up because of that." I said: "Whoooa! Calm down, Mick! What's happened?"'

McCauley's unofficial job description had always been to source the best grass, pack it in the exact same way he always had, and then transport it to Mick, or to Wayne, or whoever had ordered a shipment, by a certain specified time. If Mick needed the marijuana for a flight to somewhere, then there was a very strict turnaround time. The deadline was in place because the product always needed to be repackaged at Mick's end and properly prepared before departure. What Mick did with the marijuana had never really been McCauley's concern. He knew about Bali, but he didn't give a rat's ass. And why would he? As long as the grass was the usual top quality and it arrived on time, he'd fulfilled his part of the bargain. 'On this particular day, it became my concern because my courier hadn't arrived on time,' he says.

When McCauley finally managed to get a word in with Mick, he attempted to reassure him that Eastwood could only be a matter of minutes away: 'You know she's never late, bro'—I'm sure she's not too far. Let me put a call in. Stay put, have a beer and I'll get straight back to you.'

'Make it fucking quick!' yelled Mick before hanging up.

The moment the line went dead, McCauley dialled Granny Eastwood's number several times. It rang out on each occasion. 'I couldn't bloody raise her,' he says, adding: 'I tried and tried, but nothing. I thought, "Where the fuck is she?" Because it had never happened before, I had to consider the possibility that maybe there'd been an accident. Or, worse still, she'd been nabbed by the cops.'

McCauley's heart sank when he considered that particular scenario. He wanted to keep calling, but then again, maybe it was best not to. If the cops had caught Eastwood, then they no doubt had her phone too. A barrage of missed calls was the last thing he needed the police to see.

When Mick Corby got back in touch, he was even more irate than before. 'He was banging on about the time. He was saying: "It's [the hooter] got to leave here at this time today because it's flying out from Brisbane in the morning. You've fucked up everything."'

McCauley had to be honest and upfront: 'Can't raise her, Mick. It's a mystery. She'll be coming round the mountain when she comes. Let's try and remain patient, for everyone's sake, eh?' McCauley didn't need to raise the possibility that the police might have intercepted Eastwood because he knew, instinctively, that Mick had already contemplated it: 'It went on and on. I paced around the house and sank a few coldies. It was the longest wait.'

It would later transpire that Granny Eastwood had not been arrested, nor had she been involved in a car accident. She had in fact pulled over somewhere on the highway for a nap and then, somehow, passed out for most of the afternoon: 'When I got hold of her, several hours later, she was like, "I missed a couple of calls. Sorry, must have gone to sleep for a while."'

When asked how far she was from Corby's house at that particular point, McCauley replies: 'To be honest, I can't remember. But I wasn't really interested—it was a massive fuck-up. When a guy says this day at this time, he means he wants it there and then—bang. Did I read her the riot act?

Absolutely. Did I stay mad with her forever? No. It wasn't laziness on her behalf. The journey's a fucking long one. Under normal circumstances, what would it have mattered? Hooter arrives a few hours late, people wait.' Then, gesturing with his hands as though they were an aeroplane flying upwards, he adds, 'But when the hooter is leaving the country, there are flights to catch, a plan in place, a very strict plan.'

Did Granny Eastwood know where the hooter was going after it had arrived at Mick's? 'No way—it wasn't any of her business,' replied McCauley, adding, 'She was just a driver. Her job was to drop it on time, pick the money up and come straight home.'

McCauley says that while he was thankful the marijuana eventually arrived at its destination, he was only too aware of the drama it had caused and the repercussions it had on Mick's plans: 'Mick had been running around like a headless chook because the whole system was out. I know this because I bloody well spoke to him. The whole system was out.'

McCauley had been privy to dozens of dope drop-offs in his time and, in his own words, it never ceased to amaze him how nervous people became in the build-up, regardless of how many times they'd done it before: 'Your guts are going. You're sitting there waiting for the delivery. In Mick's case that day, he's thinking when it does get here, I've got to repack it because it's going somewhere else . . . But I can't hurry the driver up by telling them this.' He adds: 'Everyone's sitting around waiting and waiting. You're meanwhile thinking when it does arrive, am I going to pack it in here? No, I'll pack it out there. But it's still not here. Then you start panicking . . . and when three o'clock becomes five o'clock and still nothing, you're not panicking any more. You're ropable.'

McCauley said that, even with a tight deadline, Mick would never have dared pack the ten heat-sealed bags he'd received as they were. It would have been sloppy; it would have been suicide. 'And he didn't. He had to take a Stanley knife to the lot, fluff it back up to its original state, then re-do it all—something which should have happened four or five hours before. He then had to go through the whole process of spreading the hooter out into a bigger bag—which looks a lot like a suit bag until it's had the air sucked out of it in the heat seal. He had to make sure there were no leaks. It also had to resemble the boogie board bag in shape. That's not a half-hour job, I can tell you.'

McCauley says he also now realises there was the added issue of 'those going for an innocent holiday and those who knew there was a bit of business taking place'. 'The shit had hit the fan and yet none of it could be discussed out in the open, because them other girls had no idea. You telling me that wouldn't have been adding to the stress levels? Them girls that were travelling with Schapelle, they would have sensed something was wrong from the very start. If you were to get one of those sheilas to talk honestly, you'd find out what the true mood was that evening. Euphoric would not have come into it.'

Mick Corby claimed in several television interviews that, on the night before Schapelle's flight to Bali, he had had to fix her boogie board bag: 'There was a strip missin' off the boogie board thing, and it was just a little plastic strip, so we stuck that on. We stuck it in the bag. I put it in the car.'

Schapelle claims that she'd been an enthusiastic boogie board rider for years. Although Mercedes had progressed over the years with her surfing skills, right up to becoming a competitive surfboard rider, her little sister preferred to stick with her childhood boogie board. One of Ros's favorite photographs is of a young, carefree Schapelle posing in a tight wetsuit with her now-notorious bright yellow boogie board and flippers.

But, contrary to this story, her brother Michael once admitted in an interview that 'Schapelle doesn't really boogie board too much here [Gold Coast] but, well, 'cos of work, she doesn't have the time. But over there [Bali], well obviously you would.' At Bali's popular Kuta Beach, a boogie board costs less than five Australian dollars a day to hire. Despite the hassle of carrying extra baggage and the abundant avail-ability of boards for rent in Bali, Schapelle curiously decided to take her own boogie board on the trip.

The Corbys' version of events surrounding the board is that, after Mick fixed the boogie board at home in Tugun, Schapelle then left to go and stay overnight with Ros at the family home in Loganlea because that house is closer to Brisbane Airport. Their Sydney-bound flight was scheduled to leave at 6.05 am the next morning so, given the early start, travelling buddies Katrina and Ally had also arranged to stay overnight with Ros.

The night before the flight, Schapelle says she picked up Katrina on the way to Ros's house. Katrina later said that she was squashed against the boogie board in the back of the car. She said, 'Her car's only a small car, and it was fully packed. I was leaning on the bag so, if it was in there, you would have been able to smell it, for sure. But nothing.'

The four young travellers all have an identical story about what happened the next morning. They got up at 4 am, met in the garage and started packing their bags into Ros's van.

Katrina was feeling nervous about her first overseas flight and decided to put a lock on her bag. Schapelle actually mocked the first-time traveller for doing this. Ally had packed a small bag and planned to buy a few cheap clothes in Bali: 'I, um, sort of packed really light because I knew that I would buy stuff over there.'

Katrina and Ally both noticed the large size of Schapelle's bag. Ally told the documentary crew: 'She had this big, black suitcase thing. Like, it was like a . . . it was huge and her boogie board and her like airplane bag too. So I was like "Okay, you've got a lot of stuff!" I think she was taking stuff over for Mercedes though, like vitamins and stuff. Her dad gave her heaps of stuff to give to Mercedes.'

The group was leaving Brisbane on a Qantas Airways domestic flight to Sydney, to connect with their Australian Airlines international flight to Bali. Despite the hassle of having to transfer from the domestic to the international terminal, Schapelle and her friends only needed to check in their luggage once—at the Brisbane domestic terminal. When they arrived in Sydney the bags would automatically be transferred to their connecting international flight.

Alyth McComb recalls that everyone was worried they were going to miss the flight to Sydney: 'We were all in a rush to get there, 'cos we were running late.' The boogie board and suitcases were hurriedly packed into Ros's van and she drove them to the airport in the silent pre-dawn darkness.

In 2006, two years after Schapelle's arrest, James was interviewed by the documentary film crew. Nervous and mumbling incoherently, he stumbled over the details of what happened the night before the group departed for Bali. His version of events resonates with Malcolm McCauley's claim that Granny Eastwood had run late with her cannabis delivery to Mick Corby: 'We just packed our bags. I packed mine that night and, um, I dunno where the . . . I can't remember where their bags were. We put them in, 'cos I think the boogie board came late.'

CHAPTER 12

Drunk and Disorderly

'Schapelle said she got really drunk on the plane . . . she never gets drunk.'
—Ron Bakir, former Schapelle supporter

Rosleigh Rose has always been her family's unofficial photographer. Wherever she went her little camera went with her and no family event was ever deemed too boring to document. So it wasn't particularly unusual that Ros took a happy snap of Schapelle and her three travelling companions at Brisbane Airport before they boarded QF501 bound for Sydney. These days, looking at that photo can easily bring Ros to tears. She had unconsciously captured a scene that literally froze her daughter's last moment of freedom in Australia.

In the photograph, Katrina, Ally, Schapelle and half-brother James are bunched together outside the domestic terminal just minutes before they boarded their flight. Schapelle looks glamorous, showing plenty of cleavage, her dark hair draped across her shoulders falling across a summery, light white blouse. She has a deep tan and stands confidently with her right shoulder forward, making room for Katrina, who has a cheeky smile, to squeeze in. Ally has her arm dangled around James and looks the happiest of the four, like she's laughing at a joke. James almost manages a smile, but he is looking away from the camera, momentarily distracted.

On the back of the photograph, Ros wrote: '8th Oct. All happy go to Bali.' The photograph was later handed out to the media as proof that Schapelle and the others were all feeling relaxed as they set off on their tropical holiday. The photo of smiling Schapelle was not the face of a stressed-out drug trafficker.

Originally James was scheduled to take a different flight, which would have been annoying because he'd have had to find the other three travellers at Sydney Airport. However, after some last-minute special pleading at the airport by Ros, James luckily scored a seat on the same flight as Schapelle and the girls.

Ally's memory is that James carried the boogie board to the check-in counter at Brisbane Airport: 'Me and Schapelle and Katrina all checked in at the same time. James went to a different counter and put the boogie board up there to go through first and they're like, oh no, that goes in a different section—that goes over to oversize baggage.'

But apparently James didn't carry the boogie board across to the oversize baggage counter—Schapelle did. During her trial in Bali in 2005, Schapelle said: 'We all walked together from the check-in counter to the conveyor, the oversize conveyor. I put it in—everyone saw me put it in.' Katrina also remembers Schapelle checking in the boogie board: 'Schapelle actually put her bag through the oversize counter—it just looked like a normal boogie board bag. How it would normally—no marijuana in it.'

Not long after 6 am the group was finally up in the air,

beginning their holiday adventure on the ninety minute flight to Sydney. Once they arrived there, they found their way to the international terminal, where they had a couple of hours to kill in the transit lounge. Schapelle had a few beers in the airport bar with her good friend, Jodie Power, who was booked on a later flight to Bali. Jodie later claimed that, while they were having a drink and a smoke, Schapelle kept pointing at the security cameras, saying 'There's one and there's one over there' and that the ill-fated traveller's last words to her in the bar were, 'We'll see you round the pool.' But it didn't quite happen the way they had planned.

Australian Airlines flight AO7829, scheduled for departure from Sydney at 10.30 am, was full with the usual Bali crowd—mostly tourists with a mix of business people, surfers and a few expats heading back to their low-cost, exotic lifestyles. Schapelle and Ally then helped themselves to more drinks on the flight. While most people were having a morning coffee, it seems Schapelle drank solidly from Sydney all the way to Bali. She later wrote in her book *My Story*: 'Feeling tipsy, I think we spent most of the flight laughing at nothing . . . I was well into the holiday spirit.' A photo taken by Katrina on the flight shows the girls laughing and holding up their cans of beer.

The group may have thought they were discreetly having fun, but Schapelle's heavy drinking hadn't gone unnoticed by others on the plane. After her arrest in Bali, a person claiming to be a flight attendant on flight AO7829 posted this blog on the internet:

Those Crocodile tears. Seen 'em from Schapelle before. She was a total bitch on the flight to Denpasar—even jumping up on descent and demanding another beer—her ninth for the trip: 'If I wanted fucking water you would give it to me! Why not another beer?' Then the tears. She almost had to be physically taken back to her seat. We [the cabin crew] cheered about 3 hours after hearing about the arrest. And yes . . . I have considered all along she could be really guilty. Just got caught this time after having paid off officials in the past.

Gail Burgess was senior cabin purser that day, overseeing the flight attendants who served Schapelle's group on the flight. While Schapelle insists she couldn't have been more relaxed on the plane, Ms Burgess recalls a different story. In an interview for this book, she said the blog was 'completely genuine' and confirmed Schapelle had been at the centre of a 'major drama'.

'As the cabin manager in charge that day,' she recalls, 'I was mainly working towards the front of the plane, so didn't really know what was going down until the passengers had all stepped off and all the crew were talking about it. I was briefed about a woman that was heavily intoxicated and creating a scene around her area. Consequently, the attendants were forced to cut off her alcohol.

'As a flight attendant, you have to consider the fact that the Bali run is a mixed bag in terms of customers. You have business travellers, holidaymakers and your fair share of Bali locals also. For that reason it's essential that everyone is as comfortable as they can be—in what is basically a cocoon. She [Schapelle] was compromising all that. She was annoying people. The exact words used by staff were "angry", "tense" and "agitated", to the point where surrounding passengers kept on complaining that she was being too aggressive and loud.'

Ms Burgess said it was 'rare' to ban people from drinking, regardless of the route. 'How many times have you seen it occur onboard a plane? We're fair and open people. We like a drink ourselves. We don't cut alcohol off because people are enjoying themselves or speaking too loudly. It only happens when it's obvious to everyone that it needs to happen.'

While Ms Burgess said she was notified of the incident within minutes of the last passenger exiting, she was nevertheless 'upset' her staff had not alerted her at the time. 'I remember saying after we had got off, "You know the process . . . You should have let me know what was going on down the back."' The protocol is that the captain is also supposed to be informed—and he was angry that he hadn't been advised of the situation also. If someone gets violent, there are containment procedures. The handcuffs come out and then surrounding passengers also have to be moved. She hadn't reached that point, but if you have your alcohol cut off, then you are displaying behaviour that suggests this is a possibility.'

Ms Burgess said it wasn't until the following day that she learned the same woman had been the subject of a major incident inside the airport: 'We returned to the aircraft to prepare for a shuttle run to Singapore and straight back [to Bali]. It was then that I was informed a girl, from our flight the day before, had been reprimanded due to an illegality with her luggage—and that it was drugs. It then emerged it was the same girl who had been acting so strangely on the plane. They [the cabin crew] were saying, "Now it all makes sense." The captain and I had a chat and we were like "Jesus!" It kind of reinforced our earlier point that we should have been made aware of the situation as it was happening.'

Ms Burgess said that, to this day, nobody acting in any

official capacity had ever thought to interview either herself or her staff about the flight over: 'You have to say it was a bit of an oversight. Had they [the authorities] known what had occurred, it might have proved to be an important part of the jigsaw. She certainly wasn't your typical carefree, relaxed traveller heading off on a family holiday like she claimed. She was the opposite.'

The plane arrived in Bali from Sydney mid-afternoon local time. As Schapelle's group boarded the shuttle bus to travel across the tarmac to the airport terminal they were instantly hit by the stifling heat and humidity.

After the 2002 Bali bombings holidaymakers deserted the island in droves but now, two years on, the tourism buzz was back, with over four thousand daily arrivals recorded during October 2004. When Schapelle and her travelling buddies entered the airport terminal there were hundreds of people lining up at the immigration counters to get visas and also in the customs area to collect their luggage. It was now fourteen hours since the travellers had packed their bags in Ros's garage—everyone was feeling exhausted and Schapelle herself was almost certainly starting to feel the strain from her heavy drinking on the flight.

Indonesians will tell you there are bribes to be paid for almost everything in life—getting your identity card in reasonable time, passing your driving test, avoiding a parking ticket, even getting into the police force. The experts don't disagree that Indonesia has one of the worst corruption ratings in the world. After a decade of democracy—with a newly vibrant Anti-Corruption Commission and a president who has made tackling corruption one of his key pledges—unfortunately graft still remains hard-wired into the system.

Bali's Ngurah Rai International Airport is no exception

and foreign tourists are often asked to pay a 'fine' for almost anything—having too many bottles of wine or some other banned imported product. Sometimes customs officers will invent small fines and first-time travellers will get stung somewhere between $20–$50 for a 'fee'. Despite having a visible security presence at the airport, customs checks are particularly lax and not everyone's bags are inspected. As with how most things work in Bali, there are at least two levels of service.

Ordinary tourists wait in long queues to get their entry visas and passports stamped before entering the nightmare of long lines and crowding in the customs area. With corruption rife in Indonesia, however, there is an alternative for the well-heeled travellers staying at five-star luxury hotels—a special VIP service fee that ensures a quick and easy passage through all the processes and surrounding mayhem. Those travellers usually receive a 'meet and greet' service—a person who ushers them through the tedium and fuss of customs checks. Rarely, if ever, are their bags checked or scrutinised by customs officers.

When Mercedes Corby was later interviewed by journalist Sian Powell for the *Australian*, she claimed that no one in their right mind would dare smuggle cannabis into Bali. 'Usually stuff gets found inside surfboards with the glass resin over it,' she told Powell. 'You wouldn't even be able to sell the stuff; you'd be caught before you sold your first bag.' But during Schapelle's trial, it was common for television camera crews to arrange payments for fixers to ensure equipment would sail through customs without any checks. Yet, as we all know, pretty girls can get away with a lot at airports; on this particular day, Schapelle was dressed to impress and showing plenty of cleavage. Perhaps the plan had never been to use a fixer, but instead to use the happy travelling group as her 'protection'. They certainly blended right in.

There were no problems when Schapelle's group queued at the immigration counters to pay the arrival tax and get their holiday visas, nor when they lined up again to get their passports stamped. Next they all passed through the hand-luggage x-ray checkpoint and walked through to the main baggage collection area. It had been quite a while since their plane landed and the queues were now starting to thin out as passengers gradually left the airport.

At this point Schapelle was very close, but there was just one final hurdle remaining—the customs inspection desk. All that was left to do was to grab her boogie board, let the customs officers check her huge black suitcase and, if necessary, flash a flirtatious smile if she was asked to open the boogie board bag. But two years after the terrible 2002 Bali bombings, security measures had increased considerably at Ngurah Rai Airport. Now Schapelle Corby was playing Russian roulette with her life.

CHAPTER 13

Welcome to Bali

'I love my family, I love my dad. My dad lives with me. I wanted to take a holiday. I don't like drugs and I know there is a big penalty in Indonesia and all over the world if you have drugs.'
—Schapelle Corby

On the afternoon of 8 October 2004, customs officer I Gusti Nyoman Winata was on duty checking luggage from international flights arriving in Bali, including the Australian Airlines flight that Schapelle was aboard. I Gusti Winata was a twenty-year veteran on the job and a devout Hindu who was proud of the meticulous care he took with his work.

As the bags came up the conveyor belt and through the x-ray machine, something caught Winata's eye. He later told the documentary crew: 'I saw dots—brown reddish, I think. It was orange dots—the boogie board is not like usual. I must suspect something is wrong with the boogie board.' Winata decided to take a second look at the x-ray image of the boogie board, so he rewound the picture on the x-ray machine and pulled the snapshot image of the board back into view. The boogie board bag appeared to have something inside that looked like a door mat lying between the board and the flippers.

Winata then left the x-ray machine and walked into the baggage collection area. Placing the boogie board on the ground about three metres from the luggage carousel, he warned his fellow officers to be on the lookout for its owner. In his recorded interview, he says: 'I had a strong feeling, a conviction, that something is wrong.' He had decided not to put a chalk mark on the boogie board, to avoid alerting its owner.

When James walked into the baggage collection area with the girls, he was confused. He later said: 'We couldn't find the boogie board—that one took a while to find.' Ally's memory of events is that she saw Schapelle struggling with her heavy suitcase and the boogie board bag, so she asked James to carry the board bag: 'I was like, "Oh, James, do you want to help your sister with her bags." However, Winata says it was James who first picked up the boogie board: 'The male took the bag; the female took the luggage—they both walk to the counter. Because the male took the bag, I thought he was the owner of the bag.'

James and Schapelle both later said they didn't notice the extra four kilo weight of the bag when they picked it up. During Schapelle's trial she said, 'I'd never dreamed that there was anything else in my boogie board other than what I just packed, so it didn't enter my mind if it was heavier or not.'

To Winata, the young man with the dark skin carrying the boogie board fitted their target profile for drug couriers they had arrested many times before—from South America, Africa and India, Thailand, Malaysia and Hong Kong. Schapelle, in contrast, didn't look like a typical drug smuggler and, for a moment, Winata thought that he'd made a mistake about the boogie board being suspicious: 'She looks like a good person. I mean, normally drug traffickers like Africans look tough or their faces have tough features, but this one is pretty.'

Schapelle was wearing a light summer blouse and the customs officer on the desk, Komang Gelgel, was immediately struck by her enticing looks. In his interview for the documentary, Gelgel says: 'She didn't look nervous at all. She was wearing a tight top. She looked sexy, she looked beautiful; and the more we became very friendly, the more she became more and more friendly as well.' Gelgel confides that, if he had followed his own judgement about Schapelle, he probably would have let her go through the gate unchecked. But, unfortunately for Schapelle, the junior customs officer was ordered by his boss, I Gusti Winata, to take a closer look at the boogie board bag when it came to the customs inspection desk.

Schapelle and James headed straight to the green channel at the customs inspection area, indicating that they had nothing to declare. When James was about to place the boogie board on the customs desk for inspection, the officer asked Schapelle and James who owned it. Schapelle said it was hers. Winata recalls, 'James was going to hand it over, was going to put it forward, and then Corby said, "Oh, that's my bag." Corby took it from James and put it on the counter.'

From this point on, the customs officers showed no further interest in James. Winata says: 'I did not even speak to James, I spoke to Corby. James was silent, not a word.' James was off the hook, but Schapelle's life now hung in the balance.

When she was asked to open the boogie board bag for

inspection, Schapelle claimed she was happy to do so. In her autobiography, she writes, 'I cheerfully picked the bag up off the floor and placed it on the counter saying, "No, no it's mine. Here you go . . ." Almost in the same movement I went to unzip the bag. He didn't ask me to; I just did it. It all happened fast as I had nothing to hide.'

But the police and customs officers say that at the crucial moment when Schapelle was asked to open her boogie board bag, she hesitated and instead opened a small zipper on the front. Winata remembers it this way: 'With a boogie board bag, there is a bigger zipper but she actually opened the smaller front zipper, put her hands in and said "Nothing". Of course, inside that smaller pocket there was nothing.'

Maybe the pretty young woman from Australia had misunderstood him? Winata thought it was odd that she'd only opened the smaller zipper, which was designed to hold a wallet or keys. He then asked Schapelle to open the large zipper, which would open the bag right up. He says: 'When I wanted to check her bag, she said "No". I said "Why?" She replied, "Because I have some!", and then she did not continue her sentence. From there I was on guard and I was suspecting her.' Schapelle's lawyers later claimed in court that she had actually said, 'There is something' rather than 'I have some'. Later, in court, Schapelle argued: 'I opened my bag and I had a surprise, and I closed it again.'

Komang Gelgel also testified that Schapelle refused to open the boogie board bag. He said she unzipped the large zipper a tiny fraction, and then stopped and panicked: 'She tried to open a little bit, she was hesitant, she actually stepped back.'

James remembered the look on his sister's face: 'I looked back. I just saw her shocked, she was just shocked.' Schapelle claims the reason she refused to open the larger zipper on the boogie board was because she saw something inside the bag that frightened her. Later, in court, she recalled the dreaded moment: 'Well, when I opened the boogie board bag, and I seen a plastic bag containing something and it was half opened, and when I didn't know what it was, and when I closed my boogie board up, a strong smell came out and I was very scared. I didn't know what was going on.'

Schapelle was seconds away from disaster. Initially, she managed a fake smile but then she lost it. I Gusti Winata asked: 'Do you know what is in that bag?' The customs officer says that Schapelle then answered, 'It's marijuana.' As Winata tells it: 'So I asked her again how she knew about it, and she said "Because I smell when you open."'

Neither of the customs officers noticed any odour coming from inside the boogie board bag. The inner plastic bag was not half opened as Schapelle claimed in her testimony. Says Winata: 'It could be that she was nervous, anxious and then the word just came out without her thinking. She wasn't showing any anger or anything like that and you know she was like admitting to her fate of being found out.' But Schapelle later denied ever saying the word 'marijuana' and claimed that the customs officers' poor English had resulted in them misunderstanding what she had said.

When the customs officers dragged the clear plastic bag full of marijuana out of the boogie board bag, it was completely flat and tightly moulded to the shape of the board. Customs officer Komang Gelgel recalls: 'It was shaped neatly as some sort of flat plate, in transparent plastic.' Winata was impressed by how well the compressed bag had been expertly shaped to fit the boogie board: 'They had gone to meticulous care to mould the marijuana in the plastic on the surfboard, that it looked like a lot of effort had gone into to make sure this had fitted correctly. I found it nicely sealed, shaped neatly as the boogie board—it now looks like a pillow, when it was actually flat at the time.'

The compressed marijuana was in fact packed inside two plastic Space Bags—an inner and an outer bag. Having two layers of plastic reduced the risk of a stem breaking through the airtight seal and the smell leaking out and alerting sniffer dogs or a customs officer. After they'd inspected the package, the customs officers popped both of the vacuum seals on the Space Bags. Immediately, the pungent smell of fresh hydro filled the room.

Winata remembers the chaotic scenes that followed. Within minutes of the discovery, customs officers and police started sending text messages and photos to reporters at the local Bali newspapers. Soon afterwards a horde of journalists with cameras began arriving. News of the big drug bust spread fast and video images were sent around the world by the Balinese media, showing the now uncompressed marijuana bag looking like a giant pillow.

Meanwhile Schapelle tried unsuccessfully to shield her face from the prying camera lenses. News footage shows her placing her head in her hands; her eyes are puffed up from crying. She looks manic; her hands are shaking as she keeps changing her hairstyle—one moment it's up in a bun, the next it's cascading down her shoulders, with long brown strands stuck to her forehead. Her yellow boogie board lies on the floor with the plastic bag of cannabis displayed on top, almost like a trophy.

Ally and Katrina finally cleared their customs inspection after encountering problems for bringing in too much duty-free alcohol. According to Ally, for at least half an hour she and Katrina were unaware of what had happened to Schapelle and James. Thinking that they might have been held up with similar excess duty-free issues, Ally left Katrina outside the airport to wait with the luggage while she went back into the customs inspection area.

After struggling to make herself understood to the customs officers, Ally was finally taken to the interrogation room where Schapelle and James were being questioned. 'Schapelle was sitting on a seat crying and really stressed out, and just trying to answer their questions,' she recalls. James looked like a statue, standing against the wall, seemingly shocked, as Ally remembers it: 'He wasn't saying anything.'

Ally says she tried to comfort Schapelle, but her friend had grown hysterical: 'She was becoming really upset and, like, hyperventilating and I was, like, oh my God, I hope she's got like some Panadol or something in her bag.' According to Ally, a couple of the customs guys were laughing at Schapelle. Ally did her best to stay composed: 'I just knew I couldn't lose it, and I had to save face with Schapelle, because she was getting really upset. And I was, I was trying to calm her down and basically tell her that everything was going to be OK.'

While Ally was trying to calm Schapelle down, the police were testing the marijuana. Soon they began asking her questions about whose marijuana it was, and after they failed to get answers the young Australians were all bundled into vehicles out the back of the airport and taken to the main customs office in the airport precinct. I Gusti Winata distinctly remembers that from that point on, James, Katrina and Ally kept their distance from Schapelle: 'They left her to defend herself. They stayed silent and did not at any time protest or cry out that she was innocent. It was like they were leaving her to her fate and to deal with it alone.' He also recalls Schapelle's meltdown: 'When the policewoman had to take off all her clothes to check her body, she cried and appeared very unsettled.'

As more Balinese media arrived on the scene, the police and customs officers began probing the decompressed plastic bags which contained the marijuana. Ally said: 'One of the guys not in uniform had the marijuana on top of a table and were like pulling bits out.' The inner and outer plastic bags were not fingerprinted at the time of the arrest, and Schapelle's legal team and the Corbys would later portray this as a major miscarriage of justice. But the police and customs officers didn't care about fingerprinting—as far as they were concerned, Schapelle had admitted that the boogie board bag was hers and this was all the evidence they needed. After the bust, the customs officers didn't even bother searching the bags of Katrina, Ally or James. Despite the widespread availability of cheap tuna on the island, James had brought a stack of tuna tins in his bag. Nobody noticed or cared—he later explained he had done so because the fish carried protein for his bodybuilding.

The holiday booking made at the Coolangatta Flight Centre shows that a courtesy car was booked to meet Schapelle and her group on arrival, and take them in air-conditioned comfort to the Grand Istana Rama Hotel in Kuta where Mercedes's husband Wayan planned to meet them. Wayan says that he drove his van to the hotel to meet the group but, when they didn't turn up, he simply returned to the up-market villa that had been rented for Mercedes's party.

Young Michael Corby had arrived in Bali two hours before Schapelle on the flight from Perth with his girlfriend, Hamita. At the time of Schapelle's arrest, he says he was hanging out at the villa with friends. He has a clear memory of Wayan returning to the villa without Schapelle, but the laid-back Splint was apparently unconcerned about his sister and why she wasn't at the hotel. He later told the film crew that he decided to go surfing and convinced Wayan to come with him: 'Wayan's come back and we've gone: ".Well, let's go surfing . . . they can find their way—I'm sure they're going to be around. She's been here before." '

Mercedes remained relaxing by the pool at the villa with her close friend Tracey Brown, another Australian woman married to a Balinese surfer who often babysat Mercedes's kids. Meanwhile, back at the airport, Ally instructed Katrina to call Mercedes on her mobile and get her to the airport fast. Recalls Katrina: 'I just said to her, "Schapelle's been caught with marijuana", and she [Mercedes] is like, "What? You're joking!" I said, "No, I'm not", and she could hear in my voice that I wasn't joking.'

Mercedes claims that in the beginning she wasn't too concerned: 'At first I actually thought it must have been a crumb, or someone just put a little bit in a bag. Even though I knew Schapelle never touched the stuff, maybe someone had left a little bit in her bag or someone had a little smoke and put it in there.' But savvy to the ways of Indonesia and having worked in an immigration office arranging visas for foreigners, Merc's friend Tracey was familiar with local 'customs'—she handed Mercedes a small amount of cash. Mercedes said, 'I actually got a million rupee, put it in my pocket and off I went to the airport thinking, "I'm going to sort this out with my million rupee", which is like $180 Australian.'

When she arrived at the customs area, Mercedes almost collapsed at the sight of the enormous clear-plastic pillow of exposed marijuana sitting in the middle of the room. At that moment, she gave up any thought of paying a small bribe to sort out the problem. She recalls: 'I thought a million rupee would do the trick. And then, once I saw that big package, it was, like, that vanished. It never came out of my pocket.'

CHAPTER 14

Damage Control

'Schapelle's not naïve; she's not silly. She's very clever; she's very calculating. She knows exactly what's happening all the time.'
—Vasu Rasiah

In the first 24 hours after the bust, Mercedes was desperately trying to get the situation under control. She needed to get Ally, Katrina and James out of the customs' holding cell at the airport and, more importantly, she had to make sure Schapelle didn't sign any documents until they had found an English-speaking lawyer. The police and customs officers were trying to get Schapelle to sign a confession. In *My Story* Schapelle writes, 'I didn't have a clue what my rights were, but had seen enough movies to know that you don't sign anything without a lawyer present.' Ally says there was no chance that Schapelle was going to sign anything: 'I think it was a good idea for her at the time to say "No, I'll wait until I get a lawyer." See—she's smart enough to say that.'

Mercedes later convinced the police and customs officers to let Ally and Katrina go, but she decided that James should stay with Schapelle. She later recalled on film: 'I was thinking to push for James, but then I didn't want Schapelle to be by herself. And I said to James, "Is it all right if you go with Schapelle?" And he said "Yeah". So I didn't push for James.'

Mercedes later said that several police officers gave her their personal mobile phone numbers. She claimed that she didn't understand why at the time but then later interpreted this as meaning the police were willing to take a bribe.

At the height of the crisis, Michael and Wayan were apparently still out surfing and couldn't be contacted. Despite speaking only passable Indonesian, Mercedes received no help from her husband or any of his relatives with the vital translations and negotiations with customs officers and police at the airport. Wayan later said there was nothing he could do to help at the airport: 'I not deal with customs. I don't know. I don't know who I am dealing with.'

It was now almost midnight, and the four young travellers had been in Bali for about eight hours. After finally being released from questioning, Ally and Katrina climbed into a taxi and the driver followed Mercedes on her motorbike back into town. The local media gathered as James and Schapelle were escorted into waiting police cars to be taken to Polda police headquarters. Their faces were obscured from the flashing cameras. 'They told us to cover our faces and we did, and then hopped in this car,' recalls James.

As they weaved their way through the mayhem of noisy motorbikes and chaotic drivers ignoring red stoplights, the culture shock began to hit. They were in a different country now, with different rules and different laws. James kept a close eye on the direction the police vehicle was heading; he told the documentary: 'I was just trying to remember the way back to the airport, just in case we had to do a runner or something.'

At Polda police station, James and Schapelle were given a relatively soft landing by being allowed to sleep on lounge chairs in the main office, instead of a cell. James says that one police officer offered to take him out partying—he assumed so as to get him to confess: 'I remember one police officer was saying, "Do you like girls? You like drinking? I'll take you out tonight." That's what he was saying to me.'

As they sat side by side contemplating what lay ahead, James says he finally asked his sister a question that would be asked by everyone in the coming years about the marijuana: 'I go, "That's not ours, is it?" Like, um, she goes, "I never . . ."' James finished by saying, 'Like we just . . . it's all so fucked.'

Someone had to break the news to Ros and Mick and, like everything else, that responsibility fell to Mercedes. Several hours after her sister's arrest she called her mother, who in turn dropped the bombshell on Mick. In a 2005 interview published in Sydney's *Sun-Herald* he recalled: 'I was asleep at home when the ex-wife phoned and told me Schapelle had been arrested in Bali, that they'd found this bag of marijuana in her bag. My medication was knocking me around a bit back then. Anyway, I must have dozed off again because when I awoke, my first thought was, what a strange bloody dream. A short time later the phone rang. It was a television journalist. That's when it hit me it was true.'

One of the first to be immediately included in the loop about the drug bust was Mick Corby's best mate living further up the coast, Tony Lewis. Lewis says he found out about Schapelle's arrest from watching the TV news, but his former lover Beth Lavender claimed to a television producer that Tony received an urgent phone call several hours after the bust.

As the situation unfolded, Beth felt helpless; her immediate reaction was to write down her feelings about Schapelle in a poem which was published in the *Gold Coast Bulletin*'s letters pages fifteen days after the Bali arrest. It was titled and credited very simply as: 'A poem written for Schapelle Leigh Corby by friend Beth'. It began: 'Candle Candle burning so bright/ Let Schapelle see your guiding light' and included the fervent hope that 'Her truth and innocence will shine through/ So she may surf again in those waves so blue'.

They say that certain memories remain etched in the mind forever. Malcolm McCauley recalls sitting at home in Degree Road, Salisbury North, with his feet up in front of the box. The evening news came on and details emerged of a major international drug bust involving a young girl from Queensland. McCauley recalls: 'It took a while for everything to register, and then it hit me like a bolt out of the blue. Schapelle? Corby? Bali? Oh, Jesus Christ, it's Mick's daughter! And well, for a number of reasons, I panicked big time.'

The television news bulletin continued on with the story of a boogie board bag containing 4.2 kg of marijuana, but by that time McCauley had zoned out. He was privy to the finer points—he knew the story inside the story, 'the whole bloody lot'.

Over in Bali, Schapelle's arrest was also headline news and splashed across the front pages of the local newspapers. The Indonesian press was quick to dub Schapelle the 'Ganja Queen'—*ganja* being the local word for marijuana—and one of the first news articles reported 'The Ganja Queen was depressed and screamed hysterically'.

Far more frightening than the nickname she was given, however, was the news that Schapelle was potentially facing the death penalty. Most foreigners naively assume that the death penalty only applies to drug mules caught smuggling harder drugs, like heroin, and they are surprised to learn that it can also be applied when large amounts of marijuana are brought into Indonesia. Most Indonesians are happy to see drug dealers and users sentenced to death. When former president Megawati Sukarnoputri first implemented her fierce war on drugs in 2002, she called for the execution of all drug dealers. 'For those who distribute drugs, life sentences and other prison sentences are no longer sufficient,' she said. 'No sentence is sufficient other than the death sentence.'

The current president, Susilo Bambang Yudhoyono, also has a zero tolerance drugs policy and is in favour of the death penalty for traffickers. Most drug smugglers sentenced to death in Indonesia have been caught importing heroin, but not all of them. You can also be shot by a firing squad for trafficking cocaine or, as Schapelle Corby had just discovered, marijuana. At this very time an Indonesian man had been sentenced to death by firing squad for smuggling 58 kilos of marijuana into south Sumatra.

Ironically, with the way Indonesian drug laws work, Schapelle Corby would have been better off if she'd killed someone. When she was arrested there were 54 people on death row in Indonesia, 31 of them convicted of smuggling or possessing drugs and only 19 convicted of murder. Twenty-two of the death-row prisoners were foreigners who had been caught smuggling drugs into Indonesia. Most were from Africa, and had no money to pay a bribe. When Africans, Indians or South Americans were executed for smuggling drugs into Indonesia, they got less media coverage than a weather update.

Schapelle's 4.2 kilo drug haul was the biggest single importation of cannabis by a foreign tourist in Bali's history. Wayan later said, 'The first time I saw the words "death penalty" in the newspaper I thought, "Shit!" Sometimes we are crying at night, and hug to sleep and we don't want to wake up from our sleep. Sometimes Mercedes is crying, and I push her to get stronger. It's very hard.'

Mercedes was too stressed to turn her phone off, even though the constant calls from the press were driving her crazy: 'I was too scared to turn my phone off, because what if it was the police or Schapelle or something happened? I couldn't sleep or eat for a week . . . I was forcing myself to have a bite of food and vomiting in the mornings.'

Michael said his first reaction to the news of Schapelle's arrest was also to throw up: 'I was thinking about the death sentence. But then I'm like, no, she can't get the death sentence, because she didn't do it.'

Mercedes finalised arrangements for James's release from the Polda police station the day after Schapelle's arrest. Ally and Katrina, meanwhile, were understandably still in shock. In the hours following the arrest, Ally said Mercedes was constantly hammering her and Katrina with endless questions: 'She's just asking like more questions—about what happened—and just trying to go through the whole thing again. And it was upsetting me and Katrina. We were crying, and I think James went to the bedroom—he wasn't really saying much.'

The stark reality for them all was that Schapelle was now a prisoner, incarcerated without a lawyer and undergoing continual interrogations. She was alone in a tiny, suffocating, stinking hot police cell, staring aimlessly at the yellow cement walls. The cell was filthy and smelt horrible; with little light and no mattress, she quickly became sleep deprived. In the first few days after her arrest, the constant thought of a potential death penalty sentence plummeted her to new lows. The elevator to hell had arrived.

In Schapelle's own account of this time, she writes: 'I wanted to be questioned. I had nothing to hide and I wanted to tell these people that I didn't do this and it was all a terrible mistake.' The local newspapers, however, tell a very different story. Five days after her arrest, a local Balinese newspaper ran the headline, 'Marijuana Courier is stressed at Bali Police HQ cell'. The newspaper reported: 'The suspect is experiencing a great depression. She often screamed and she took hours in the bathroom.' The Indonesian police told the newspaper: 'For the meantime we will not examine her until there is a confirmation from the medics that the suspect is ready to be examined.' The newspaper also said, 'When examined the lady gave a statement that in Australia marijuana is being used for animal feed.'

The director of Bali police narcotics division, Bambang Sugiarto, told one local paper that interrogators had experienced some difficulty in examining Corby, who was stressed out and refused to be examined. He said, 'The suspect often screamed hysterically, even locked herself up in the bathroom for hours.'

Back in Canberra, news of Schapelle's plight had barely made it onto the political radar. The Minister for Foreign Affairs, Alexander Downer, and the Minister for Justice and Customs, Chris Ellison, were informed of the arrest, but it looked like just another sad story of an Australian drug trafficker who had done something stupid overseas and got busted. At this time there were 192 Australians imprisoned in foreign countries around the world, and a further 39 being held under arrest. Of those held in jail or under arrest, 112 were in trouble for drug-related offences. As in all such cases, officials from the Department of Foreign Affairs in Bali gave Schapelle the standard visit and afforded her their advice about engaging legal representation in a foreign country.

The initial reports by the Australian media about Schapelle Corby were mostly negative. Four days after her arrest, she was paraded in front of the media by the Indonesian police outside Polda police station, where she was being held. She yelled out, 'Help me, help me! Tell my mum and dad I love them!' Given the seriousness of the situation, she looked surprisingly sheepish rather then terrified.

Despite the negative reports and doubt about her innocence at the outset, this unusual case had everyone intrigued. In what was soon to become a battle of the television networks in Australia, Channel 9 moved faster than its rival Channel 7 and scored an interview with Schapelle on a mobile phone. She said, 'I'm innocent, I'm innocent. I put my suitcase and board cover on in Brisbane, you know, and I arrived in Denpasar and I had the shock of my life!'

But the Australian media correspondents working in Indonesia weren't buying Schapelle's story that a stranger had stashed the drugs in her unlocked boogie board bag. Veteran television reporter Mark Burrows told the host of Channel 9's *Today Show*, Steve Liebmann, 'I think the case is extremely strong against her.' The television host then asked Mark Burrows, 'She says she's been set up—obviously there are not many people where you are who believe that?' Mark Burrows answered, 'I don't think there's anybody. Certainly none of the Indonesian police or prosecutors or detectives believe that at all.' Burrows also explained that the plastic bag containing the marijuana had been shaped perfectly to fit the boogie board. This was a simple and accurate observation that would soon go missing from all of the Australian media reports once Schapelle hysteria began to build momentum.

The early news reports in the Balinese media made it clear that the Australian Federal Police were working closely with the Indonesian authorities. In the wake of the Bali bombings, the AFP had developed a close working relationship with its Indonesian counterpart, providing forensic specialists and establishing a joint police investigation to try to track down the bombers. By the time Schapelle was arrested in October 2004, the AFP and the Indonesian National Police had never enjoyed closer ties.

On 2 November 2004 a Balinese newspaper ran the headline, 'AFP Trace Corby's Network in Australia'. With the secondary headline 'Minutes of Investigation of the Marijuana "Queen" is Handed-over', the paper quoted Senior Police Commissioner AS Reniban as saying: 'Corby's case received serious attention from the Australian Government. The AFP are also tracing the suspect's network abroad . . . An effective coordination and exchange of information is one of the main points of the MOU [memorandum of understanding] between Indonesian Police and the AFP in combating narcotic distribution to the general population. A number of drug cases successfully unveiled by Bali Police are admitted to be of AFP's assistance. AFP awaits Corby's Minutes of Investigation to trace inter-country narcotic distribution.' Despite frequent mentions in the Bali newspapers about the AFP sniffing around the Corby case, nothing had yet emerged that looked damaging for Schapelle.

For the first time Alexander Downer is now prepared to open up about the early days of the case. In an interview in 2009 for this book, he recalled attending a meeting not specifically about Schapelle Corby, but where the Australian Federal Police were present. At that meeting, he raised the issue and requested feedback on Schapelle's claims that she was innocent: 'I asked the AFP what they thought, and they thought in all probability that she was guilty.'

Former Foreign Affairs Minister Downer had dealt with many Australian parents whose children had got into trouble overseas. He said, 'And you know she was hysterical and people vary in situations of great adversity and she was out there in the more hysterical wing. But you know the Federal Police didn't volunteer any information or send me a letter or come and see me about the Schapelle Corby case, I just asked them once in a meeting what they thought and their view was she was guilty. You don't just get arrested at an airport with 4 kilograms of marijuana every day—I have never known it to happen before and, by the way, it hasn't happened since.'

After news of Schapelle's arrest reached Australia, the Queensland police did a few checks on the now infamous 'Ganja Queen'. A detective from the Queensland state drug squad explained: 'We checked the whole passenger list for Schapelle's flight and her mobile phone records going back 24 hours before she left Brisbane.' Schapelle's mother Ros had given her a pre-paid mobile phone for the holiday, but the Queensland police's check of phone calls made from the mobile didn't reveal anything suspicious. The Australian Airlines flight passenger manifest didn't turn up anyone of interest either.

Several days after Schapelle's arrest, McCauley's eyes

nearly popped out of his head as he witnessed his marijuana being paraded for all to see on national television: 'There it was—the Bali cops, they had their mitts all over it. And there was Schapelle . . . she weren't looking too hot.'

A series of hypothetical scenarios were rattling around McCauley's head. Each of them related to Schapelle's detention, and what she may or may not have said to the Indonesian authorities. While the Australian media clamoured for more information about the vulnerable young Queenslander, McCauley was in two minds about whether to contact her father, Mick, or not: 'On the one hand, I wanted to know what was going on; but on the other hand, it might have been too risky to call him. I was worried anyone could be listening in.'

Mick Corby's first instinct was to bribe the Indonesian police to get his daughter out of trouble. He was a realist, and he knew in this kind of situation only money talks. Mick's old schoolmate and lifelong friend Noel Vinall, in his interview for this book, made a claim not heard before— that, after Schapelle was arrested, 'a plan was in motion for Mick to sell his property at Tugun and then to pay a bribe to get her out'. According to Noel, Mick wanted to keep Schapelle's arrest as quiet as possible. That meant his family keeping a low profile and hanging back in the shadows. Unfortunately for Mick, his plan of action never came to fruition as there was a major problem—he'd never been able to hold sway over Ros.

Ros was understandably distraught that 'my baby' was now locked away in a Bali police holding cell. She took matters into her own hands when she yielded to the overtures of a particularly convincing television producer who told her that the only way to ensure Schapelle came home was to make a public plea to the Australian government. An emotional Ros subsequently appeared on the Nine Network's *A Current Affair* program, declaring that her daughter was innocent and that she never had anything to do with drugs. With tears in her eyes, Ros told television host Ray Martin that not only was she worried about Schapelle, but she was also frightened for all her family in Bali. She said, 'The Indonesians have got my children!' It was a prime-time, high-rating show and suddenly the Corbys were all over Australian national television.

Noel recalls: 'Rossie went right in over the top of him [Mick] and, within days, it then became a circus.' He added: 'Mick was not happy with the way she carried on. He was furious. He wished to Christ she'd have shut up, stayed out of the limelight and said nothing. Unfortunately, Rossie's not that sort of woman. He had a plan but, due to everything that transpired, it never even came close to happening.'

The chance of cutting a quiet deal with the Indonesian police was gone forever.

CHAPTER 15

The Brother-in-law

'Well, there's so many reality TV shows . . . The way I sort of see it, is you spend a year in Thai jail and you come out with say $100,000. You wouldn't like to come second and spend twelve months there and get nothing. But I think people would do that . . . $100,000 to spend a year in a Thai jail . . . I think people would try that. But they could probably go out when they want . . . Schapelle can't.'

—Michael Corby Jnr

Lily Lubis is a softly spoken, gentle young Balinese lawyer, and she was about to bite off more than she could chew. The Schapelle Corby drug trial would be the biggest case of her life and for seven months she would devote her every breathing moment to a foreigner she hardly knew but instantly liked and felt compelled to save. Lily was the first to admit that she had little experience in defending drug matters—in fact property law was more her speed—but her legal firm, Bali Law Chambers, had been on the Australian Consulate's list of recommended lawyers for travellers in trouble. She had been the first English-speaking lawyer to respond to Mercedes's frantic telephone call for legal representation for her sister late on that Friday night after the drug bust.

Dressed professionally in a conservative dark suit and smart high heels, the petite Lily knew her way around Polda police headquarters, but navigating through the media contingent now camped outside the building waiting to get pictures of her new client was an entirely novel experience. As western reporters vigorously questioned her about Schapelle's mental state, Lily politely declined to comment, apart from what was to become her standard response to most questions: 'Schapelle is innocent.'

Schapelle's innocence mattered deeply to Lily. Although a modern career woman, she was also a devout Muslim and staunchly anti drugs. She said that she never had any interest in legally representing drug defendants—that is, until she met Schapelle: 'I look at her expression, her body language. Every time I ask her questions, or when I ask her to do something, I try to study her to convince myself that I am representing an innocent person. The impression that I get from her in the beginning is, yes, I believe this girl. And I know she didn't do it.'

Schapelle immediately felt comfortable with Lily and the two formed a strong bond. In her conversations with Lily inside the jail, Schapelle was always tearful and emotional, continually protesting her innocence. After visiting her in prison, Lily would often break down and cry. The case had become a personal one for her, ever since she had broken the news to Schapelle that she would be facing the death penalty.

Although Lily was inexperienced in drug matters, she had a savvy business partner, Sri Lankan born Vasu Rasiah. Vasu was a flamboyant property developer with a penchant for wearing a petal behind his ear; he claimed that his speciality was contract law, even though he wasn't a qualified lawyer. What Vasu brought to the table was an uncanny ability to make connections—he was a Mr Fix-it and soon he appointed himself as Schapelle's 'case coordinator'. In Indonesia case coordinators are commonly hired to liaise with the police and courts to help smooth things out. They are people with good police contacts and, although it is never discussed in public, some case coordinators often know a thing or two about how and when to pay a bribe.

Due to the language barrier, foreign media despatched to report on the case missed most of the details about the unfolding investigation that were written in Bahasa in the local newspapers, and hence the Australian public never really got the full story. It was widely reported that the drugs were of the type commonly known as 'Lemon Juice'—a code-name used for a specific type of marijuana not usually found in Indonesia.

Narcotics chief Bambang Sugiarto told the Balinese press that, 'Police have strong proof of the suspect's involvement in the marijuana business in Bali.' He also said, 'There are informants who knew Corby.' Another Balinese newspaper reported, 'Her arrival in Bali is suspected to have connection with marijuana distribution on the Island of the Gods.' Sugiarto added, 'According to some of our informants, the suspect Schapelle Leigh Corby is a dealer and a distributor.' Although Schapelle's passport proved she hadn't been to Bali for four years, the narcotics chief was keen to talk up the prosecutor's case; he insisted there were informants in Bali who knew the young Australian woman.

Vasu's first big challenge was to get the Bali police and the local media off Wayan Widyartha's back. Much to Mercedes's annoyance, the local newspapers had shifted focus on to her husband Wayan, who in turn was terrified of being arrested and annoyed that the local reporters were starting to include him in their news stories. He later told the documentary makers: 'We are scared what everybody thinks about us: "If that was Schapelle . . . If that's Schapelle's stuff, who's she going to bring it for?" I'm the brother-in-law. I'm Balinese. They're focusing on me.' The speculation in the local newspapers was so intense that Lily and Vasu eventually escorted Wayan to Polda police headquarters to make a statement denying that he had any involvement with the drug trade. Lily Lubis recalls, 'One of the rumours is they say that Wayan is one of the drug dealers in Kuta. So I call Wayan and explain to him, "Please come to the police station and I will introduce you to the police."'

As Vasu Rasiah sums up the situation: 'If we delayed and covered him up, it will give more opportunity for them to go and dig up something. But we said no, straight away—let's go there and meet and sit down. This is the guy you are saying is a drug trafficker! If what you are saying is true, arrest him now.' Wayan adds: 'They never come to search my house or anything. I go to them and say, "This is my sister-in-law and I am the brother-in-law." I don't want them to come to me; it is better I go to them. After one week, we go and see the big police in Bali, and I said, "Whatever the papers say, I am not the connection. This is me. Am I wanted?"'

Persistent rumours were also being posted on the internet about Wayan's connections to the Bali surf scene. Many bloggers were incredulous that Schapelle had taken a boogie board to Bali when her brother-in-law was a local surfing champion and could easily have provided a board for her holiday. Mercedes worked relentlessly to distance herself and Wayan from the surfing industry, presumably because she judged that the image of surfie hippies was not going to play well in the media. 'We don't own a surf shop in Bali' was the mantra she repeated over and over to the press, and this was true. But Mercedes and Wayan's link to the surf scene was close—as well as working as surf guides for tourists, Wayan sold Dakine merchandise to surf shops and Mercedes also occasionally worked in a surf shop as a book-keeper. Dakine, founded and based in Hawaii, is owned by Billabong and is a popular surfing brand with the young fashion-conscious surf crowd.

Schapelle's lawyers were becoming increasingly concerned that the judges who were going to be presiding over her court case would know that this foreign woman had a Balinese relative. It didn't matter that Wayan said he had nothing to do with the marijuana trade, the association with Schapelle looked bad. Wayan even volunteered to undergo a blood test to be cleared for drug use. He says, 'I was worried about that too, because of what the papers say. They can check my blood, because I am not doing this.' Unfortunately a blood test would have been useless—if he had been taking drugs at the time of Schapelle's arrest, they would have already passed through his system.

The chief government prosecutor for the Corby case, Ida Bagus Wiswantanu, had a fearsome reputation. He boldly stated that in 90 per cent of the more than two hundred narcotics cases he had handled, he had obtained the sentence he sought. In more recent times, he had been responsible for the conviction of three of the terrorists involved in the 2002 Bali bombings.

Commenting on the possible brother-in-law connection, in a 2010 interview Wiswantanu explained that despite the rumours in the local newspapers about Wayan, the police had nothing on him: 'I didn't think the police had developed

Corby's case that far because, if it's true that the case had something to do with Wayan, the police would have put it in Corby's file before they gave the file to me. It's not that we didn't want to go after the wider organisation—the problem was Corby didn't want to say anything at all, she didn't admit that the marijuana belongs to her, the chain had broken.'

Over time, the speculation about Wayan in the local papers fizzled out. Mr Fix-it had smoothed out the potentially damaging problem. When asked how that happened, Vasu smiles enigmatically and replies: 'They [the police] just couldn't. They just couldn't.' He refuses to explain why. Throughout the high-profile trial Wayan managed to stay out of the Australian media spotlight—suddenly his poor English was a plus and no one wanted to interview him.

Meanwhile, back in Australia, Mick Corby and Tony Lewis were agitated and pre-occupied with a sickening, ever-present dread that either the police or the media would make a connection between Schapelle's arrest and the drug bust on Tony's property three weeks earlier.

To everyone it seemed unlikely that the former beauty school student, who'd been sitting around on the Gold Coast watching daytime American soaps, could possibly have come up with an estimated $20,000–30,000 to buy the 4.2 kilos of pot in Australia. Furthermore, Schapelle had borrowed money from both her parents for the trip and she was driving around in an old car. Even if the hydro was given as a loan to be paid back after it was sold in Bali, it was obvious she wasn't capable of carrying out the whole operation on her own.

Three days after his daughter's arrest, Mick Corby came bursting out into his front yard to greet the media pack gathered there. He looked wild in his singlet, shorts and thongs, his bright blue eyes flashing above his bushy beard. He told the waiting media that the boogie board bag had been unlocked and that Schapelle had been framed. He said, 'My daughter has never been involved in anything like that. She was just going on a holiday. She knows you cannot smuggle drugs—she was stitched up!'

Mercedes told the *Age*: 'If someone was going to smuggle drugs, they would hide it, put a lock on their bags. They would not have their name and address on the label.' Mercedes also said, 'She knows she's innocent; she's not depressed.'

Curiously, it would be many months before Mick would make a personal visit to Bali to see his beloved daughter. The family's explanation was that he was too sick to travel, due to his prostate cancer.

Malcolm McCauley, on the other hand, had no hesitation about heading towards the epicentre of the disaster.

CHAPTER 16

The Man on the Plane

'You don't accidentally step on someone's foot on a plane and then suddenly become best mates by the time you've landed. I mean, that's just bloody ridiculous.'

—Kathleen McCauley

Kathleen McCauley was in a state of shock. During 36 years of marriage, she had never once managed to drag her lazy husband on an overseas excursion. That's not to say she hadn't tried. She had begged and pleaded until she was blue in the face. On one occasion, she had even gone travelling without him.

Trouble was, Malcolm always seemed to find an excuse not to go. If his back wasn't playing up, his legs were. If he couldn't successfully feign injury, then he would exaggerate his fear of flying. If all else failed, he'd simply ask Kathleen why she or anyone else would ever want to leave Australia in the first place. 'We live in God's own country,' he would say. 'Everything you need is right here on your doorstep.'

But on 26 October 2004, the unthinkable was finally about to happen. The McCauleys were boarding a flight bound for Bali. It was eighteen days after Schapelle Corby's arrest and Kathleen was well aware that this was the underlying reason for Malcolm having booked this overseas trip. The irony that another woman had finally succeeded where she had failed was not lost on her. She reassured herself with the knowledge that, once Malcolm had decided to go, he had practically begged her to join him.

He was a crafty old bugger. He wanted Kathleen to accompany him, of course. But make no mistake—her inclusion on the travel itinerary was also an insurance of sorts. If anyone ended up asking questions, he could pass the expedition off as an innocent husband-and-wife holiday to Bali.

The McCauleys had now been separated for more than eighteen months but, when it came to making the booking, Malcolm had pitched the trip as a perfect chance to mend some bridges and to rekindle the spark they once both shared. Deep down, there was nothing Kathleen wanted more. As the plane departed the runway at Adelaide International Airport that afternoon, she relaxed back into her seat, closed her eyes and visualised the candlelit dinners and beautiful sunsets awaiting them both.

She should have known it was all too good to be true. Malcolm had failed to mention something significant prior to departure. It wasn't that it had slipped his mind—he simply knew that his ex-wife would never have agreed to travel had he told her the truth. Seated approximately twenty rows behind the McCauleys was a man named David Trevor McHugh.

McHugh was a 46-year-old former postman who had grown up in the Adelaide suburb of Mitchell Park. After leaving school, he had moved to nearby Mansfield Park to live with his grandmother. During his late twenties and early thirties he roamed from state to state, living in multicultural Darwin for a while and then later tropical Queensland. In the early nineties he returned to Adelaide and had become stuck in a rut.

In recent times McHugh, a large imposing man with short dark hair and a deep booming voice, had preferred to be known by his self-appointed nickname, which was 'Smoothie'. One family member says: 'He'd tell our kids to call him "Uncle Smoothie".' She added: 'If you ever dropped by his local pub, the Marion Hotel, to look for him, you'd ask whether David had been by and they'd say "Who?" So you'd then say, "Sorry, I mean Mr Smoothie." And they'd go, "Aaaaah yes—Mr Smoothie. He was in a while ago." '

It is fair to say there had always been two sides to David McHugh. Most of the time, he was a likeable enough bloke. He was also, however, one of those people who could lose his cool and explode at the drop of a hat. When McHugh did snap, often without thinking, he was capable of saying and doing quite literally anything. His friends warn that on such occasions, it's always advisable to disappear fast until the tornado has run its course—which more often than not, it did.

As McHugh edged closer towards 50, he had started to suffer from agonising bouts of arthritis in his knees. A large network of unsightly varicose veins had also started creeping up his ankles. While most people these days usually have them surgically removed, McHugh came up with a rather bizarre alternative. He blanketed them all with enormous tattoos—a big tiger on one inside leg and a Red Indian on the other.

In recent years he had developed into something of a loner. Sure, there were his drinking buddies at the Marion and the local RSL. A lot of his time, however, was spent alongside his beloved racing greyhounds, many of which he had loved from pups and proudly trained into top champions. He had owned and raced dozens of dogs over the years and, in doing so, had become a well-known face around the local traps at Gawler and Angle Vale, both outlying suburbs of Adelaide. But while other trainers enjoyed mingling and sharing stories, he always shied away. Generally, he would arrive trackside just in time for his own race on the program. Once it had finished, he'd then bundle his dog into the back of his car and away he would go. 'It's sort of like a job,' he explains. 'And, like all jobs, you don't hang around at work when there's no need to.'

In subsequent interviews, McHugh and McCauley both denied ever having met each other—until supposedly a chance meeting on the plane they were now both travelling on. 'I got out of the seat to get another beer, 'cos I don't mind beer, and, um, happened to run into Dave,' said McCauley. 'We got on the beer, and then what does he say—better come down and join me in the back of the plane, 'cos that's the last bit to hit the ground. Anyway, he said, uh, meet up with you tomorrow and we'll have a couple of beers. So he came around to the motel we were staying in.'

McHugh trotted out a similar tale: 'I just met him on the plane going to Bali. I was actually going up the back of the plane to get a drink, and he was right behind me. I sort of turned around quickly and run into him, and that's how it started.' He added: 'He [Malcolm] told me where he was staying and I just said, "What I'll do is catch up with you in a couple of days and we'll do a bit of a pub crawl." Which we did, but I think we got as far as one bar and that was it—he lost his thongs. Yeah.'

For the first time, it can now be revealed that both men were lying—and for good reason. As McCauley points out, 'It was vital we distanced ourselves so nobody down the track smelt a rat.' Aside from racing greyhounds, McHugh had another hobby, which was financially far more rewarding. He was an Adelaide-based commercial marijuana grower—a gardener, and one of McCauley's regular suppliers. Not only that, McHugh was the same 'mutual contact' who originally helped McCauley secure the Gold Coast run. It is also claimed that he supplied a significant portion of the 4.2 kg found in Schapelle's bag. 'Dave was the link and that's why we were both there on the plane,' he said. 'Dave had been helping to transport the hooter on the domestic flights [to Queensland] until that all went pear shaped. Then he introduced me because I had the established road runs interstate.' McCauley explained that once he became involved McHugh still remained a central supplier, although he often struggled to source the amounts required. 'I, on the other hand, was able to offer continuity because I had the contacts. So I said to Dave, "If you can't always do it, I know a man who can. Moi." It was all very amicable.'

Within minutes of the seat-belt signs having been switched off on the flight to Bali, McCauley decided it was time to stretch his legs. He left Kathleen in her seat and slowly strolled down towards the rear of the plane. He found McHugh slouched back in a left-hand side window seat, and greeted him with a wink and a smile: 'I see there's acres of room down here, mate.'

'It's practically first class,' replied McHugh.

'Give me half an hour with the missus and I'll be right back.'

McCauley shuffled back to his seat. He went through the

motions of playing Happy Couples, but his mind was now focused on a free beer session with his buddy down the back. He waited patiently as Kathleen flicked through the in-flight movie program. Then, once she had become engrossed in watching one, he made his escape.

Poor Kathleen had been abandoned less than halfway to her dream destination. When she finally realised it, she was seething. She says: 'Malcolm knew a lot of people who I didn't know, and it wasn't immediately obvious that Dave and him were associates—because he never told me. For several days, he kept insisting it was all just a random meeting.'

Kathleen describes the unexpected addition to her travelling party as 'a bit odd'. Initially she feared McHugh was a cop: 'I thought he was a federal police officer. He never spoke about his family or about anything that mattered to him. He was very quiet on detail about himself. He didn't answer many questions. I just felt there was something fishy about him and the whole situation of him suddenly being with us. I mean, I sat alone for most of the flight. Then, once we got to Bali, Malcolm kept vanishing all the time. Eventually it all slotted into place—he and Dave knew each other. I was really, really angry and I gave it to Malcolm big time. We were supposed to be fixing our marriage.'

Kathleen had picked up on McHugh's reluctance to talk about his relatives and, with hindsight, it's perhaps easy to see why he might not have had much to say. His parents, to whom he was close, had long passed away. He had a pair of teenage twins, a boy and a girl, from an early marriage that had ended badly, and was in touch with neither of them. After years of simmering tensions, he had also had several major bust-ups with his siblings and was no longer on speaking terms with them.

McHugh's sister Sharon said that aside from personal differences, she and her other sister Vicky had slowly distanced themselves from their brother because he was 'growing drugs for a living'.

Vicky confirmed this: 'He showed me a big hydro set-up in a room in his old home at Morphett Vale. There were lights and plastic sheets everywhere, and the plants were chock-a-block—that's when I found out that David was in the drug trade. That was about fifteen years ago.' She says she scarpered straight out of the house after seeing his set-up.

Later down the track, Sharon found herself in a similar situation: 'He took me inside his place at Mitchell Park. It was packed full of marijuana plants. He then had the cheek to ask me if I would tend to them while he was away overseas. I said, "You must be kidding." It's how he's always made his money . . . I know for a fact he's certainly never smoked the stuff. He hates it—he can't even stomach the smell of cigarette smoke.' Sharon adds: 'Put it this way, he is a man completely motivated by money and yet he hasn't worked in years. He supposedly lives off a disability pension, and yet he still finds enough cash to head off to Bali every year.'

Official flight records show that Bali was indeed McHugh's favourite holiday destination. He travelled there twice in 1999 for vacations that, intriguingly, lasted less than a week. He made similar pit-stop visits in 2000 and 2001. Now he was heading back, but with something at stake. As McCauley later described it, 'There was more than just one head on the chopping block, and Schapelle was holding all the cards.'

The first few days in Bali followed a recurring pattern. Kathleen and Malcolm would wake up and have breakfast somewhere close to the hotel they were staying in. They would then join all the other tourists slowly shuffling their way through Kuta's narrow alleyways. By early afternoon, Kathleen was happy to sit by the pool, read a book or do some shopping. That was the cue for McCauley to exit stage left and rendezvous with McHugh.

Together, the drug associates embarked on some low-key snooping around to try to gauge the potential fall-out from Schapelle's bust. 'It was red hot—and I'm not talking about the weather,' said McCauley. 'It was like, "Don't make a move; this is serious here."' He adds: 'Schapelle was massive news and the local atmosphere was hostile towards her to say the least. As far as the natives were concerned, she was a drug dealer and she was bringing their culture down. You couldn't shut the cunts up. To be honest, there was little Dave and I could do so we kept well out of the way and just tried to gain a feel for what was happening.'

The two men found themselves in something of a holding pattern. Within a week, McHugh had packed his bags and headed home. McCauley, meanwhile, had some major crawling to do to make up with Kathleen, so the couple stayed on a few extra days.

Schapelle was now stuck in a classic Catch-22 situation. If she gave up the names of people back in Australia involved in the drug syndicate in order to try and cut a deal with the Indonesian police, she would first and foremost have to give up her father. Then, potentially, the whole syndicate would unravel and more questions would be asked. Who was she delivering to? Who were the suppliers? Who were the clients? And the most fundamental question of all was: could she trust the Indonesian police to reward any such confession with her freedom?

As her weeks of incarceration dragged on, Wayan was worried that Schapelle might try to commit suicide. He told the documentary crew, 'I thought she was going to kill herself, because we can't help.' He said he desperately wanted to swap places with her, but he knew it was impossible: 'I want to be there instead of Schapelle, but it doesn't work like that, because we can't do that. I could be strong, but she is just a girl.'

But loyalty to family ran thick through Schapelle's veins. They had always been her lifeline, and dobbing in Dad just wasn't an option. She wasn't going to 'sing' for anyone—there was way too much at stake. When asked who she trusted, Schapelle's answer was a stoic 'I trust only my family'.

Police prosecutor Ida Bagus Wiswantanu explained that Schapelle's refusal to talk stopped the Indonesian police from broadening the investigation and he suggested that that was frustrating for them: 'We can say that she didn't tell us anything—she didn't admit her ownership. She made the situation difficult—it's hard to track down anyone else. We never know who will receive marijuana from Corby. She never put forward any name—this made the situation a bit difficult for us. It's 4.2 kg of marijuana—that's a lot for her to use it by herself. So there was a strong indication that the marijuana would be distributed to others—but who?'

Alone in her cell at night, the overwhelming fear of being executed by firing squad tormented Schapelle. She told the documentary crew: 'I just can't imagine a bullet going through my heart.'

Perhaps, in many ways, it already had.

CHAPTER 17

Praying for a Miracle

'Lord set me free to be all you've created me to be, and follow you faithfully all the days of my life. Amen . . . Um, sorry—that was only half of it . . .'

—Schapelle Corby

Schapelle had never been particularly religious, but now she was prepared to do whatever it took to get home. If that meant praying while brandishing a new crucifix around her neck, then so be it. Her lawyer, Lily Lubis, had explained to her that Indonesia's legal system appreciated defendants who were humble, gracious and, most importantly, religious. ' "I believe that you are strong enough—that's why God let this happen to you." I always say that to Schapelle,' Lily said in the documentary.

Heeding Lily's advice, Schapelle turned to religion and was baptised in Kerobokan Prison. She then took to constantly reciting the 'Forgiveness Prayer', though she was quick to point out that she wasn't praying to God for forgiveness: 'I haven't done anything wrong to ask for forgiveness. But I thank him for choosing me 'cos he . . . he has to be chosen, and, uh, I think that he's . . . he thought that I was so arrogant, and I've always believed there was something there. But I've just been so arrogant to realise if there's something there, why can't it be God?'

While Lily was convinced that her client was innocent, her business partner Vasu Rasiah was far more cynical and he avoided teary personal meetings with Schapelle wherever possible. 'I leave all that to Lily,' he said. 'You know I never really wanted to do the bloody case, but I did it for Lily. She wanted to defend Schapelle,' Vasu said.

Schapelle's decision not to confess to the crime left Vasu and Lily with no choice but to start investigating alternative theories to present in court as to how the marijuana came to be in her boogie board bag. In November 2004, the pair flew to Queensland and met with Qantas Airways officials to try and obtain security video of Schapelle and her group checking in their baggage at Brisbane Airport.

Unfortunately, by the time they arrived in Australia to investigate, it was too late. The images had been recorded onto a computer hard drive and, as a matter of internal practice, after one month the security video was automatically recorded over by new images. The former head of Qantas Airways Security, Geoffrey Askew AM, says that Qantas went to great lengths to get technicians to recover the vision, but even the experts couldn't do it: 'Normally it's a maximum of about thirty days in any organisation. Thirty days is the unwritten standard, if you like, for the length of recordings; and then that technology is used again and recorded for the next 30 days. And that's what happened in this case.'

Vasu and Lily were also hoping to find a record of the weight of the boogie board bag when it was checked in but, in line with the procedures of all international airlines, the bags were not weighed individually. In the end, the pair's flight to Australia was a waste of time as there was nothing that Qantas could provide to help her case. On the upside, however, at least there was no record of a boogie board that should have weighed just 3 kilos weighing 7 kilos, being the combined total weight with 4.2 kilos of marijuana inside the bag.

While the Balinese press may have been hostile towards the 'Ganja Queen', and the Australian media reports weren't much better, word had got around newspaper circles and television headquarters that the prisoner was a stunner, and good for a front-page story or headline news: she was a young Aussie female traveller busted for drugs in an Asian country. Schapelle ticked all the boxes for selling newspapers and boosting television and radio ratings back home. The Australian media were starting to take a greater interest in her.

Right from the very beginning, it appears Vasu was shrewd when it came to the media, the spin and money. He encouraged Schapelle to keep diary notes in case she one day wrote a book, so she diligently started writing diary entries every day.

While Schapelle was still in the Polda police cell she posed for a photo beside the word 'Cobra', which had been scrawled on her cell wall. The Bali bomber, Amrosi, had apparently written the word using his very own shit. A family friend later let slip, just weeks after her arrest, that the photograph was taken for 'Schapelle's book'.

The Nine Network in Australia was determined to own Schapelle's story for prime-time broadcast as a television exclusive, so Vasu was constantly courted by *60 Minutes* producer Kathryn Bonella, who would later become a major player in the Corbys' inner sanctum. But back then, she was just another media identity, albeit armed with a hefty chequebook.

Just three weeks after Schapelle's arrest, *60 Minutes* paid $10,000 for an exclusive undercover 'police cell' interview. With the knowledge and approval of Mercedes, the money went directly to pay the legal bills. Veteran reporter Liz Hayes asked Schapelle: 'Are you telling me you've never ever taken drugs?'

SCHAPELLE CORBY: (Laughs nervously) People have experimented when they're in, like, Year 8, Year 9. I did experiment in Year 8 and Year 9, but I get really, really paranoid. I can't . . . I can't . . . I can't be around it.

LIZ HAYES: So you did take drugs as a teenager?

SCHAPELLE CORBY: Oh, I experimented. And I'm pretty sure most, maybe 90 per cent, 80 per cent of teenagers actually do.

LIZ HAYES: So you're not a drug taker now?

SCHAPELLE CORBY: No, not at all. As my tests prove.

LIZ HAYES: You're not a dealer?

SCHAPELLE CORBY: No, I'm not a dealer.

LIZ HAYES: You've never sold drugs?

SCHAPELLE CORBY: Never sold drugs.

LIZ HAYES: Never bought drugs?

SCHAPELLE CORBY: No, never. Not even when I was experimenting, I never did, no. So as I say, I shouldn't be here. And it's just really, really hard to sit in that cell for three days straight, not getting let out of the cage once. Um, it's really hard to keep strong and not think—well, you just think, 'Who? Am I ever going to find out who did this?'

The biggest problem with the story was that Schapelle looked shifty and manic—she chewed gum and spoke too fast. By the end of the program, very few Australians were convinced that a stranger had put 4.2 kilos of marijuana in her boogie board bag. Mercedes also appeared on the program. She was asked by Liz Hayes, 'If Schapelle didn't put the drugs in the bag, then who did?' Mercedes didn't hesitate with her reply and blamed the Indonesians: 'Oh, everybody is just saying, "Ooh mafia sabotage."'

Although the early media coverage was overwhelmingly negative, the prospect of a pretty young woman receiving the death penalty had intensified the intrigued Australian public's interest in the unfolding story. But for Schapelle's Indonesian legal team the growing media interest was a double-edged sword—while it gave the defence case a public profile, it also made it extremely difficult to 'manoeuvre the case' behind the scenes.

The Indonesian judicial system is notoriously corrupt, especially in connection with large civil cases, but no charges of corruption had ever been levelled against the three judges appointed to Corby's case. Head Judge Linton Sirait was a member of the bench that sentenced the chief Bali bomber, Imam Samudra, to death. His personal record in matters of drug smuggling is stark. 'I've handled many cases,' he reminded everyone on 24 May 2005, just three days before handing down his verdict. 'Not hundreds or 200, but over 500 since I became judge. As far as I remember, for narcotics cases, I haven't yet set anyone free.'

Vasu had one networking ploy up his sleeve. He obtained the services of veteran court performer Erwin Siregar to support the inexperienced Lily in defending Schapelle's innocence in the upcoming court case. The charming and deep-voiced Siregar was close friends with Judge Sirait—they both hailed from the same village in Medan in north Sumatra. In Bali, they were also actively involved in the same church, so Vasu calculated there would be many informal opportunities for the likeable Siregar to gauge the mood of the trial and have the ear of the judge.

Even so, Siregar had deep reservations about taking on the case—that is, until he met Schapelle. 'Every drug case I have been involved with, I have lost; but I believe her,' he told the documentary makers. Although one side of Siregar was genuinely moved by Schapelle's intoxicating combination of beauty and tears, his rational thinking side was somewhat perplexed. He thought innocence was impossible, given the shape of the plastic bag that contained the marijuana. He assumed someone had taken a hell of a lot of time to make sure it was moulded exactly to the same shape as the boogie board.

Over and over Siregar wrestled with the same question in his head: 'How can the boogie board bag and the marijuana bag be the same size? So sometimes I'm thinking, "Does this truly belong to Schapelle, or not? But if not belong to Schapelle, how come the plastic bag is same?" That's why I ask again to Schapelle, "This is yours or not?" She say no! Now the truth is in God.'

While Erwin left the question of innocence to God and networked the case with legal mates on the ground, Vasu's focus turned to Schapelle's travel companions, Ally and Katrina. He had to know what their evidence would be about the packaging of the boogie board bag on the morning they left Brisbane.

The Corbys said firmly 'that everyone had seen the bag being packed'. Ally and Katrina agreed. They both could clearly remember the exact moment Schapelle zipped up the bag, and they would say there was no bag of marijuana inside it. Who could blame them, even if they had not been able to recall it? They'd been told Schapelle faced the death penalty if they couldn't put together a credible defence. Katrina recalled on film: 'The boogie board was already packed. In the morning Ally, as we were about to leave . . . we were all under the shed and Ally, um . . . had Schapelle's flippers. And Ally handed the flippers to Schapelle, and Schapelle opened the boogie board up. Everyone seen, and she just chucked the flippers in and closed up and just packed our bags in the car and off we went.'

The two young women each went over and over the story again and again. They had exactly the same version of events.

CHAPTER 18

The Singing Lawyer

'She needed a defence and she needed a defence quickly.'
—Robin Tampoe, Schapelle's former lawyer

Schapelle's trial finally got under way in January 2005 and played out over a five-month period with one court hearing scheduled per week. Attending court days was bitter-sweet for Schapelle. She resented being handcuffed to her fellow female prisoners and being herded into the prison van like sheep for the sweaty twenty-minute trip to the Bali District Court in Denpasar. As the van ducked and weaved through the traffic with sirens blaring, the only comfort was the passing scenery—a blurry glimpse of the world outside Kerobokan Prison grounds.

During her first days in court the media presence was relatively low-key compared to the circus it would eventually become. As she and the other prisoners were roughly escorted by their guards into the court's holding cell, Schapelle masked her nerves by talking through the bars to the waiting camera crews and reporters. She came across as a friendly, chatty girl-next-door type and certainly didn't look like a drug dealer.

Everyone noticed that she had taken care with her make-up, and in particular how she had plucked her eyebrows into perfect arches above her dramatic, spectacular eyes. News photographers marvelled at how beautiful Schapelle looked as she peered through the bars. The cameras loved her, and it was impossible to take a bad photo of her.

But the first day inside the stifling hot courtroom turned out to be a complete disaster for Schapelle. As she sat with her defence team, it became overwhelmingly clear that the chief government prosecutor, Ida Bagus Wiswantanu, was going to go hard on the case. His key witness was the quietly spoken, highly regarded customs officer I Gusti Winata. In meticulous, unembroidered detail, Winata explained how Schapelle had panicked at the customs checkpoint and confessed there was marijuana inside her boogie board bag before it was opened.

Schapelle could feel the eyes of the reporters on her as they waited for her reaction to Winata's damning account of that day. She was forced to stare at the huge bag of marijuana that had been inside her boogie board bag. Since the vacuum-sealed plastic bags had been opened during the bust, the pungent dope smell had trailed along with them. Now the stench consumed the courtroom; in a dramatic show, the prosecutor extravagantly covered his nose with a handkerchief whenever he made reference to it.

Schapelle was called to the floor and asked by the judges to demonstrate how her flippers were placed inside the bag. She refused to stand near the plastic bag of pot—'I'm not going to touch it. It ruined my life,' she told the judge.

When Ally's turn came to testify, she sounded irritated and flustered when questioned under oath.

After the day's hearing was finally over, Schapelle was duly escorted back to the court's holding cell to wait for the other prisoners' hearings to be completed so they could all be bundled into the police van and escorted 'home' to Kerobokan.

The media contingent covering the case had by now all rushed from the court grounds to meet their various news report deadlines, so no one noticed Malcolm McCauley's mate, Dave McHugh, as he sidled up to the holding cell and called out Schapelle's name. McHugh had flown from Adelaide back to Bali without McCauley for the hearing. This time he had no problems in making direct contact with Schapelle.

McHugh originally claimed the meeting was a chance encounter: 'I was actually going in to the court, just to sit in the back in the court, and I got there too late. I asked someone, "What time is the hearing?" And he'd said, "Nah, it's finished," and he just took me around to these holding cells. And there was four or five police there, and I just said, "I've come to see Schapelle Corby," and there she was in the holding cell. She heard me say her name, and she just came to the door.'

Dressed in a singlet, shorts and thongs, McHugh looked like any other nondescript Australian tourist in Bali. He claims they chatted briefly, and he promised Schapelle he would be back later in the trial to support her. Strongly affected by her glamorous vulnerability, McHugh felt as if he was in the presence of a movie star. For the first time in his life he felt important, nervous and fascinated all at the same time—drawn by the silent connection he knew they both had.

As the court hearings progressed over the following weeks, time was running out for Schapelle's Indonesian defence team. They had nothing—no evidence, only family and friends for witnesses. No strategy—nothing. Since the Corby case had landed in his lap, Vasu often visited his village's Hindu temple to pray for inspiration, although realistically, he knew, divine intervention was highly unlikely. He suspected he had a solid chance of getting Schapelle off 'death row', but immediate freedom was an impossibility.

There was no doubt about it: Schapelle was in deep trouble. She couldn't claim to be a drug addict who was carrying drugs for personal use—no one was foolish enough to believe that 4.2 kilos of pot could be used by one person on a two-week holiday. Claiming to be an addict was a popular defence strategy for people facing drug charges in Indonesia and later worked well for the Australian model Michelle Leslie, who served a three-month prison term in Bali after being caught with two ecstasy pills. But, unlike Michelle Leslie, Schapelle was busted with a large-scale commercial importation of top quality 'skunk', not something you could fit in a handbag.

Privately Vasu figured that it was achievable to aim for a 15-year sentence. He then planned to appeal to the High Court to reduce the sentence to ten years, and appeal again to bring it down to five. Given the media attention now surrounding the arrest, this was a best-case scenario. However, he still needed a plausible defence if Schapelle was going to plead innocent. Vasu said later, 'I wanted to be able to open a door for the judges to walk through, so that the sentence could be reduced later on. They needed a feasible defence to work with and a reason to give her a low sentence.'

Just as the future of Corby's case was looking bleak, Vasu's prayers were answered and the heavens delivered to his doorstep two unlikely miracle workers. Together they would spin, manipulate and create a defence strategy so strikingly audacious that it would end up convincing 97 per cent of the Australian public that Schapelle Corby was innocent.

Former Gold Coast lawyer Robin Tampoe nearly died as a result of the Corby case. Later, with the aid of hindsight, he would come to see his near-death experience as a sign from God that he should never have got involved.

After years of living and working in Asia, Tampoe was an enthusiastic karaoke devotee with a yearning for singing the blues. He was also renowned for spontaneous sing-ing performances with live bands, with whom he would improvise and for fun change lyrics to popular songs. During the Corby case, Robin Tampoe's favourite tune was Michael Bublé's hit song 'Home'. He would sing it with his own personal twist to the lyrics: 'Pelle, we're going to get you home . . .'

Often Robin Tampoe's back-up singers were lawyer Lily Lubis and the beautiful Eka, who became known to millions of television viewers as Schapelle's alluring dark-haired court translator. Eka's voice was as captivating as her physical presence and, when the trio performed, it confirmed to everyone that Schapelle's legal team included an array of colourful characters straight from Central Casting.

It was at a defence team gathering held for family and supporters at the Bali home of Vasu Rasiah that the charis-matic Tampoe nearly died on the family and Rosleigh Rose. In what could have been a scene straight out of a movie, one minute the glowing Ros was gushing and fussing around him, and the next moment Mercedes was giving him 'the kiss of life'.

Tampoe was about to hype up the party with a live band performance. He was standing in bare feet at the edge of the swimming pool and had only just started to scream the first words to 'Stand By Me' when suddenly his body jolted and went into spasm. He flew up high into the air and landed straight in the swimming pool with a live microphone clenched firmly in his hand. It took the partygoers a little time to realise that Schapelle's new defence lawyer was actually being electrocuted in the swimming pool.

Lily desperately tried to pull Tampoe out of the water, and also received a shock from the live current in the pool. Quick-thinking Eka immediately ran and shut down the power to the house, while Tampoe was now being resuscitated by Mercedes. Tampoe's heart had literally stopped. He later recalled: 'I died and rose again, all in the space of ten minutes. Not a bad effort. Apparently Rosleigh Rose was sobbing—she must have liked me at some point.' By the end of her daughter's court case Ros would hate him, and Tampoe would publicly describe Ros and her family as 'ungrateful trash'.

Given the acrimony and sheer hatred that now exists between Tampoe and the Corbys, it's particularly poignant to note that, back in 2005, as he lay dying on the pool deck, it was Mercedes Corby who brought him back to life with her own desperate, urgent breath. These days, it's hard to imagine him entrusting Merc with his life—'I'd rather die than have her anywhere near me,' he says only half-jokingly to friends. But during the early months of the trial, Tampoe and the Corbys enjoyed a brief but passionate mutual lovefest that included flamboyant Gold Coast mobile phone entrepreneur 'Mad Ron' Bakir, who entered the scene with his best friend Robin Tampoe.

Locals on the Gold Coast knew Bakir from his outlandish television commercials, which ranged from setting himself on fire to jumping out of aeroplanes—all in the name of selling mobile phones. Schapelle and her family were well aware of his fame—they'd watched his zany TV commercials and he was a well-known identity on the Gold Coast scene.

When Bakir first met Schapelle inside Kerobokan Prison in Bali, she told him that she'd gone to one of his mobile phone shops to buy a new phone before the trip to Bali. The local store manager had knocked back her application because of bad credit. 'Well, love, you can have all the phones you want once we get out you out of here,' was Bakir's optimistic reply.

Bakir was only 28 years old when he joined the Corby defence team. He'd migrated to Australia from Lebanon as a five-year-old child, and by the age of 23 made a meteoric rise from a member of a poor migrant family to mobile phone entrepreneur. But his financial track record was unfortunately patchy—he'd crashed and burned more than once, and had also been declared bankrupt. He always denied that he'd joined the defence team for the publicity and told *The Hidden Truth* documentary team, 'I could have picked something else. I could've gone and built a children's hospital ward if I wanted to.'

Schapelle was already making front-page news in the *Gold Coast Bulletin* when Bakir became inspired to help her. He told the documentary crew: 'My PA called and said, "Have you read the paper? There's this girl who's been caught with drugs in her bag and we should help her." I said, "Are you feeling okay? Why would we want to help someone who's been trafficking drugs?" I said, "Deb, if the girl's guilty, she deserves to get whatever penalty she gets." ' For reasons he still can't explain, four days after this conversation Bakir decided to fly to Bali to meet Schapelle: 'Something said, "You've got to meet this girl." I don't know why.' He said that five minutes after meeting Corby, he was convinced without a doubt that she was innocent.

Corby case coordinator Vasu Rasiah wasn't impressed when out of the blue he was instructed by Mercedes Corby to attend a meeting with Ron Bakir and Robin Tampoe. 'I really didn't want anything to do with them,' he says. Vasu was annoyed that another lawyer had turned up in Bali— particularly an Australian lawyer. He was very protective of the case and feared it was about to be hijacked. But within a few hours of meeting the pair, Vasu was simply bowled over by Bakir's optimism and spirit: 'He reminded me of myself at his age. I love him like I love my own son.'

It was inside the confronting grounds of Kerobokan prison that Ron and Robin first met their 'damsel in distress'. Bakir told the media that he felt compassionate towards Schapelle because she 'reminded him of his sister'. Schapelle was constantly in tears as she described the appalling third world conditions. Opened in 1979, Kerobokan was initially built to house about 500 inmates, but in 2005 there were more than 700 prisoners crammed inside its cells. Schapelle frequently protested her innocence, both verbally and later in cards and letters she wrote to Bakir. She took to writing rhyming poetry to him—poems that were rich with metaphors about freedom and innocence. Bakir was impressed with her writing skills and didn't realise until much later that her self-described 'original' words had actually been copied from the pages of one of her many positive thinking books.

During his visits to Kerobokan, Schapelle playfully flirted with Bakir as they sat together outside the prison church. Often, to his embarrassment, she would drag him away from the rest of her visitors to whisper conspiratorially in his ear. Bakir asked his beloved sister to buy expensive make-up and skincare products for Schapelle, and he quickly fulfilled her bizarre request for a plastic wading pool to sit in.

Like her mother, Schapelle was a shameless flirt when the occasion called for it. She was particularly dramatic when saying goodbye to Bakir after his long prison visits. Her farewell hugs lingered longer than they needed to. The barbed wire, the prison guards and the beautiful girl with the tearful blue eyes were a mesmerising mix that rendered Bakir incapable of believing the Gold Coast beauty could possibly be guilty. He later told the documentary crew: 'If I had actually seen her open the boogie board bag and grab the four kilos of marijuana and stick them in the bag, I would have hesitated to believe that she did it. That's the honest to God truth. That's how convinced I was. I said to Robin, there is no way in the world this girl is guilty.'

When Bakir and Tampoe first met with Mercedes Corby she was with her friend Jodie Power. 'They seemed nice enough, although they had previously been concerned about the Indonesian lawyers. Mercedes was very nervous, she seemed to me like a girl under pressure. It was obvious that all the decisions in relation to Schapelle's defence had been left up to her, a pretty big ask for anyone. I suppose she saw us as able to take some of the pressure of the decision-making away from her,' recalled Tampoe to *The Hidden Truth* team.

Bakir was particularly concerned about the background of the family, and wanted to know whether there was any history of drug use or convictions that related to any family members. According to Tampoe, Mercedes confirmed to Bakir that 'Schapelle didn't do drugs, didn't sell drugs and was a victim.'

After receiving advice from several confidants back on the Gold Coast, who warned him not to become involved with the case, Bakir promptly hired a private investigator to check out Schapelle's history. But the investigator didn't find anything incriminating, just some unsubstantiated rumours about the family. The young entrepreneur decided to follow his gut instinct about Schapelle and ignore the insidious claims. 'You can't turn your back on a person due to rumours, and I don't believe in guilt by association,' was his common mantra to anyone who provided him with scuttlebutt about the family.

Meanwhile, Vasu was becoming particularly paranoid about keeping Mick Corby and Michael Jnr hidden away from both the media and the court hearings. 'Her bloody brother looks like a drug dealer,' Vasu fumed to one journalist who was keen on interviewing the mysterious Michael Jnr. 'Have you seen what he looks like? I don't want him anywhere near the judges!' When the journalist insisted that a story on the father could be sympathetic because he 'was dying from cancer', Vasu was annoyed and said, 'He can still walk around all right. That story won't work.'

Ros discussed the case with Bakir only a couple of times and yet, without hesitation, she described him to the press as Schapelle's 'White Knight'. By this stage, Mick had retreated quietly into the background. 'Looking back I guess it was strange the parents didn't ask us any questions about the strategy we were going to take,' recalled Bakir in the documentary. 'I think I only spoke to the father once. I remember

I asked Vasu, "What do you need?" and he said, "Get me witnesses and evidence." So that's what I did.'

Within days of meeting Schapelle, Bakir declared his commitment to her cause: 'I will do whatever it takes, at whatever cost, I will utilise all the resources, all the funds that I have access to, to ensure her release, because I believe her.'

Robin Tampoe was less enamoured of Schapelle's protestations of innocence. But taking on the Corby case was like an adrenalin rush to the 39-year-old lawyer. The challenge of creating a reasonable doubt, thinking up a defence that would overcome the case's glaring weaknesses was his ultimate dream gig. At the age of 25, the ambitious solicitor had opened his own law practice, Hoolihans Lawyers, on the Gold Coast. He remembers fondly: 'The practice flourished. We were young, hungry and not afraid to work, more importantly we kept winning. We took on national law firms and won. We took on cases that no one else wanted and challenges that seemed impossible. I suppose that was the attraction of Schapelle's case. It was a challenge and it had been a while since I had been challenged. The challenge was to beat the death penalty.'

Robin Tampoe doesn't recall the details of how Mercedes Corby saved him as he lay dying by the swimming pool, but as he opened his eyes and regained consciousness the architect of what would become famously known as the 'baggage handler defence' was back—alive, on top of his game and ready for the biggest struggle of his professional life.

CHAPTER 19

God's Plant

*'I don't know what's in the bag, because it was never tested. It could
be bloody lawn clippings for all I know.'*
—Mick Corby

Having obtained no evidence from Australia that could
possibly help their case, the Indonesian legal team originally
thought they had little choice but to run with a defence that
attempted to prove drugs had been placed in Schapelle's boogie
board bag by corrupt customs officers on her arrival in Bali.

Lily Lubis and case coordinator Vasu Rasiah were the
first members of the legal team to travel to Canberra to
meet with Foreign Affairs Minister Alexander Downer and
plead Schapelle's cause. It was a major coup that the duo
had secured a meeting with such a high-profile government minister. Downer remembers Vasu challenged him by
asking, 'Do you know anything about Indonesia?' Downer
was insulted! 'It's not a very polite thing to say to a Foreign
Minister. I said, "I know a bit about it." He said, "Well, you
know how these schemes operate." And I said, "Well,
describe the scheme to me." '

Vasu then proceeded to tell Downer that they believed Indonesian baggage handlers were stuffing marijuana inside the bags of tourists when they arrived in Bali, so that customs officers and police at the airport could extract bribes from them. Downer recalls Vasu telling him: 'Police arrest the person; they go to a watch-house. And that's when the police say, "Give us ten thousand dollars, and we'll let you go." And that's what's happened to Schapelle.'

Downer remembers saying to Vasu: 'How can you prove that? Did the police ask her for money? That would be the proof.'

And Vasu replied, 'Well, no, they didn't.'

Then Downer said, 'Well, your whole scheme has collapsed, and there obviously isn't an explanation.'

The meeting with Downer hadn't gone well—he thought their theory was bullshit. Lawyer Robin Tampoe thought it was bullshit too and he immediately dumped the strategy. Tampoe always believed this defence would have the potential to upset the Indonesian judges and said, 'They'll be particularly cranky, because we're accusing Indonesia of setting up this poor Australian girl for this horrific potential death penalty crime. It was a stupid idea.' It also didn't make any rational sense to him that corrupt authorities would use 4.2 kilos of cannabis to set Schapelle up in order to extract a bribe, when in theory they could have obtained the same result with a simple gram.

He adds: 'The quality of the cannabis also concerned me. If the cannabis was tested and proved to be hydroponic, this defence would fail, as hydroponic cannabis is extremely hard to come by in Indonesia and is incredibly expensive. This fact is contrary to the way we ran our ultimate defence in the media. We asked: why would anyone bring coal to

Newcastle? Answer: When it is worth more in Newcastle than where it is sourced.' He privately made this argument to the Indonesian lawyers.

In Bali, the medicinal properties of marijuana are fabled. 'We call it God's Plant,' Mercedes's husband Wayan told the documentary crew. 'It's not a dangerous drug, and it can help sick people with cancer.' During a defence strategy meeting in Bali, Tampoe and Bakir were given an up close and personal view of 'God's Plant' when it was placed in the middle of a table in front of them. The cannabis was a sample that had been 'souvenired' from Schapelle's boogie board stash by an anonymous, but reliable, member of the defence team. 'Knowing what I know now about the tough penalties for drugs in Indonesia, we should have run the hell out of that room,' recalls Tampoe.

For members of the Indonesian defence team, the origin of the cannabis was a puzzle to be solved. But Robin Tampoe's initial gut reaction was that it probably wasn't a good idea to go investigating its DNA—'Be careful where it leads,' he warned. There had been plenty of speculation in the Indonesian press that this was what was known on the streets of Kuta as 'Aussie Gold' or 'Lemon Juice'. Bali's narcotics chief, Bambang Sugiarto, told a local paper: 'The dried marijuana that was found by officers in the bag belonging to Corby is considered unique. It gives out a very strong odour and is shorter compared to marijuana from Aceh or Medan. The marijuana is believed to be a foreign product.'

Before Tampoe joined the case, Vasu and Lily had made inquiries about getting the marijuana DNA tested to try and identify where it came from. If they could prove that it was not from Australia, or at least not from Queensland, then they believed that might help Schapelle's case. Vasu says:

'You know, originally we went to Canberra and met experts, and Adelaide experts. And they said by testing the marijuana you can identify exactly where it is grown and then they can give a DNA sample, all those things. And we even got a couple of samples from the Bali police for this testing.'

In the end Schapelle signed a letter giving her consent to have the marijuana DNA tested, but it never happened. Vasu says that Mercedes then contacted the Australian Consulate in Bali to get advice about the test. The AFP's liaison officer, Paul Hunniford, wrote a letter to the Indonesian defence lawyers advising that 'the AFP has no jurisdiction nor does it have any role in facilitating such testing. Any engagement of Australian foreign experts would not include AFP and is a matter between you and the Indonesian authorities to arrange.' The Indonesian police were also unwilling to help Schapelle's lawyers.

Desperate to obtain a result, the legal team wrote to Dr Lynne Milne, a leading palynologist and forensic scientist based in Perth who was famous for having solved a murder case through her meticulous forensic work with pollen. In a letter to this distinguished scientist, Lily Lubis admitted that the legal team had obtained an 'illegal sample' of the drugs Schapelle was arrested with, and they wanted to fly Dr Milne to Bali to carry out secret forensic tests. Lily indicated that if the results were not 'favourable' to the case they would not be used. Dr Milne, dismayed that she would be required to work with an illegal cannabis sample in Bali, declined the offer. But the defence team was equally reluctant to fly to Perth with the stash for scientific examination there, and thus chance their luck with customs in two countries.

When they were in Australia, Vasu and Lily had investigated the origins of the inner and outer transparent plastic bags that Schapelle's marijuana had been tightly packed in. The brand name of the bags found inside Schapelle's boogie board bag was 'Space Bag' and each bag had an individual serial number. Space Bags are commonly used to pack bulky winter clothes in during summer, after the air has been sucked out.

Drug dealers particularly love Space Bags because, when packed down in them, marijuana can be tightly compressed and moulded into a shape. When Vasu and Lily tracked down the Space Bag manufacturers, they discovered that the serial numbers on Schapelle's two plastic bags showed the bags had been produced in the US and shipped to a warehouse in Melbourne from where they were distributed to two major supermarket chains in Australia. In 2005 Space Bags were not available for purchase anywhere in Indonesia, which made it harder for the legal team to argue that the marijuana had been snuck into Schapelle's boogie board bag after she arrived at Denpasar Airport.

During discussions with senior Queensland police officers, Vasu and Lily also showed photographs of the marijuana found inside the boogie board bag. The police said it looked like hydroponic marijuana, probably from South Australia. The cops told Vasu there'd been some big busts of hydro trafficked from Adelaide to Queensland shortly before Schapelle's arrest in 2004.

While the defence team was busy speculating about the origin of the marijuana, Malcolm McCauley sat tight and hoped that the Australian public would remain forever in the dark about the popularity in Bali of his South Australian home-brand hydro.

One of the most effective pieces of spin from Corby supporters was the 'coals to Newcastle' argument. Why would anybody take marijuana to Bali when it's not worth anything over there? As one of the many 'Free Schapelle' websites put it: 'No one would try to do that, it's like taking coal to Newcastle or sardines to Scandinavia.'

Not so, says McCauley, keen to provide a compelling motive for Schapelle's risky drug run: 'While Indonesia might be stinking hot, the general conditions are amongst the worst for growing good dope. People think, "Ah, Bali—it's sunny and nice. The hooter surely thrives everywhere." Well, as any grower would tell you, it ain't as simple as that.' He explains: 'The weed is shit in Bali, and it's all down to the humidity. Once the plant buds up, the moisture content in the air gets inside. It saturates the flower and very quickly, long before it has had a chance to bloom, it begins to rot. The buds rot. They go a grey-black colour. Once that happens, forget it. The ratio, in terms of strength, is about five to one compared to South Australian hydro. It's weak—you have to use more and, consequently, it's worth shit.'

McCauley argues that, if the two products were placed side by side, even someone who doesn't smoke could tell, just by looking, that one is far superior to the other. 'South Australian hydro has very high THC content. The heads form bigger, brighter and tighter—they grow to the size of donkey's dicks. It's trimmed up perfectly and there's zero waste. Whereas the stuff over there is grown outside—it's dull in colour, it's leafy, full of stems and, because of the humidity I just referred to, there's very little THC and bugger-all strength.'

McCauley adds that seasoned dope smokers in Bali are no different to anywhere else. 'Everyone and his dog wants good hydro and they're prepared to pay that little bit extra, because it goes further and gets you to where you want to be. Not only that—the high lasts a helluva lot longer. I haven't been over there in a little while but, last time I knew, a j-bag [a small transparent plastic bag] of the local bush would cost you, say, $30, whereas the other person, selling the same quantity of Aussie hydro, would be selling at $50. If it means paying an extra $20, hell, it really is a no-brainer. You're getting five times the strength.

'If people still can't get it round their heads why someone would go to the trouble of transporting it from Australia, well then consider this: you get at least ten j-bags out of every ounce of hooter and, of course, there are 16 ounces to every pound. That's 160 bags at, say, $50 dollars a pop. Maybe more. Now, do your own calculations—once you start breaking it up into those small quantities, you're up big money. You can be making $8000 or more from every pound. Mick was buying it at $3000. That's pretty big dough.'

Independent investigations back up McCauley's claims. The ABC's Triple J radio station had plenty of listeners with experience of drugs and host Steve Cannane decided to ask his audience about the market for pot in Bali. He says: 'We put a call out to our listeners, asking the question "Is there a market for hydroponic dope in Indonesia?", and we subsequently found out that there was. So to me that put a big question mark over one of the Corbys' key arguments.' One caller to Triple J said, 'There is quite a strong market for good pot in Bali; there is a good reason to bring it into the country. Hydro sells for at least $20 US per gram, or $20,000 a kilogram.'

Many westerners have been busted taking drugs like cocaine, hashish and ecstasy into the Bali tourism market.

However, western tourists don't bother smuggling speed into Bali, because Indonesia is awash with various forms of amphetamines. Unlike amphetamines, Aussie Gold is in demand and there's a very good reason to take it to Bali. One young Australian surfer, a long-time traveller to Bali, explained that Indonesian pot is mostly not worth buying: 'I know people who can get weed over there, and it's grown on the neighbouring islands like Lombok. The local grass is full of seeds and not very strong, and the westerners don't want it. They also don't want to buy pot from the Balinese in case they are cops.' The price of Aussie Gold varies, depending on who is buying it: 'The Japanese pay the most—they get the most ripped off and can pay up to $50 US per gram. The Australians pay less than the Japanese, and the European tourists—maybe $20 to $30 US per gram. When it's hard to get in Bali, the price goes up.'

Around this time the ABC's Indonesian correspondent, Tim Palmer, told Triple J: 'I have spoken to people who have put prices on this and, if you look at prices in Australia by the pound for hydroponic marijuana, it's currently dropped as low as two and a half thousand dollars. I previously valued the amount of marijuana carried in the boogie board bag as being worth maybe $30,000. It was suggested to me that it might only have been worth $25,000, because of a glut in the market. Here [in Indonesia], from the best estimates that we've got, selling it in smaller gram quantities it could come out to about $60,000 US—that's $80,000 Australian. You could triple or quadruple your price potentially— certainly make a premium on the value of the marijuana from Australia. To argue that there could not possibly be any motive to bring high-grade marijuana into this country, and that this was always "coals to Newcastle" and there was never any reason for this prosecution, simply flies in the face of [the] facts.'

Matthew Moore, the then Indonesian correspondent for Fairfax newspapers, also made some calculations about the value of Schapelle's marijuana in Indonesia. When the plastic bags were opened in court, he wrote, 'It was clear it was made up of buds the size of bananas, which emitted a powerful smell whenever the plastic was opened.' He asked around Bali and estimated that the marijuana inside Schapelle's boogie board increased in value, in Aussie dollars, from around $20,000 to $25,000 in Australia to somewhere between $80,000 and $96,000 in Bali.

If Schapelle had cleared customs on 8 October 2004, it was an easy $60,000. If pot was in short supply at that time, then the profit could have been as much as $100,000. The young Australian surfer says: 'I thought Schapelle Corby was guilty from the get-go. I knew there was a market in Bali and a reason to take it there. I'm sure they thought they could just walk straight through the airport. I usually go straight through without my bags being searched—the customs guys rarely bother checking your bags.'

As Malcolm McCauley so eloquently puts it, there is no shortage of buyers 'in party town'. 'You've got the expats—huge market there. The surfing crew and the beach mob—they live off the stuff. And, like I said, they're willing to part with good money for good gear. To the non-smoker, you have to put it this way: "Would you rather eat a piece of leather—or a decent piece of steak?"'

CHAPTER 20

Creating the Baggage Handler Defence

'They can't find her guilty. It's impossible. Her bag was unlocked.'
—Mercedes Corby

One of Robin Tampoe's favourite lines was 'I'm in the business of reasonable doubt'. Now he was on the hunt for it. He recalled on camera to the documentary team: 'Schapelle needed a defence, and it was my job to give her one. Without something mind-blowing she was just the same as every other drug courier. And who remembers their names? Not me, not anyone. And who cares? Not me, not anyone. Why? Because they are drug dealers, and we don't care about drug dealers. Drug dealers get what they deserve. Can you name one of the 150 Australians languishing in foreign prisons around the world? I didn't think so. We had to make everyone believe that Schapelle wasn't like the rest of them—she was innocent, and she was a victim.'

The defence team wrote the facts of the case up on a whiteboard. The reality of the situation was depressing.

Young love. It's Christmas 1971 and a 26-year-old Malcolm McCauley proudly poses with Kathleen, 21, at a function held at the Finsbury Hotel in Woodville North, South Australia.

Where it all began. Malcolm McCauley takes a trip down memory lane in March 2010 and surveys the remains of his old sausage skinning factory at Gawler River in South Australia. The property housed his first hydroponic crop fifteen years earlier in 1995.

The odd couple. Malcolm McCauley (left) and former AFP drug cop Roger Rathjen (right) enjoy a day at the greyhounds in March 2010.

Left Living the high life. Malcolm McCauley poses alongside a red Porsche acquired during the course of business in 2001. *Right* Partners in crime. Jeff Jellese (left) and Malcolm McCauley share an ANZAC Day drink at their local, Salisbury RSL, in April 2005. Six months later both men were arrested as the chief organisers behind a million dollar marijuana syndicate operating between South Australia and Queensland.

Left The Pig Shooter. Prior to his arrest in October 2005, Wayne Williams controlled the hydroponic marijuana supply along the North Queensland coast line. (*The Northern Miner*) *Right* Inside the cutting room. One of Malcolm McCauley's former growers and couriers, Peter Dudley, posing with a batch of freshly cropped Aussie Gold in 2001.

Busted! Gladstone Detective Sergeant Troy Lehmann with some of the marijuana plants found during the raid on Tony Lewis's farm. Kim Moore tipped off police about his marijuana-growing business and his associate Mick Corby running drugs to Bali. (*Gladstone Observer*)

And there was more. Apart from the 197 cannabis plants found on Lewis's farm, detectives also seized bags of stockpiled vacuum-sealed cannabis stored in freezers. (*Gladstone Observer*)

Left Mick's best mate. Tony Lewis leaves Rockhampton Magistrates Court in 2005 with partner Beth Lavender after being charged with numerous offences relating to the marijuana seizure on his property. (*Gladstone Observer*) *Right* Happier days. Mick Corby and Schapelle proudly pose for a beachside snap in Queensland. (Supplied)

Oblivious to what lies ahead. Happy travellers (from left) Katrina Richards, Schapelle Corby, Ally McComb and Schapelle's half brother, James Kisina, pose at Brisbane Airport before their flight to Bali. Seven years on, it remains the last picture of Schapelle taken in Australia. (Supplied)

Unwanted celebrity. With a hungry media pack looking on, Schapelle Corby turns to her family during her trial. (AFP/Newspix)

Staying positive. Schapelle receives a welcome visit from her mother Rosleigh Rose in Kerobokan Prison in 2005.

Carrying the weight of the world on his shoulders. Mick Corby reveals Schapelle is 'suicidal' during an interview with the author in April 2005.

Meeting Father Christmas. Mick Corby showed the author this photo of an excited Schapelle (far right) during an interview in 2005 and then took it to Bali several days later to lift his daughter's flagging spirits. Mick said, 'I found it while I was packing and the moment she sees it, I know it's going to light up her face. She has such a beautiful smile, and this will bring it back.' (Supplied)

Unexpected company. Kathleen McCauley arrived in Bali in October 2004 to discover an additional travelling companion, Adelaide pot grower Dave McHugh.

With the supporters. Ros and her partner Greg Martin pose with Malcolm McCauley and Dave McHugh outside Kerobokan Prison in May 2005.

First contact. Malcolm McCauley and David McHugh meet Schapelle at the holding cells prior to a court hearing in May 2005.

The photograph that created the storm. South Australian police stumbled upon this photograph of Malcolm McCauley and Schapelle Corby in Kerobokan Prison during a police drug raid on his house. When the shot was later leaked to the press, the question was asked: what was he doing there?

Jailhouse visit. Pot grower Dave McHugh poses with Schapelle Corby inside Kerobokan Prison two weeks before her verdict was handed down in May 2005.

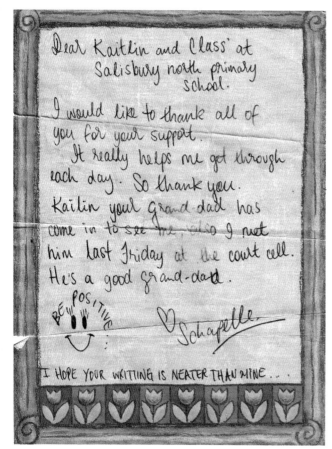

Dear Kaitlin and Class' at
Salisbury north primary
school.
I would like to thank all of
you for your support.
It really helps me get through
each day. So thank you.
Kaitlin your grand-dad has
come in to see me, also I met
him last Friday at the court cell.
He's a good grand-dad.
BE POSITIVE
♡ Schapelle.
I HOPE YOUR WRITTING IS NEATER THAN MINE....

Alibi. After the jailhouse photos were leaked in December 2005, McCauley produced this handwritten letter from Schapelle to his granddaughter Kaitlin in an effort to divert attention away from their links to marijuana.

Inside the Secret Garden. Ros enjoys a drink with Corby supporters David McHugh and Malcolm McCauley at the Secret Garden bar, Kuta, during the lead up to Schapelle's trial.

Old Blue Eyes. Schapelle's father Mick in Bali in 2005. (Glenn Martin)

Courtroom drama. A distressed Schapelle collapses onto the shoulder of her translator Eka Sulistiowati after fainting in court. Mercedes was quick to the scene to comfort her sister. (Glenn Martin)

Left A sister's support. A dishevelled Mercedes arrives at Kerobokan Prison with supplies for Schapelle in 2005. (Glenn Martin) *Right* The journalist. Former *Gold Coast Bulletin* journalist and Corby crusader Tony Wilson was sacked for unprofessional conduct relating to the saga.

The defence team. From left to right, Lili Lubis, Ron Bakir, Vasu Rasiah and Robin Tampoe discuss Schapelle's case in May 2005. (Lukman S Bintoro/Newspix)

The surf loving brother. Michael Corby Jr poses at the family's fish and chips shop, the Rox Seafood and Takeaway at Southport, in the weeks before his sister's verdict. (Steve Holland)

Lying on camera? When interviewed for a documentary in 2006 Malcolm McCauley and Dave McHugh claimed they were mere 'supporters' of Schapelle.

The Customs officer. I Gusti Nyoman Winata was thrust into the spotlight after discovering the 4.2 kg of marijuana in Schapelle's boogie board bag.

Ganja 1. Indonesian police parade Schapelle's 'ganja' before the media prior to it being destroyed in March 2006.

Ganja 2. Taken out of its packaging, police douse the marijuana with fuel before they destroy it.

Ganja 3. The marijuana goes up in smoke.

Breaking the pact. A battle-scarred Malcolm McCauley opens up to the *Sun-Herald* in July 2008 revealing it was one of his couriers who delivered the drugs to Mick Corby the day before Schapelle left for Bali. (David Mariuz)

Pipe down. Mercedes Corby smokes marijuana from a penis-shaped pipe during her self-confessed 'silly teenager years'. The photograph was submitted to the NSW Supreme Court in March 2008 as evidence in her defamation trial against Channel 7. Mercedes won.

Two worlds collide. Schapelle holds a copy of the January 2009 edition of *Ralph* with her sister Mercedes on the front cover. Mercedes was reportedly paid $50,000 for the eight-page spread. (Lukman S Bintoro/ Newspix)

The only thing they had going for them was the fact that Schapelle's boogie board bag was unlocked. In theory, this meant it was possible to argue that someone else had put the drugs inside the bag.

The Indonesian customs officer who had busted Schapelle, I Gusti Winata, believed that Schapelle had purposely chosen an unlocked bag as insurance in case she was caught. He said that she could always later claim that someone else put the drugs inside her boogie board bag. His view is: 'She seems to know the loopholes of our law and, when caught, how she can get away—bringing it in a transparent plastic bag and that the bag is not locked. In court these two things can actually lighten up her sentence, as it cannot be proven that she intentionally hid away the marijuana. She knows that, if she's caught, she might get a lighter sentence.'

Winata was right—the unlocked boogie board bag left a door open for Schapelle's defence team to exploit. They started talking about 'reasonable doubt' and 'lack of evidence' in the case against Schapelle. The Indonesian police couldn't prove who put the drugs in Schapelle's bag.

The spin coming from the Corby camp was that the Australian government was withholding information that could free Schapelle. Tampoe's first target was Qantas Airways. He got on the phone and started pressuring the Qantas lawyers. 'I asked why they couldn't provide me with the x-ray images of Corby's suitcase or board bag when they were checked in at Brisbane airport. She reluctantly advised that, because this flight was technically a domestic flight, her suitcases were not required to be x-rayed, as Qantas didn't [require] the x-raying of luggage that was destined for the hold of the aircraft on domestic flights, only hand luggage. And that, in any event, only something like one

SINS OF THE FATHER

in one hundred bags destined for Indonesia were x-rayed. But she proudly told me that 100 per cent of bags bound for the United States and the UK were x-rayed. I would have thought, though, that after the Bali bombing, Marriott bombing and the Australian Embassy bombing, the x-raying of 100 per cent of bags coming from or going to Indonesia would have some sort of priority.'

Tampoe's next question to the Qantas lawyer would be echoed in newspapers and throughout the media in the coming weeks, bringing much unwanted attention to the airline. 'I said to the Qantas lawyer: "Is this right? I could put a bomb in my suitcase and no one would know because it isn't x-rayed? Is it possible that it would then be loaded into the aircraft luggage hold, and I could then remotely detonate it from my mobile phone, either as a passenger on the aircraft or from another destination?" Her answer to me was "Yes."'

Tampoe hung up the phone in total disbelief. He could not get over what he had just been told. He looked down at the notes that he'd scrawled during the conversation. He had circled the words 'bomb' and 'no x-ray', and underlined 'domestic flights'.

Finally Tampoe had the ammunition he had been looking for and he quickly rang a media contact at ABC Radio in May 2005 to let fly on air: 'Isn't Qantas the safest airline in the world? Don't we hear every day how much money is supposedly spent on securing our borders? After September 11, isn't security of our aircraft of paramount importance? Obviously not! I can't believe how badly the Australian public has been conned into believing how lucky we are that our government is continuously upgrading security to protect its citizens,' he explained during the fiery interview.

196

The story took off like wildfire. 'Suddenly Australia was listening. Australia was pissed off. Qantas and our politicians had been lying to us. Not only were they putting our lives at risk by not giving a rat's about our safety, they wanted a subpoena before they would provide basic information to Corby's defence,' Tampoe recalls.

The reality of the situation was that the Corby defence strategy would now expose two significant inadequacies in Australian airport security: there were no x-ray images, because they didn't x-ray domestic luggage, and there was no CCTV footage, because the CCTV system had been experiencing technical problems during this period. They also drew attention to the fact that there were no individual baggage weights of Schapelle Corby's suitcase and boogie board bag when she'd checked her luggage into Brisbane airport. It seemed to Tampoe that air passengers should have an absolute entitlement to know what their baggage weights are when they check in to an airport. 'It's commonsense. That way, if you arrive in Indonesia, or any other country for that matter, and you find drugs in your bag, you can compare the weight on checking in to the weight on arrival. And, if there is a difference, then someone other than the passenger must have placed the drugs in your bag. Qantas told me it wasn't necessary to give individual baggage weights. They comply with an international standard and that's good enough. Just because a standard is international doesn't mean it's a good standard.'

In Schapelle Corby's case she was travelling with three companions and, because she was the first at the counter with her friends, the combined luggage was weighed together and ticketed to her; essentially what this means is that she would be deemed the owner of the luggage on arrival.

As Tampoe delved further, looking for more evidence, he concluded that the only way forward was to somehow turn the overwhelming lack of evidence into a positive: 'None of the evidence existed—through a combination of system failures, pathetic airport and aviation security, and large organisations that did not want their inadequacies exposed. Ron and I were yelling and screaming in the media about all the problems we were encountering—the barricades that were being put up by big business. The media was watching and loving it; the politicians were watching and hating it, which was a good thing because suddenly doors started opening.'

But the clock was ticking. Tampoe and Bakir literally had three weeks to pull together a case that would help the Indonesian legal team. Then finally a breakthrough arrived. Tampoe received a phone call that would change everything: 'I received a phone call from one of my best mates, Marc. He told me that his partner Veronique was tuned into the ABC's Triple J radio station and was listening to presenter Steve Cannane, whose program that day centred around baggage handlers and drugs.' Tampoe immediately went online to listen to a recording of the program. 'Could baggage handlers be the ones who put dope in Schapelle Corby's boogie board bag? That's one theory that's come through to Triple J's *HACK* website.' Cannane had had a flurry of emails and calls from people with information about baggage handlers. Almost all callers said that Schapelle was innocent and had been used by baggage handlers to transport drugs.

One caller said, 'It's kind of known that domestic baggage handlers are putting it in passengers' bags to ship it between the states.'

'OK, why would they do that?' asked Cannane.

'Because it's away from where they inspect the bags—doesn't go through to any of the customs areas. It's put on board by a particular baggage handler and then obviously coordinated for a shift worker who is on when that plane arrives and takes off.'

Robin Tampoe continued listening to Triple J and heard the following: 'It's not hard to imagine that Schapelle's luggage was used for this purpose on the domestic end of her flight, with the Sydney baggage handler unable to remove the pot from her bag prior to flying to Indonesia. It certainly makes more sense than a non-user smuggling pot into South East Asia.'

In the blink of an eye the baggage handler defence was born. It was a beautiful thing—there was no need to blame the Indonesians, and it sounded believable. Robin Tampoe later summed up the attractiveness of this proposition: 'It's feasible. It's feasible that some dodgy baggage handler at Brisbane was shifting his pot to Sydney, and he put it in her boogie board bag and someone was supposed to pick it up on the other end, and he missed the pick-up. And you paint a picture that this happens all the time.'

Tampoe says that the baggage handler story 'gave Australia someone to blame'. For the first time since Schapelle Corby's arrest in October 2004, the Australian media now began to portray her as an innocent victim. The story was beginning to turn around—it was the baggage handlers who were to blame. Schapelle was now being seen as an 'unwitting mule'.

As journalists started focusing their attention on the lack of security at Australian airports, their scrutiny became a big problem for the Howard government. The baggage handler story was growing bigger and bigger every day.

199

In April 2005, the media went into a frenzy when a baggage handler was photographed parading around in a trolley on the tarmac at Sydney Airport wearing a giant head from a camel costume. This baggage handler had taken the camel suit out of a passenger's bag and put it on. It was 'proof' that someone could have put the drugs in Schapelle's bag.

The Australian media was now publishing stories about security cameras being tampered with and criminals paying dodgy baggage handlers to pick up drugs. Australian travellers even started having their baggage shrink-wrapped, particularly after the arrest at Sydney Airport of some cocaine traffickers.

Despite all the carping from the Corby camp about Qantas being uncooperative, the company in fact undertook a major internal investigation into claims that its baggage handlers had put the drugs inside Schapelle's bag. According to Geoff Askew, who was head of Qantas security for fifteen years and was also in charge of security for Australian Airlines when Schapelle flew to Bali in October 2004, Qantas questioned all of its baggage handlers at Brisbane Airport and put a whistleblower program in place, asking for anonymous tip-offs about any employee anywhere who might have been involved in the Corby case. 'We specifically targeted the baggage handlers in Brisbane, and told them if you know anything then come forward. But we did not get one report saying this particular colleague of mine is acting strange or did act strange.'

Like the background checks on the baggage handlers, the protected disclosure facility produced nothing. 'I really did think, if anybody had thought "Hang on a minute, this lady might lose her life", if they had known something, then they would have come forward,' recalled Askew. 'And that didn't happen—we didn't get one. We didn't get it from anywhere; but specifically we didn't get anything from Sydney or Brisbane. There was absolutely no evidence identified from any investigation that suggested that a Qantas baggage handler or any other employee may have been involved. And we went public and said so.'

In the course of creating the hype surrounding the baggage handler defence, Bakir and Tampoe made some powerful enemies. They had forced the Australian government into a situation where it had to take some sort of action. Ron Bakir and Robin Tampoe travelled to Canberra to meet with Australia's Foreign Affairs Minister. In a candid scene filmed mid way through the trial under cover in Kerobokan Prison, Bakir informs Schapelle: 'You know what I said to Alexander Downer? I said to him, "If you don't make a particular thing happen, I'm going to do everything in my power, and spend as much money as it takes to make sure you guys lose the next election." '

Downer vividly recalls his first encounter with the passionate Ron Bakir. 'He screamed at me about how you've got to get her out—he just screamed. And I thought, "You've come here to see me, which is fair enough. I've agreed to see you—presumably you want me to help. Well, screaming at me isn't going to encourage me to help as best as I can possibly help." So he toned down and Robin told him to stop screaming. It was abominable behaviour, really vile and feral people. And now they had a new theory. It was that the marijuana had been stuffed in a boogie board bag by baggage handlers in Brisbane who were part of a racket to smuggle it down to Sydney. Unfortunately the baggage handlers in Sydney, who were part of the racket, didn't pick the right bag and that bag went on to Bali.'

Downer wasn't buying this new theory and he remembers saying to Bakir and Tampoe: 'Why would you need to smuggle marijuana from Brisbane to Sydney? You'd just put it on a Pioneer bus, or just put it in the boot of your car. There hasn't been a customs post since 2001 between Brisbane and New South Wales.' He said, 'I don't believe that—I don't believe they'd go to that much trouble.' The Foreign Affairs Minister was not impressed—the theory had now changed, but the second explanation was no better than the first. Downer recalls saying to Tampoe and Bakir: 'You guys have got to come up with some explanation here that will encourage us to look more sympathetically at her. Because, on the face of it, she turns up at the airport with four kilograms—it was a hell of a lot of marijuana, and it's in her bag. What can you possibly conclude?' The meeting hadn't gone well. Alexander Downer says, 'I don't recall seeing them again.'

Although the mobile phone salesman and the defence lawyer may not have impressed the Foreign Affairs Minister with their theory about how the drugs got inside Schapelle's bag, their mission to bring Schapelle home was far from over. The baggage handler story had yet another twist. At a critical stage in Schapelle's trial, a Victorian prisoner named John Patrick Ford came up with a fantastic story. Ford had been charged with rape and burglary, and was languishing in Melbourne's Port Phillip Prison awaiting his trial. He claimed that he'd overheard two prisoners joking about how a bag of marijuana had gone missing between Brisbane and Sydney at the same time that Schapelle had flown to Bali. When this new 'evidence' came to light, the Corby legal team insisted that the Australian federal government fly the prisoner all the way from Victoria to Bali so he could appear in court.

The media coverage of Schapelle's trial was now so feverish and the heat on the Australian government so intense that they simply couldn't afford to ignore this demand. Incredibly this prisoner, facing rape charges, was flown to Bali to testify. The then federal Justice Minister, Chris Ellison, said publicly, 'The Australian government has pulled out all stops to ensure that Ms Corby's legal team is given the opportunity to present the evidence that it considers important to its case.'

It took weeks to overcome the enormous legal hurdles involved in sending a prisoner overseas. A political staffer explained: 'Our department and advisers were working night and day on this for weeks. It was just a herculean effort to do it. To my knowledge it was unprecedented.' In the court of popular opinion the Australian government was now under the pump and it had to deliver.

John Ford arrived at the Bali District Court in Denpasar on 29 March 2005, sporting a crisp white shirt to hide his tattoos. He told the presiding judges that Schapelle was an innocent victim of criminals in Australia who'd been using travellers as drug mules: 'It's not uncommon knowledge where I come from about how the drugs got into her bag and how they ended up over here.' But Ford would not say exactly who put the drugs in Schapelle's bag because, he claimed, it could get him killed. 'All I can say to the court is there's no way on God's earth that Miss Corby is a drug trafficker.'

Schapelle cried and looked shocked throughout most of Ford's testimony. She later told the documentary crew: 'Being used as a mule is disgusting and embarrassing and ugh. But to know that they know that I had nothing to do with it, and they sit there knowing that my life is on the line here for something I didn't do, and they're sitting and talking about it and laughing. Do they have a heart? Is it made of stone?'

After the court hearing, Vasu Rasiah announced to reporters outside the court, 'With Ford's testimony, the Australian government cannot sleep any more. They have to investigate. So there's another road opening towards freedom.'

Although the Indonesian judges were unmoved by Ford's testimony, support in Australia for Schapelle Corby was mushrooming into something bigger than any of her lawyers or family could ever have dreamt of. Ron Bakir told the documentary at this time: 'We're trialling her by the media. That's the only way to get her out and we've got 87 per cent of Australians on our side. If we lose that, we got a problem—because then the government won't do anything.'

Vasu Rasiah also kept an eye on the public opinion polls back in Australia: 'Originally, less than 20 per cent of the Australian public believed in her. And it is due to the combined effect of Bali Law Chambers, as well as Ron Bakir and Robin Tampoe, that nearly 90 per cent of the Australian public supported her.' Ron Bakir put it more bluntly: 'When I originally came onto the scene, I did not find one journalist that believed Schapelle Corby was innocent. Not one. The spin was a big thing—the spin that not everyone that's sitting in a jail is guilty.'

For Robin Tampoe, the master of spin, life didn't get much better than this. In truth he had no idea why John Ford had volunteered to give evidence and, while he had to admit it was all hearsay, it added immeasurably to the world of smoke and mirrors he was creating for the case. Tampoe relished the prospect of drafting the defence team's closing address. But, smiling to himself, he also knew what its underlying emotional message to Australians was: 'Poor Schapelle, we could all relate to her. This could have been any one of us. She is a victim—a victim of baggage handlers, a government that didn't care, of lax airport security and airlines and, even worse, of those evil Indonesians that are keeping our little girl locked up in their dirty little prison for a crime she didn't commit.'

Tampoe lounged back in his chair, satisfied. 'Nice,' he thought to himself. 'We have the case by the balls, and we are squeezing hard.'

CHAPTER 21

Help Me, Australia

'I haven't seen the stars and I haven't seen the moon for . . . a long time. I try to look out of my cage, but there seems to be no stars. There are stars all over the sky but there's none in front of my cell. Where did they go?'

—Schapelle Corby

Somehow, against all odds, Schapelle Corby was now being portrayed in the media as a modern-day Joan of Arc. On court hearing days the press and all the TV cameras would wait expectantly at the Bali District Court's front gates for Schapelle's prison van to arrive. As the dishevelled and less attractive other prisoners were unloaded from the van, Schapelle would often sit by the window praying, a single tear falling elegantly down her cheek. The press photographers would go into overdrive.

When she left the relative safety of the van, Schapelle then faced a media barrage as she braved running the gauntlet to the court's holding cell. She was often bruised and battered as the guards pushed her down the path through the front-line of camera crews. Always by her side was big sister

Mercedes, who would try to comfort her—constantly reassuring her ('It's okay, Schapelle, don't look at them') as they linked hands and struggled through the sea of cameras into the courtroom together.

'Super Merc' was always good in a crisis—brave and feisty, her sister's protector. On one occasion she famously hurled herself into the middle of the media pack, screaming madly, wielding her handbag in wild circles and striking a cameraman. Another time, when Schapelle fainted during one of her court hearings, Mercedes leapt over a barrier in a single bound and sprung past the police guards to revive her sister.

Since the creation of the baggage handler defence, Schapelle was no longer friendly to the reporters following her case—she had been instructed by her minders not to give spontaneous comments unless there was a deal in place. Schapelle was now an elusive 'prize', a silent princess who only granted an audience to the highest bidder. When she did speak, no matter how inane her utterance, it often made the front pages of Australian newspapers accompanied by a dramatic photo—usually in the praying position, or staring with helplessness and fragility into the camera lens.

Before each court appearance, Ron Bakir would come up with a calculated headline. His most spectacular success was the simple phrase 'Help me, Australia'.

Schapelle was a willing pupil. In one sequence in *The Hidden Truth*, she asks Bakir: 'Will I say "Help me, Australia" or "Australia, help me"?'

'We've got the government on the back foot, everyone wants you home,' he tells her.

'I know,' she replies. 'Everyone loves me.'

'You had better believe it, love. We just drip feed the

press,' he explains as he juggles his mobile phones and media quotes.

But while Bakir had carefully created Schapelle the Superstar, he had little time to make-over the entire Corby clan, whose members had each been hurled into the spotlight with varying degrees of success.

Dad Corby had been cleaned up—the bushy bikie beard was gone, and he now sported a new clean shirt and pants and mostly kept his mouth shut around the cameras. However, when he did speak to journalists, he inevitably stuffed it up. On one particular occasion, when surrounded by baying reporters, he was asked a simple question—what did he hope the outcome of the trial would be?

'I wish they would just find her guilty and then let her get on a bloody plane and come home,' he replied. Then, quickly realising his faux pas, he corrected himself: 'I mean bloody innocent—find her *innocent,* and let her bloody come home.'

At this stage Mercedes furiously dragged her father away from the press pack and let rip at him: 'Just shut the fuck up, Dad. Don't say anything! They're trying to trick you.' She later blamed her father's cancer medication for his muddled answer. 'He gets confused and he can't hear properly,' she said.

Berated publicly by his daughter, Mick Corby now sat obediently in the middle of the courtroom, effectively tamed but increasingly frustrated. Privately, he was pissed off by the ever-growing media circus that the rest of the family seemed to be revelling in. 'No one listens to me,' he moaned openly.

Rosleigh Rose was proving herself to be quite a co-star in the whole sorry saga and was now on first-name terms with Australia's most popular Logie-winning journalist, Ray Martin. Two months after Schapelle's arrest, she had announced to the media that she might have to sell her home at Loganlea to pay for her daughter's legal fees: 'I'm not good with money. Anything over $1000 boggles my mind.' But Ros's money worries were soon eased. After making her emotional plea on camera, *A Current Affair*'s producers drew up a contract agreeing to pay all her airfares to Bali plus accommodation costs. The deal was said to be valid 'until Schapelle comes home'.

The program's producers immediately warmed to Ros, because she was low maintenance and never took advantage of the deal. One Channel 9 insider said, 'She always chose cheap accommodation. We liked her for that.' It was also easy for the producers to whip Ros up into a frenzy for a 'good grab'. Her high-pitched voice was grating, but she spoke in exaggerated sound bites, continually blaming the Australian government for Schapelle's plight. In the world of tabloid current affairs shows, she was 'great talent' if you didn't have her on camera for too long. And besides, Ray Martin thought 'she was a good old stick'.

You couldn't blame him for thinking that. During the early days of Schapelle's trial Ros was seen down on her hands and knees, scrubbing the court's squalid holding cell with bleach and antiseptic—trying to make it clean before her daughter's arrival from prison. 'It's filthy,' she sobbed as she worked her way through the dried faeces and dirt. Later she would be seen throwing water over pro death penalty protesters baying for Schapelle's blood.

On court hearing days Ros didn't say much. 'I'm signed to *A Current Affair*,' she would boast to any reporters who weren't aware of the deal, and then, as if handing out a secret gift, she would give them 'a little grab' on the side. Many of the journalists commonly mistook her plain-speaking direct- ness as a sign that she was a clueless Aussie battler, an 'open book' with absolutely nothing to hide. In truth, Ros managed to make a lot of noise without really saying much. Pushed for detail, she would play her cards close to her chest. She knew how to put on a show for the tabloids and television crews—play it dumb, play it poor. Do whatever it takes, and hope like hell it all works out.

Most of the time, she got through the continuing drama by being in a constant state of denial and by planning her daughter's homecoming. Ros was a woman of routine. Every morning she would visit Schapelle at the jail and then fight her way back through the press pack waiting outside Kerobokan so she could be home by noon to numb the pain with Bintang beers.

Unlike Ros, Mercedes hadn't struck an exclusive deal with any print or broadcast media. She liked to make it clear to the press that 'I'm not with anyone'. She was free to sell the photographs she took of Schapelle in jail and, in fact, did deals with magazines like *New Idea*. She was flying under the media radar. In her mobile phone she had an impressive contact list of Australia's most influential reporters and producers, all of whom were desperate for an angle—anything from a Corby that would keep feeding the Australian public's hunger for this story.

Over a very short period of time, the Corbys felt they had developed leverage when it came to dealing with the insatiable Australian media pack. If any TV reporters or newspaper journalists dared to produce negative stories about Schapelle, they could get lost—they'd get nothing from Schapelle or the family. In the coming months and the years that followed the

Corbys would become savvy and successfully learn how to control the media, how to give access to friendly reporters and cut off those who asked difficult questions. For a family with no media experience, they soon learned how to play the game and play it well.

One month before the day of the verdict, the defence team still appeared to be on top of the case and was boldly inventing different media angles to help their cause. On 14 April 2005, Schapelle was in court to learn what penalty the Indonesian prosecutors would recommend if the three judges found her guilty. The death penalty was still very much on the table at this point. Shortly after Schapelle arrived in court, she appeared to become faint and suddenly collapsed onto the interpreter's shoulder.

A local doctor, Conny Pangkahil, who had been called to the court by the Australian Consul, examined Schapelle in the courtroom and said she was suffering from extreme stress. The doctor explained to the gathered media: 'She became hysterical, and then the blood pressure was suddenly up, and then she fainted—that's all.' After her assessment, Dr Pangkahil said that Schapelle needed rest.

The chief judge asked that a full medical report be provided the following week to establish whether the trial could continue. It was the second time in two weeks that Schapelle had claimed that she was too sick to face the trial and the chief judge was clearly irritated at the further delay, saying: 'You were sick last week. You present here again—you're sick this week.'

Ron Bakir told the Australian media contingent that Schapelle had become suicidal and that the Indonesian authorities were not treating her depression. 'She's lost hope, she's completely, completely lost hope,' he said. But, in reality, the defence team was pleased that Schapelle's illness bought them time to come up with further witnesses. 'There's more than one way to get an adjournment,' quipped Robin Tampoe in a later interview with the documentary team.

While Schapelle was being treated by the doctor at the hospital, her lawyer Erwin Siregar suggested that they take advantage of the situation and make a last-minute attempt to convince the judges that Schapelle had gone insane. As a close friend of Judge Sirait, Siregar knew things were not going well for them. He argued that appealing to the judges' sense of compassion might get a shorter prison sentence. If Schapelle was not prepared to plead guilty, she could at least appear to be insane and less responsible for the drug importation—that would explain her lack of remorse and failure to plead guilty. But Vasu Rasiah didn't like the idea of an insanity plea at this late stage in the trial as it would look fake, and a few days later all talk about Schapelle's mental state was suddenly dropped. There would be no more discussion about her going crazy for another four years.

With the media obsession for Schapelle's story now at a peak, chequebooks were opening wide in Australia. Channel 9 and Australian Consolidated Press, who together had won the Battle of the Chequebooks and bought exclusive access to the Corby family, were now working overtime to portray her as an innocent victim.

With just days to go until the Indonesian court handed down its verdict and sentence, Ron Bakir was at the apex of his influence as the maestro of media spin; he expertly negotiated a sympathetic *60 Minutes* special titled 'Schapelle's Nightmare: The Untold Story', involving a studio audience and featuring the 'Worm', an electronic device previously used to measure audience reactions during political debates. Hosted by Mike Munro on the Nine Network, this was Australia's version of the trial that had been unfolding in Indonesia—a kind of make-believe television court that would expose the apparent flaws in the Indonesian judicial system.

Ron Bakir made sure the program not only had the Worm but also a phone poll, so that Australian viewers could participate by phoning in and voting for Schapelle's innocence. There was an overwhelming response—91 per cent of viewers who phoned in believed that Schapelle was innocent; only 9 per cent thought she was guilty.

Although the Worm TV special was a great triumph, Ron Bakir's favourite form of publicity was milking radio. This medium was quick and rarely delved deep, but unfortunately it also revealed the racist underbelly of Australia. Sydney's 2GB radio announcer Malcolm T. Elliott, for example, likened Indonesia's president and the three judges to banana-eating apes. Also feeding the rampant xenophobia was Sydney's highest rating radio host Alan Jones. His listeners were hungry for regular Corby updates. At the time Jones was then Prime Minister John Howard's broadcaster of choice for getting his political messages out. Bakir was impressed and flattered by the powerful radio host's support, and decreed that all radio exclusives should go to 2GB.

One day Robin Tampoe was doing a telephone interview from his Gold Coast law office with Jones's arch-rival, 2UE's heavyweight broadcaster John Laws. So loyal was Ron to the Jones camp that he ran into Tampoe's room and dramatically put an end to the live on-air discussion by pulling the telephone cord mid-interview. Although Laws probably didn't know that Bakir had pulled the plug on his interview, it had become obvious that all the Corby exclusives were going to his bitter rival. Bakir was now on Laws's hit list, and Laws paid him back by regularly slagging off at him over the months that followed.

As Ron Bakir got closer to Alan Jones, he privately confided to the radio host that people representing the Indonesian prosecutor on the case had asked for bribes so he would recommend a lower sentence for Schapelle to the panel of judges. Jones allegedly urged Bakir to go public with the allegation and convinced him that, if the Australian government knew that people in Bali were seeking bribes, the politicians in Canberra would put more political pressure on the Indonesians to allow Schapelle to return home. Jones personally promised Bakir that he 'had the ear of the Prime Minister'.

Bakir was convinced that Jones was right, even though the Indonesian legal team had made it clear that all talk about bribes had to be kept secret. One morning on his show, the persuasive Jones asked Bakir: 'Has there been any move in the prosecution to approach the defence team about how the defence team's concerns might be met?'

Bakir answered: 'Yes, look, um, it's been addressed two or three times now.'

Jones: 'The prosecution team have approached the defence team?'

Bakir: 'Absolutely.'

Jones: 'Are the prosecution saying things to the defence, like well, if you want this result, you might have to do something to get it?'

'Yes. I'll say yes to that. To be honest with you, it's an absolute disgrace—but anyhow, that's the way it works,' Bakir replied.

Alan Jones then said: 'Perhaps we shouldn't say any more here. My listeners can work out for themselves what's behind all of this.'

The story was a bombshell in the Australian media and inevitably a big exclusive for 2GB, but back in Bali it was an absolute disaster for Schapelle's legal team. The Corbys and their lawyers were furious that Ron had spoken publicly about bribes.

Ron Bakir retracted the statement and took the rap for the 'bad strategy', but it was too late—the damage was already done. Vasu later said, 'I wanted to hit him. He's half my age, he's like my son—I wanted to slap him. That's what I wanted to do.'

Robin Tampoe was also furious, and immediately distanced himself from the comments. Bakir told Vasu that the Indonesian judges were 'all a bunch of turkeys' but it didn't wash with Vasu, who knew how dangerous it was to embarrass both the Indonesian prosecutor and the judiciary, who were about to decide Schapelle's future. Vasu retorted: 'Mate, they can be turkeys; they can be childish; they can be whatever it is. But if you push them to the wall, if you push them to the wall—they will strike back.'

Shortly after 2GB broadcast the story about the bribe allegations, the Indonesian government prosecutors recommended to the judges that Schapelle receive a life sentence. Although—and with great relief—the death penalty was now effectively off the table, Schapelle had been constantly promised she was coming home by everyone involved in the case. Everyone had been expecting a much lower sentence guideline from the prosecutors, but now they were showing no mercy and many Australian reporters in Bali felt that the bribery allegations had pushed them into a corner.

Back in Canberra, Foreign Affairs Minister Alexander Downer also thought the comments made by Bakir on Alan Jones's show were a complete disaster. In his interview for this book, he recalled: 'They were abusing the Indonesians; abusing the Indonesian judicial system; abusing the Indonesian police. Stop and think about who you need on side here. Why do people go to court in suits? Think about who you are trying to keep on side. Going around and abusing the Indonesians is at best not going to influence them, and at worst they are just going to get their backs up.'

In the end, only Alan Jones and 2GB benefited from the bribery revelation. To this day, despite his damaging and pivotal role in the debacle, Alan Jones continues to be the Corbys' radio announcer of choice when it comes to promoting their campaign. His famous 'pick and stick' club of good mates still includes the Corbys.

CHAPTER 22

The Badger

'I kind of liked Clinton being in jail because I knew where he was . . . before I'd worry about him, always expecting the phone call—he'd pinched a car and rolled off a cliff.'
—Rosleigh Rose

Ron Bakir's implicit belief in Schapelle's innocence was strengthened by the views of respected Queensland criminologist Professor Paul Wilson. Bakir had paid for Wilson to travel to Bali and give his expert opinion on the likelihood of Schapelle being a drug trafficker. In the course of his research work over the years, Professor Wilson had interviewed hundreds of drug couriers stuck inside foreign jails around the world. He concluded that most drug traffickers are usually drug addicts and, as far as anyone knew, Schapelle was not an addict. Wilson told the lawyers that it was highly unlikely Schapelle was a drug dealer 'because dealers don't travel with their family and friends'.

Ever mindful of public perception and keeping the positive media spin going, Bakir arranged for James Kisina to be interviewed by the Nine Network's *60 Minutes*. This TV appearance was stage-managed from beginning to end, with Bakir frequently stopping the interview to 'help James'. Despite the conservative jacket and tie, James unfortunately came across as being inarticulate and dumb.

When asked who he thought had put the pot inside the bag, James gazed at the ceiling and then looked down before mumbling 'the baggage handlers'. Ron Bakir later said of James's appearance on *60 Minutes*: 'We weren't trying to cover anything up. I was just trying to make sure that his inability to express himself didn't come across as guilty.' But James was soon to be the least of Bakir's worries. Another half-brother, who was at this time fairly unknown to the public, was about to create havoc with damaging effect.

It all started with what was supposed to be a relatively harmless interview. Ron Bakir suggested to Mercedes that she agree to an on-camera interview with Ross Coulthart, a hard-hitting investigative reporter who back then worked for the Nine Network's now defunct *Sunday* program. Bakir and Tampoe had spent considerable time briefing Coulthart about the intricacies of the baggage handler defence strategy, and Coulthart had pursued his own investigations into airport baggage handlers. Although he had come up with nothing that was directly linked to Schapelle's case, he had been able to uncover massive security problems at Sydney Airport.

Mercedes was originally nervous about being interviewed by Coulthart, but Ron assured her that, 'He is one of the good ones. He's on our side.' It would be one of the few interviews Mercedes would give without requesting a fee.

Coulthart's style wasn't to entrap or railroad Mercedes, so he frankly warned her about the questions he was going to ask before the cameras rolled: 'I don't personally believe all the rumours, but I have to ask you about them.'

'Okay,' replied Mercedes.

Midway through the interview, the following exchange took place.

Coulthart: 'Are there any drug dealers, drug traffickers, any crims at all in the . . . in the family or in the family circle of friends?'

Mercedes: 'No.'

Coulthart: 'I mean, is there anybody in your family, either a stepfather, a distant relative . . . Is there anybody who has ever been convicted or involved in the drugs trade?'

Mercedes: 'No. Not that I know of and . . . nah. There wouldn't be.'

This interview with Coulthart would soon come back to haunt Mercedes. Three weeks later, in May 2005, the *Australian* ran a sensational front-page story headlined: 'Meet the Corbys'. The newspaper had finally discovered that Mick Corby had been arrested for possessing marijuana in the 1970s, when he was about the same age as his 27-year-old daughter now facing the courts in Bali. Mick Corby denied that the marijuana had been his and told the newspaper: 'I got a fine for $400 for about two grams of marijuana, which wasn't mine. Some girl had it, and they busted the whole joint and I had to go along for the ride.' Mick then said: 'The charges were all scrubbed, because it was the Bjelke-Petersen days where, if you had an ugly face or you were in the wrong place, you got pushed around.'

It was now eight months since Schapelle's arrest and this was the first time that the Australian media had made any connection between a member of the Corby family other than Schapelle and drugs. But the article in the *Australian* contained more bad news for the Corbys. For the first time a mystery half-brother, Clinton 'Badger' Rose, was revealed to the Australian public. The 'Badger' (the family nickname for him) had a criminal history as long as his arm and was locked up in a Queensland jail at the time Schapelle was busted.

On 26 August 2004, just six weeks before Schapelle's arrest in Bali, Clinton was found guilty of break and enter, fraud, stealing and the unlawful use of a motor vehicle; he was sentenced to twelve months' jail at the Woodford Correctional Centre near Brisbane. It wasn't his first time in jail—Clinton had been before the courts before and was going through the prison system's revolving door. The Badger's record includes a crime spree on the Gold Coast which resulted in him pleading guilty to 62 offences. During one court appearance, Judge Hall had clearly had enough of Schapelle's half-brother and told him, 'Your campaign of crime shows a complete lack of respect for other people's interests or for their property.'

Like his half-sister Schapelle, the Badger had also run into trouble with drugs. In January 2002 he was busted for drug possession and possessing drug utensils but the court documents don't give any detail of the type of drugs or the amounts. In February 2003 he was also charged with possessing a dangerous drug and convicted without punishment.

Clinton's father, Michael Rose, has always been elusive, maintaining a low profile throughout the whole of Schapelle's drama and never appearing in the media. Nothing is known about him except that Rosleigh kept his surname 'Rose' because she liked the sound of it. But the 'Meet the Corbys' article reminded readers of Mercedes's repeated denials, during her interview on the *Sunday* program, that anyone in her family had any connection to illicit drugs—it now appeared that she and Schapelle had both regularly visited Clinton in jail in Queensland.

When Mercedes was asked by the *Australian* about her comments on the *Sunday* program and her father's drug history, she said that she was not even alive when that happened and 'wouldn't even bloody know'. However, she did know about Clinton's criminal record, which included drug charges, and had now been caught out lying on national television.

Ron Bakir and the legal team allege they were completely shocked by the revelations about Mick and Clinton, although Mercedes insists she had told the defence team about the problem half-brother. 'It was never a secret. Never,' she told the media in June 2005. 'They always knew.' The *Australian* was widely criticised for revealing Dad Corby's drug possession convictions and Clinton Rose's criminal history so close to Schapelle's verdict day.

From this point on, the Corbys described Clinton as the 'black sheep' of the family. Mick made the following statement in the *Australian*'s 'Meet the Corbys': 'We don't talk about him. We don't want to know about him. We don't know where he came from—he's not like any of us. He's in the slammer—he gets out in two months, but he'll probably end up back there. He should be a con man or a politician, he lies so beautifully. He doesn't realise how much he's hurting the family.' Later, in *My Story*, Schapelle devotes barely a paragraph to Clinton, but she writes, 'He has a problem, he's a kleptomaniac. My family still tries to look after Clinton, because we love him and we're hoping that one day he'll learn and change.'

Before now, Schapelle had looked like a cleanskin but, as the police back home began to dig deeper, alarm bells were starting to ring. The Queensland Police had found something and passed it on to the Australian Federal Police. It wasn't long before federal government ministers and their staffers in Canberra found out more about Mick Corby's past. Before Schapelle's verdict had been delivered, according to a former Coalition political staffer, the AFP held a meeting with several government ministers and said that there was an 'intelligence holding' on a person associated with Schapelle and it was about drugs. The staffer explained in strictest confidence: 'I can distinctly recall a conversation where Police Commissioner Mick Keelty told us that there were intelligence reports which had been forwarded to the AFP from Queensland Police, and Keelty basically urged extreme caution in terms of making public statements in support of Schapelle Corby because of the intelligence holdings about a member of her family. I remember that very clearly. We were told that, if this came out, it would be more than embarrassing for Schapelle Corby.'

It's unclear if the statement made by Kim Moore about the alleged Bali drug runs had been passed from the Queensland Police to the Federal Police, but news that Schapelle's father had drug convictions, no matter how minor, went down like a lead balloon. The political staffer said the intelligence holding was 'like a fucking flashing red light. It went beyond the innocent dupe here—it was like these guys are involved in some criminal conspiracy of some kind. Downer was very close to Keelty, and Keelty would have given him the same message that he gave us, I have no doubt.'

Although the *Australian*'s explosive article had inferred that Mercedes was a liar and revealed that Mick Corby had once been arrested for possessing marijuana, at the time of Schapelle's verdict, in May 2005, the full extent of Mick Corby's drug past still remained hidden. That dirty secret was yet to unravel.

CHAPTER 23

Jailhouse Visit

'My greatest fear was that she [Schapelle] would cave in and spill the beans. I wanted to see her, I had to talk to her. So that's exactly what Dave and I set out to do. We went there and we talked to her.'

—Malcolm McCauley

Seven months after their original visit, Malcolm McCauley and Dave McHugh were back in Bali. This time around, there would be no cautious tiptoeing through the back streets of Kuta. They were there for some one-on-one time with Schapelle. The sooner they could make contact with her the better.

Both men were present at one of the final court hearing days before the verdict was due. They were heartened by the latest public opinion polls indicating that the majority of Australians now believed Schapelle was innocent. 'Compared to the last time I was there, the dust had settled,' remembers McCauley.

In the time that had elapsed between their two trips, McHugh had managed to squeeze in a solo visit by himself. McHugh explained to Schapelle that he would be back later in the year to see her and, sure enough, there he now was with McCauley—two faces in a courthouse crowd, low-key and blending in, or so they thought.

They didn't know it at the time, but throughout Schapelle's trial a documentary crew had been filming the Corbys every move. As the camera rolled back then, McCauley and McHugh would have been viewed as insignificant faces through a lens constantly trained at members of the family. Mercedes, however, appears to be treating them as 'supporters'. As she enters through the gate to the courtroom in one sequence, she acknowledges them and says, 'Hi'. It's a tentative 'Hi' and a 'Thanks for coming'. In one screen grab that eventually did make it to air, it is unclear exactly what he meant but McCauley turns to Ros, Greg, Mercedes and Wayan and says, 'I'll try and organise some smoke for next week'. None of the family respond; it is unclear if they have heard him or not.

Footage also exists of McHugh and McCauley meeting Schapelle for the first time together in the holding cells, prior to her hearing. A film crew member recalls: 'Dave struts up to the holding cell as if he knows Schapelle, and certainly in all the time we were filming I have never seen her just hang out at the court holding cell and talk to strangers. Usually she would hide.'

During the trial the Secret Garden, located on a popular side street named Poppies 1 in Kuta, was where the Corbys loved to hang out and drink. They had become good friends with the manager and could be found there most evenings, huddled around a table, dissecting the day's events while planning their next move. McCauley remembers that, after initially hooking up with Ros at the Secret Garden, he and

McHugh were taken to see Schapelle in the holding cells. In further gatherings at the same pub, the Adelaide men then discussed the 'importance' of getting inside the jail to visit Schapelle privately, away from journalists and prying eyes. Ros agreed to take them in the coming days. One of these meetings at the Secret Garden was captured on video by McHugh. Mal is absent during the session but Ros sends him a greeting yelling: 'Hi, Mal!'

McCauley recollects that, with so many Australian tourists around them, the Corbys were constantly recognised as they drank away in the bar. He adds that, while the family was by now well aware of its celebrity status, there was also strong suspicion amongst them that they were being monitored and tailed by undercover Australian Federal Police: 'They were being photographed, but Dave and I . . . we were being photographed too, even when we were on our own. Bloody oath. Was there a sense of paranoia? Yes, I accept maybe there was.'

McCauley said there were occasions when the whole group became so spooked, they would drink up and move on from the bar. 'We would walk down to Ros's place, watch, then double back and check if anyone was coming in after us into the forecourt. You know, we'd wait and then we'd go to their bungalow.' But on the day Mal and Dave were finally given access by Ros to visit her daughter at Kerobokan Prison, she, Mal and Dave didn't seem at all concerned about being seen together. In fact they asked a stranger waiting outside the jail to take a photograph of them posing as a group in front of the imposing entry doors of Kerobokan Prison.

Every day dozens of Australian tourists made the pilgrimage to Kerobokan Prison to visit 'Our Schapelle'.

They lined up in the hot sun with their Bali braids and sarongs, hoping to get a glimpse of the most famous woman on the island. They came bearing gifts of food, hygiene packs and money. Very few were let in to see her, even though many offered modest bribes to the prison guards. The only way through the ominous wooden doors to see Schapelle was by accompanying her lawyers or family members.

Visiting sessions for prisoners at Kerobokan are held twice a day. The first intake of visitors is between 9 am and 12 noon, and the second between 1 pm and 3 pm. Although visiting procedures have now changed and strict checks are made on visitors to the jail, back during Schapelle's trial period visitors were only required to write their names down on a piece of paper which was then handed to Schapelle by the guards. If Schapelle didn't recognise the name, entry was denied. However, visitors accompanied by members of the Corby family got straight through the doors with little scrutiny, apart from having to provide either their driver's licence or passport and leave their mobile phones and cameras at the door.

Rosleigh Rose had a knack for regularly upsetting the equilibrium of the jail. She and her entourage of relatives would burst through the media scrums and well-wishers, cocky and full of attitude. The prison guards were wary of the 'force of nature' that is Rosleigh Rose. Unlike the polite mothers of the 'Bali Nine' prisoners, who were always over-whelmed by the prison environment, Ros seemed right at home. She was never intimidated by the guards, or even the prison itself. She bossed everyone around, and complained loudly and often about the 'entrance money' (a few rupees) that had to be paid with every visit.

Ros was outraged when her bags were checked, so the guards always processed 'Corby mum', as they called her, quickly. Somehow she always got to keep her camera, even though the prison rules, listed on a large sign outside, clearly stated those found with a camera in the jail would be punished and the camera confiscated.

Inside, Schapelle detested posing for photographs and was paranoid that any pictures of her taken by strangers could be on-sold to magazines and newspapers prepared to pay a small fortune for any candid shots of her in jail. Ever mindful of Schapelle's celebrity, her family ensured that the only photos taken of her were usually by trusted friends and family, or media organisations that had paid for the privilege. But on the day Ros ushered Malcolm McCauley and Dave McHugh on a magic carpet ride through the doors of Kerobokan, she was brandishing her camera and ready to offer happy snap opportunities for free.

Of the now infamous summit with Schapelle inside the jail, McCauley says: 'We were all gathered beside a fishpond. I sat on the wall and Ros, her husband Greg and Dave were there too. Schapelle was facing us but she could also see over our shoulders across the main area.' McCauley described it as a deliberate seating arrangement. 'We didn't know who was who in there, but Schapelle obviously did. She told Dave and me where to sit and was then looking out to see who might be heading our way.'

Ros's partner Greg quickly took the camera out and braved taking some happy snaps while the guards were nowhere to be seen—there were shots of Mal and Schapelle together, and shots of Dave and Schapelle together. These photos, captured on the day, show them all smiling and looking happy and relaxed in each other's company.

McCauley describes Schapelle's mood as being 'quite bright' that day. 'There was growing talk that she might get back to Australia, and she was in good spirits.' He remembers saying to her, 'What's the story, love? Can you keep it together?'

Ros was constantly geeing her up, saying: 'You're strong, we can do this, we'll fight through, we'll get there. You could get sent back and then it's a different story. But you've got to stay strong.'

McCauley comments: 'A dripping tap will always wear down a stone and Ros kept on reassuring, kept on reassuring, kept on reassuring . . . ' As the conversation continued, he could see relief in Schapelle's expression. 'Put yourself in her shoes. She was a long, long way from home. And while she was maintaining to everyone she had nothing to do with the hooter, she was well aware there were others, namely Dave and I, who knew otherwise.'

McCauley claims that despite Schapelle's best efforts 'trying to convince the world she was innocent, her greatest fear was that it would all unravel back in Australia'. Now, for the first time, he was able to privately reassure her there would be no leaks from the Adelaide end. 'I said: "There's absolutely nothing to worry about from our side, I promise. United we stand, love. If anyone or anything divides us, we're gonna go down and, believe me, nobody wants that." It was the reason we were there. It was obvious she was relieved to hear what we had to say.' He concludes: 'You know what? I'm ashamed to say this now, but sitting there that day like we were . . . Well, it was the first time since her arrest that I actually stopped thinking about my own skin for one second . . . to consider someone else's. Hers.'

McCauley recalls that at one stage during the conversation, Schapelle suddenly signalled that people were approaching from behind: 'Somebody came up close to where we were sitting. There was a screw, a prisoner and some visitors. It was too close for comfort—they could have been ear-wigging—and so suddenly we had to change the topic. You know, general chitchat. That's when I said to her, "You know what, Schapelle? My granddaughter watches you every time you're on television. She's got a lot of time for you. I'd love to be able to take her a memento, an autograph." She said, "Yeah, of course."'

McCauley says Schapelle reached into a bag beside her feet and dug out a photograph of herself. She scribbled a message on the back of the picture that read: 'Kaitlin, when you are old enough to travel the world, remember the locks on your bag.'

He continues: 'The other people in the yard were still hanging around close by, so we carried on in the same manner. I said to Schapelle, "I'll get my granddaughter to take that to school, because everyone in Australia believes you're innocent. I mean that, love . . . They believe you."'

McCauley knew exactly what Schapelle needed to hear. Touched by his words, she wrote a separate note to his granddaughter and her classmates, thanking them for their support, adding, 'It's what gets me through each day.'

She also wrote about having met McCauley previously at the holding cells and again in prison that day: 'Your Granddad has come in to see me, also I met him last Friday at the court cell. He's a good Gran-dad.' Schapelle then signed off with a smiley face, adding, 'Be Positive'.

Little did anyone know at the time but, eight months on, the private jailhouse photos of Schapelle and McCauley would be exposed publicly through a post-verdict police leak.

CHAPTER 24

A Flimsy Defence

'Saya tidak bersalah [I'm not guilty]'
—Schapelle Corby to the Indonesian judges

Two weeks before the verdict hearing, Mercedes finally had some good news for Schapelle. In front of the media pack, she whispered through the bars to her little sister, 'There's been a breakthrough in the case. They've got new evidence!'

If Schapelle was shocked, she didn't immediately show it. In fact she looked bewildered. 'I'm trying hard not to be excited but I am,' she giggled to the camera crews.

It was the sort of staggering twist that makes it a great day for journalists, and an even better day for conspiracy theorists. On 8 October 2004, the same day that Schapelle flew from Sydney to Bali, 10 kilos of cocaine arrived in Sydney with a passenger on a flight from South America. This importation had been organised by the Coogee Mob, a drug syndicate led by Michael Hurley, one of Sydney's biggest cocaine importers. Hurley had been known to the police for decades; his gang had been paying baggage handlers at Sydney Airport to stash cocaine from incoming drug couriers

the letter because it didn't link the cocaine importation with the marijuana inside Schapelle's boogie board. When asked if the letter from the Australian government was sufficient to assist her client, Lily said: 'In my personal opinion, it is not.' Lily at the same time submitted to the judges a petition carrying 10,000 signatures from Australians saying that Schapelle was innocent.

A former member of Michael Hurley's syndicate had read all the internet stories doing the rounds and agreed to be interviewed for this book. Having done his time behind bars, the 50-year-old belly-laughs at the suggestion that any member of the Hurley gang would bother to set up Schapelle Corby: 'Why would a big guy like Michael Hurley deal with grass? He wouldn't go near four kilos of pot. There is no way Michael Hurley's team would have mucked around with marijuana on an airplane—it's too bulky, too smelly and there's not enough profit in it. That to me is a story made up by a defence counsel looking to confuse a jury. There is no basis in fact to linking Schapelle Corby to Michael Hurley—it defies logic.'

As someone who's been involved in importing drugs, he also has his own theory about Schapelle's drug run: 'How could you take a four kilo bag of grass and shape it into a boogie board bag at the airport? I would say the airport handlers would have nothing to do with Schapelle Corby's bag—it's a total red herring,' he laughs.

But there's no doubt that the campaign was putting pressure on Canberra. When asked if there was any minister in Canberra who believed the story from the Corby camp, Alexander Downer responded: 'No. I guess one or two people said to me, "This is politically a problem, we've got to do something about it." I am not going to say who it was—it was not John Howard. But I do remember one minister saying that to me.'

A political staffer confirmed that Schapelle Corby was getting special treatment well beyond the level of support ever given to an Australian prisoner facing trial in a foreign country. He says: 'She had every level of consular assistance available. It went above and beyond the call of duty. Politically and on a public level, because a lot of people in the public arena and some people in the media as well thought/believed/knew that she was innocent . . . It was beyond galling—it was an absolute insult to see Australian taxpayers' money used in such a fashion.'

Understandably, the Australian Transport Workers Union was also not a fan of Tampoe's baggage handler defence. Hugh Williams from the Queensland ATU said, 'Why would you want to take that grave risk of putting it in somebody else's luggage, or allowing it to be in your own luggage under all the surveillance when you can slip that amount of drugs on the back of a truck?'

Robin Tampoe's favourite newspaper cartoon of the trial depicts a reporter asking Mick Keelty why he believes the Corby baggage handler defence is flimsy. The reporter is wearing a camel head.

When the usually sanguine Tampoe learnt via the television news that the Transport Workers Union was on the warpath, he was uncharacteristically apologetic about the power of his defence. As the documentary camera rolled, Tampoe apologised to the baggage handlers. 'Sorry, guys,' he shrugged, momentarily unable to control the sheepish grin that was threatening to break into a victorious beam.

CHAPTER 25

The *60 Minutes* Verdict

'This place is teaching me things. Teaching me patience, it's teaching me tolerance. And it's teaching me about the real characteristics about human nature that's in this place. Survival tactics.'
—Schapelle Corby

Rosleigh Rose was convinced that her daughter was 'coming home', and she therefore wanted to make sure Schapelle had a lovely outfit to wear for the verdict hearing. She had chosen a conservative black shirt contrasted with pale pink slacks. 'You don't think the pants are too light?' Ros asked Schapelle as she held them up to the window in the jail's visiting area.

'They're perfect. Thanks, Mum,' Schapelle replied, hugging her. She was pleased with the selection and the mood between mother and daughter was bright and breezy, as if they were choosing an outfit for a party and not a drug trial.

'I think this will come up well on camera,' Ros raved. By now Ros was acutely aware of the opinion polls back in Australia and the fact that the majority of Australians right now believed her gorgeous daughter was innocent. Ros glowed with pride as they sat on the dirty prison mat, holding hands. 'Not long now. Everyone wants you home,' Ros assured her.

Shut off from the outside world, Schapelle was at the mercy of everyone else's opinion and actions. Ros kept saying she was coming home, but Mercedes was constantly preparing her for bad news. 'They might find you guilty, Schapelle, but that doesn't mean it's over. Just remember that. We can appeal,' Mercedes told her sister.

One week out from the verdict, Vasu and Lily called a meeting with Ros and Mercedes to discuss verdict day strategy and this was documented on film. Ros reluctantly turned up, complaining all the time as she waited for Lily and Vasu to see them. 'Why the bloody hell are we having a meeting?' she bitched to Mercedes. Ignorance might be bliss, but it didn't seem to be giving Ros much comfort. She looked puffy and exhausted and, in her determination to remain positive, she had become bad tempered and wildly irrational. 'Bloody lawyers—always wanting meetings. It's like they are deliberately trying to make Mercedes tired,' she said.

Vasu was careful in the meeting to stress that there might be a need to appeal should the trial outcome not be the one they wanted, but Ros would have none of that 'guilty talk'. 'She's coming home. I know that. Can we take her with us straight away on the day?' she asked.

'If we win, we will get her out before the prosecutor appeals,' Vasu replied.

'We'll have to make sure she gets her passport, Mercedes,' said Ros.

Mercedes bowed her head down and inhaled a deep breath. 'Mum, you won't be able to visit her at the holding cell before the hearing.'

'I'll visit her if I want,' Ros snapped.

'But the media . . . the media will be everywhere,' Mercedes argued.

As she left Bali Law Chambers Ros warmly hugged Vasu and Lily, as if they had already won the case and the verdict was just a mere formality. 'She's coming home, Lily, she's coming home,' Ros said as she waved goodbye.

Despite trying to stay level headed about it all, Mercedes was also consumed with the prospect of Schapelle's pending release. For weeks she had been planning Schapelle's flight to freedom: 'She could go via Singapore and then maybe Australia. Or maybe we could hide her on an island somewhere and not tell anyone,' she said. *60 Minutes* would be in the loop—of course. Lucrative TV deals were also very much on Merc's mind.

Freedom was on Ron Bakir's mind too—freedom from a nightmare that was consuming his very being. On the eve of the verdict, he constantly paced around the pool of his rented Bali villa. The documentary team recorded him taking a phone call from a Gold Coast informer who was concerned that Ron was being played for a fool by Schapelle. Bakir exploded: 'I'll go out publicly and say she's guilty if anybody can give me that fucking evidence. Because every cunt's been talking shit and I've got no fucking evidence.' Despite his enduring loyalty to Schapelle's crusade, Bakir was feeling edgy—he had landed in Bali for the verdict and Mercedes was avoiding his calls. Schapelle was still pleased to see him and had welcomed him with open arms, but Merc was unreachable.

In recent days, Mercedes had been wined and dined by *60 Minutes* producer Kathryn Bonella. Although Bonella had been in regular contact with both Bakir and Tampoe for back-up research regarding the baggage handler defence, she was now dealing directly with Mercedes when it came to making the crucial 'verdict deal' for the Nine Network.

60 Minutes was playing wedge politics, making sure the media middleman Ron Bakir was kept out of any media negotiations as the producers figured he had the potential to make the deal more expensive or, even worse, give the 'exclusive' to the network's main rival, Seven. Bakir suspected he was being sidelined when both Bonella and Mercedes didn't return his calls. He later asserted, 'I just wanted to make sure she wasn't being ripped off, but Mercedes went into shut-down and wouldn't tell me what was going on.'

Whether Schapelle was found innocent or guilty, plans had been put in place by Nine to interview the Corbys straight after the verdict hearing was over. Nine had allegedly agreed to pay them $80,000 if Schapelle was found guilty, or $300,000 plus if she was found not guilty. Ros was booked to do a live cross to Ray Martin back in Australia immediately after the verdict.

There was also a large contingent of Corby supporters in Bali for verdict day—close relatives, distant relatives, family friends, people Schapelle probably hadn't seen since she was a child—all desperately trying to get into the jail to visit her, and then to be interviewed by the hungry media so they could have their fifteen seconds of fame. Mercedes was concerned that some relatives and friends were selling photos of themselves with Schapelle.

Meanwhile, Robin Tampoe waited in limbo. Earlier in the day he had attempted to half-heartedly spin a yarn to radio station 2GB that Schapelle had to be immediately released because she was frightened she was going to be attacked by violent lesbians, but he had to admit his heart wasn't in it. Even he was too exhausted to 'spin'.

Earlier in the week he had visited Schapelle and was shocked to discover that her family were yet to inform her that the verdict was going to be broadcast live on television back in Australia. Tampoe decided to break the news to her before she was confronted with it on Verdict Day. 'Wow!' she had exclaimed. 'Just like Melbourne Cup!' He couldn't believe that she had been kept in the dark, but Mercedes argued that she wanted to keep Schapelle on an even keel without too many hyped-up expectations.

On the eve of the verdict Mercedes, with her hair salon-straightened for the cameras, was anxiously munching into blocks of chocolate, hoping that the astrologers were right and her sister would soon be back home in Tugun. If Schapelle was found 'not guilty', *60 Minutes* had an exit plan in place—a private plane would whisk her away to an exclusive interview location.

On 27 May 2005, eight months after Schapelle was arrested at Denpasar Airport, Verdict Day had finally arrived. Never before had a court case involving an Australian in a foreign country received such intense media attention. Millions of Australians back home would watch as the three Indonesian judges handed down their verdict and sentence.

In his cheap hotel room in Kuta, Dave McHugh was also wound up. He had travelled from Adelaide to Bali to attend the trial. He felt certain that soon the whole nightmare would be over. McHugh was so sure that he was about to become part of a momentous victory that he'd brought his home video camera to personally record the outcome. In many ways, he was like a firebug who had lit a fire and couldn't help returning to the scene of the crime to record all the action.

Meanwhile, back in Adelaide, Malcolm McCauley was one of two million Australians who tuned in to watch the live multi-camera coverage of the verdict on TV. As usual he was knocking back the beers and feeling confident: 'We were in the lounge room at Degree Road, Kathleen and I. Everyone was speculating what would she get? It was the question the whole country was asking. To be honest, I was past predicting. I was nervous for her.'

'You hope for the best,' Kathleen remarked. 'I knew she was going to be there longer than what she wanted. It was just a case of how long.'

When the star of the show finally arrived at the courthouse, she was clutching a pink handbag. A swarm of Indonesian police and camera operators snaked their way through the court's metal detector as she was carried along in the stream of bodies. The windows of the courthouse were so jammed with cameramen trying to film over the shoulders of the police that they were blocking the airflow into the courtroom.

Schapelle was marched across the white tiled floor and plonked down unceremoniously on a chair in the centre of the courtroom. She bent forward, gulping in deep breaths of air—the mad rush from the prison van had left her gasping in the hot muggy courthouse. She had her hair pinned up in a bun; her make-up was perfect and her accessories included silver earrings and the obligatory silver crucifix. Sitting next to her was her equally pretty interpreter, Eka—together they looked like a pair of beauty queens.

The Corbys were chauffer driven to court courtesy of Channel 9. Ros had her own producer, who was given the unenviable task of keeping at bay the rest of the media, all of them desperate for any 'grabs' they could get.

Old Mick, Mercedes and Wayan sat with Ros in the

front row of the public gallery. When Schapelle turned to face them, Mercedes and Ros blew kisses at her. Ros told the documentary team that she felt good and that Schapelle would be coming home. Schapelle was now the leading lady of a TV soap opera in which her family were playing supporting roles, and this was the big moment, the climax of the series.

Noticeably, despite all their hard campaigning, Ron Bakir and Robin Tampoe had been relegated to standing-room-only at the back of the crowded courtroom. The Corbys hadn't saved any seats for them. Instead room had been made for their new media mates, who were paying big money for the Corbys' time. Both men had done the hard yards for the family and, all of a sudden, they had been dumped. They wouldn't be the last. Tampoe later recalled: 'It was patently clear that we had become irrelevant. *A Current Affair* was glued to Ros, *60 Minutes* were nearby and I stood at the back like a moron, a person of no significance, after all the work that had been done to get to this point. Not so much as a wave or a smile, not even any sort of acknowledgement, I stood at the back of the court crushed into a corner with every other onlooker. It was too much. I went outside, got myself a glass of water and sat in the shade. Intermittently I would walk inside, and had to push my way past some grumpy old woman that was hovering at the entrance and didn't like moving to let me through. For the first time since I got involved, I hadn't spoken to the family or seen Schapelle. The same producers that had chased Ron were now ignoring him—how dramatically the dynamics of the relationship had changed.'

Meanwhile Dave McHugh was pretty certain he had been saved a seat in the court, but instead he was denied entry because he was wearing shorts and thongs. Undeterred and armed with his home video camera, he pushed his way through the professional camera crews to film through a court window. At one point the crowd was so thick with cameras all jostling for position that McHugh was shoved out of the way and pushed onto a shrub.

At the front of the courtroom the three judges sat imposingly in high-backed chairs with ornate wooden carvings. Their chairs looked like royal thrones compared to Schapelle's cheap swivel office chair, which looked like something from a second-hand furniture sale. If it all looked like a daytime TV soap opera, the judges were not playing their part—rather than get to the big moment, they droned on and on for an hour and a half summing up of the case.

At times Schapelle looked as if she had transported herself to another world. She stared straight ahead, constantly praying to her newly found God that a miracle would happen and that all the promises from her family and Channel 9 that she would be 'coming home soon' would come true.

Eka, sitting next to Schapelle, was interpreting as fast as she could under the immense pressure. When the chief judge said the statements from the Indonesian customs officials who had arrested her were accepted as 'truthful', Schapelle started breathing faster and looking pale. The judge then said that every single defence witness who had claimed that someone else put the drugs inside Schapelle's bag was ruled to be irrelevant.

Judge Sirait continued with his demolition of the defence case; he said that none of Schapelle's witnesses, including the prisoner John Ford, could prove who had planted the drugs in the boogie board bag. Then it got worse—he said that she 'was convincingly proved to have trafficked the drugs'. When he finally delivered the sentence of 'twenty years' in

Indonesian, Schapelle didn't comprehend it—she turned to her translator and was told 'twenty years' in English. Ros and Mercedes instantly started hurling abuse at the judge. Indonesian police waved their hands at them, but couldn't stop the attack. Ros screamed out, 'She swore on the bible that she was telling the truth and your fellow lied! You judges will never sleep!'

Schapelle turned to her family and said, 'It's OK. It's OK.' Mercedes yelled back, 'It's not OK!' Then Schapelle fought her way past the police to Ros and hugged her amidst a sea of cameras. The Indonesian police then wrenched Schapelle away from her mother and Ros yelled out, 'My daughter's coming home.' If the sound on the television sets back in Australia had been turned down, this could have been mistaken for an episode of Schapelle's favourite show, *The Bold and the Beautiful*—as the evil judges marched out of the courtroom, the glamorous heroine was taken away by the police and the family were left railing against the injustice of it all.

Inside the court, Schapelle's lawyer Lily Lubis said, 'I don't think she can survive.' Outside the courtroom, Mercedes was furious: 'To all our family and friends, we love you all. Schapelle is innocent! This verdict is unjust! We will stand by Schapelle every step of the way.' Then Mercedes started screaming as she unleashed months of pent-up restraint. 'I don't know what happened in the trial, they didn't take any of our bloody witnesses into account!'

The courthouse had descended into mayhem. Schapelle was escorted from the court to the prison van in amongst a massive crush of reporters. She looked a pathetic sight—staggering, punch drunk, her face streaked with make-up and tears. In her wake, she left collateral damage.

Robin Tampoe recalls: 'I didn't know where Ron had

gone. I went up to the defence table—Eka and Lily were consoling each other. Lily was crying; everybody, myself included, was in shock.' When he went outside the courtroom he found Ron Bakir at the back of the building, away from the cameras, sobbing. As Tampoe hugged him and led him to a waiting car, the TV cameras that Bakir had been trying to avoid were rolling. 'Ron was still crying. I had seen him go through some personally difficult times in his life and never cry. Anyone who doubted his motivation should have been in the back of the car that day.'

Rosleigh Rose was spirited away to do her live cross with Ray Martin straight after the verdict was over. Meanwhile, a *60 Minutes* producer and a producer from *A Current Affair* were arguing over who would get the first interview with the Corbys. Schapelle was back in the slammer and they had just made $80,000.

As the TV producers fought and the Corbys ran to their Channel 9 cars, Dave McHugh's camera was still rolling. He jostled with the news crews to capture his own final images of Schapelle. He looked like just another nosy tourist at the court with a video camera. Time would prove otherwise.

The verdict had been a surreal experience for the Corbys, and now they were locked away in a luxury villa paid for by *60 Minutes*. In the villa's swimming pool a Corby cousin could be seen, passed out, floating around on a blow-up air mattress, burnt bright pink in the Bali sun, a bottle of cheap champagne still clutched in her hand.

After the verdict, Schapelle didn't see her family for nearly a week. While speculation raged that she was pissed off with all the broken promises, Schapelle insisted that she told her family to stay away so they wouldn't have to endure rough media scrums when they visited the jail. But there may have been another reason for the family to lie low—*60 Minutes* had ensconced the family in the rented villa so they couldn't be interviewed by rival networks until the program's next exclusive story went to air.

Schapelle Corby was now a 'Million Dollar Baby', but with all the cash and fame, and all the attendant costs of keeping the family in Bali to support her, came conflicting priorities. After enduring the harrowing verdict—and the very real prospect of twenty years in an Indonesian 'hell hole' jail and her return to the Gold Coast at the age of 47—Schapelle cried alone in Kerobokan, still wearing the new black shirt and pale pink pants Ros had bought for her. When she needed her mother and father's arms around her most, they were both sitting devastated in a posh villa meeting their obligations to *60 Minutes*.

PART THREE

The Morning After

CHAPTER 26

The Blame Game

'Has the wrong thing been done by me, yeah, absolutely. Have I been spat on unjustly? Without a doubt in the world. Have I been treated like a scumbag? Without a doubt in the world. Has Schapelle conned me? It depends if she's guilty or not.'

—Ron Bakir

In the luxury *60 Minutes* villa in Bali a distraught Rosleigh Rose was knocking back the Bintangs and everyone was copping a serve—the Australian government, the Australian Federal Police, the Indonesian judges, airport security, the baggage handlers, the lawyers. Everyone else was to blame, and in particular Ron Bakir. 'She would've been out if they, if we didn't stuff up with those other friggin' bloody lawyers,' Ros asserted.

Those privileged enough to be included in the inner sanctum included *Gold Coast Bulletin* reporter Tony Wilson, who it seemed was now Ros's unofficial adviser. This worried Mercedes, who thought he was just another of the desperate opportunists who had recently attached themselves to the Corby bandwagon; and she was deeply concerned about his motives when it became increasingly clear he was planning to write a book about Schapelle.

Wilson was smart enough to know that if Ron Bakir remained in the picture, it was very unlikely that he would be chosen as Schapelle's biographer. Bakir was already in talks with a book publisher and Wilson's name certainly hadn't been included in the negotiations. But Ros liked and trusted Wilson, and he had become a regular, steady fixture in her life. She had always felt inferior to 'educated types who use big words' but, there from the beginning, Wilson was like an adopted Corby, the rest of the press commonly mistaking him for a relative—he wore Bintang singlets and thongs and liked to drink with Ros while they discussed defence strategy.

Wilson's reward for his loyalty was special access to Schapelle in prison and therefore plenty of front-page stories; he enjoyed the exalted status of being the 'Corby insider and expert' for the Murdoch newspaper group. Schapelle had confided in others that she 'found him revolting' and wished her mother wouldn't bring him into the jail, but the positive stories he was regularly generating about the family kept him tightly within the circle of trust.

Ros had had little to do with Ron Bakir throughout the trial and had also quite often refused to speak with Schapelle's lawyers. Apart from Ros doing her bit by giving interviews to Ray Martin, all other responsibility for the trial had been laid firmly in Mercedes's lap.

On the night of the verdict, according to an insider who was present at the villa, an emotional argument broke out between Mercedes and Ros about Ron Bakir. Merc pleaded with her mother to believe that 'Ron's heart is in the right place'. Ros's brother, Shun Hatton, was present and he argued that Harry M. Miller should be employed to assist with media deals, even if it meant that the family would have to forsake a large percentage of any income because of the notoriously high commision Miller always demanded.

This suggestion went down like a lead balloon with Mercedes. Over the months leading up to the verdict she'd watched carefully how Bakir and Tampoe had handled the media and how they'd promoted the baggage handler defence. She was a quick learner and, as far as she was concerned, from now on she would be in charge. Or at least she thought she would be in charge—her mother had always been a loose cannon and not an easy person to wrangle. And now Ros had her own media flunkies to deal with, all wanting exclusives and giving their opinions on what should and should not be done. Controlling Dear Mum would soon become another full-time job for Mercedes.

While the arguments raged and debates moved back and forth over several Bintangs, the person around whom the discussion centred was crying her heart out alone in her Kerobokan cell, dealing with the crushing blow and contemplating her twenty-year sentence. Across town, Schapelle's defence team were equally as deflated and still trying to come to terms with the trial defeat.

Robin Tampoe and Vasu Rasiah thought the sentence was a relatively good result because Schapelle could have received a life sentence or worse. They knew the Indonesian prosecutors had been disappointed. Tampoe said at the time: 'We're not happy with it as defence lawyers but in Indonesia it's an exceptional result—4.2 kilos of cannabis is the biggest ever brought in to this country and it is death.' Vasu agreed: 'It's a good result so far.' He still hoped the twenty-year sentence could be brought down on appeal to fifteen and then ten years—he wasn't fazed and believed that there was still time to cut the jail term in half.

Ron Bakir wanted to talk strategy for an appeal, but Tampoe was over it. He'd hit emotional rock bottom and wanted to quit. He'd always lived off his gut instinct, and now he could sense a changing of the tide. 'Don't you people get it?' he asked. 'They're going to blame us. Everyone is going to blame us! We get the death penalty off the table, but it's not good enough.'

Back in Australia the outrage continued—there were calls to boycott Qantas and stop all travel between Australia and Bali. In the days that followed an envelope containing a suspicious white powder was sent to the Indonesian Embassy in Canberra, resulting in the whole building being shut down after government authorities feared it might contain deadly anthrax. There was talk of a national day of protest and Foreign Affairs Minister Alexander Downer was flooded with 5000 emails protesting Schapelle's innocence.

Despite the media frenzy following the verdict, Alexander Downer recalls there was very little diplomatic tension between Australia and Indonesia: 'Well, I spoke to the Indonesians about the case a couple of times, and I said to them there was a lot of emotion in Australia about this issue. It wasn't an issue between our two governments, though, and I wasn't asking anything of them.'

But the media was spinning Schapelle a different line—in particular representatives from the Nine Network's 60 Minutes, who had enlisted the help of a former Kerobokan prisoner, Australian Chris Parnell, to help them convince Schapelle that she should agree to an undercover jailhouse interview. Parnell had spent 11 years in Indonesian prisons after being convicted of drug smuggling back in 1985, and after his release he wrote a book about his harrowing experience entitled *The Sunday Smuggler*. Parnell had always maintained his innocence. While serving his own prison sentence in Kerobokan, desperate to get out and back to Australia, he pretended to go crazy and, in taking on the part, walked around with a pineapple under his arm, telling guards that it was his best friend. The crazy scheme had worked and his 'academy award-winning' performance, reminiscent of a manic Jack Nicholson in *One Flew Over the Cuckoo's Nest*, had an impact—Parnell was transferred to Bungli Mental Hospital.

Now in a bizarre twist of a tale, Parnell was suddenly transported back to Bali and was being paid to help the *60 Minutes* team with their 'post verdict' story about Schapelle. In an interview for this book, Parnell alleges that when he was first contacted by Kathryn Bonella, 'She said to me that Mercedes had read the book and that I could be a big help to Schapelle, building her up and letting her know that things aren't that bad, and being able to help her with the case and with her appeals.'

The moment Parnell arrived in Bali, the *60 Minutes* team asked him to smuggle a camera and audio equipment into the jail so that they could interview Schapelle. He said, 'They wanted me to take the camera in, and I said, "Well, I'll ask her first and let's see what she feels about it." And when I came, she said, "No cameras, I don't want to do anything."' Parnell added that when he first met Schapelle in jail, she immediately frisked him: 'She gave me a cuddle and felt me all over, and she frisked me to see that I wasn't wearing a recording device.'

On that visit, he tried to convince Schapelle to admit her guilt in order to get a sentence reduction. His own experience with the Indonesian judicial system had taught him that pleading innocent rarely helps any foreign prisoner facing serious jail time. 'I said to her, "Look, it doesn't matter if you are guilty or not guilty, look at yourself, look at your life, look at your situation. What you've got is a definite 20 if you stick to being not guilty, or a definite 6 by saying guilty. Take the tip from me, I did 11 years . . . if I knew then what I know now, I would have pleaded guilty."' But according to him, Schapelle wouldn't have a bar of it. She told Parnell that the drugs were not hers. Parnell said, 'She was like, "It wasn't mine, it wasn't mine," and I said, "Yeah, OK, whatever! Use your commonsense—the Indonesians will not back down."'

Schapelle also confided to Parnell that the Channel 9 producers had been reassuring her they would get her out of jail. Parnell was surprised that she believed them: 'Schapelle said, "No, I won't do it . . . I'm not going to do any time in jail. I've done enough. I don't want to do any time," and then she said, "[60 Minutes] has promised me that I will get out of this, I will get out of this."' Schapelle explained to the former Kerobokan inmate that 60 Minutes had it all worked out. 'She said that [60 Minutes] had told her [it] would get behind her, and they would push and push the story, and the Indonesian government would feel the pressure because angry Australians would blacklist their country and disrupt the whole tourism of Bali, and it would cost them millions and millions of dollars.'

Parnell claims that he also spoke to Schapelle about 'acting crazy' to get out of jail. He recalls, 'I said if worse comes to worse, remember the Bungli [Mental Hospital], but don't run on the roof, don't go on the roof.' Parnell had tried to escape from Bungli by running across the roof of the mental asylum, but the roof collapsed and he had crashed back down into the prison yard.

After failing to get a camera into the jail for *60 Minutes*, Parnell went back to visit Schapelle a second time, but this time the young woman from the Gold Coast was nothing like the person the media was portraying to the Australian public. 'The next time I met her, I walked in and she said, "Yeah, what do you want?" And I said I'd contacted the prosecutor and he's happy to do a deal. She called him [the prosecutor] a monkey face. She said, "That monkey-faced bastard, I hope he dies, I hope he dies." I said, "Settle down." My mate the guard came over and had a look when she was getting angry, and she said, "What's this cunt looking at? He looks like a fucking monkey, too." And I said, "Hang on, he's your friend," and she said, "How come you're so friendly with these guards, they are all dogs, they're all cunts."'

After two meetings with Schapelle in Kerobokan, Parnell summed her up this way: 'She comes from a tough family. She's as tough as nails, but she's a good actress too. I thought, you're a great little con girl and you are carrying this through really well, but you're hitting your head up against a brick wall because you were found with the stuff.'

Meanwhile, upon returning home to Queensland post-verdict, Rosleigh Rose's opening attack on Ron Bakir came via an exclusive interview with the *Bulletin*'s star reporter, Paul Toohey. In the article, Toohey admits that Ros had a few beers under her belt before she let fly. Tony Wilson later confirmed to documentary director Janine Hosking that: 'Rossie was drunk when Toohey later called her to check his facts and to confirm what she had told him earlier in the day. She actually thought she was talking to me, but what the hell? It doesn't matter. It got the desired result and that was to get rid of Bakir.' Wilson went further and took credit for the phrase 'Black Knight' in reference to Ron Bakir. 'I told Rossie that and then she told Toohey,' he boasted. 'Black Knight' became the magazine's headline.

Ros had grown to hate Ron Bakir saying, 'Naturally he's nice, because he's a salesman and a con man. He made you feel comfortable.' She then followed up this spectacular attack with an interview on *A Current Affair*, accusing Bakir of demanding money from Schapelle to cover his costs. She said, 'He says to Schapelle . . . He touches her and says, "I've been working around the clock for you and spent $300,000."' Ros then claimed that Bakir visited Schapelle a second time in prison and told her that she owed him $500,000.

Ron Bakir denied that he'd asked Schapelle for half a million dollars, but admitted there'd been a discussion with the family: 'I said, "If I can recoup any money, then thanks. If I can't, so be it."' As Tampoe subsequently explained: 'Ron started out as the next candidate for Australian of the Year, and ended up being depicted as a shameless self-promoter. He was seen by the press as an opportunist who had come to steal Schapelle and her family's new-found wealth. I learned he had a contract with her, the contents of which I haven't seen. He was criticised heavily for this contract, which seemed ridiculous to me . . . He was spending money trying to help get a stranger out of prison. He didn't know Schapelle before the arrest; there was no obligation to help. Ron probably thought he could make her rich and famous, recoup his costs and get her home. What's wrong with that? At that point in time the Corbys were making a bucketload, and Ron was haemorrhaging a truckload. Besides, I hadn't seen anyone else offer to help.'

'Reading between the lines, what Ros really wanted to say in that *Bulletin* article was that no Lebo was going to take her family fortune,' Tampoe concluded. 'But they wouldn't just cut Ron loose—they were going to humiliate him in the process. They went from loving him to loathing him in a split second.'

After the *Bulletin* article was published, Tony Wilson decided to go in for the kill and took it upon himself to personally ring Bakir. 'I am going to finish you, you fucking bastard. What you've done to that girl is a fucking disgrace. You're a fucking . . . cunt!' Absolutely shocked at the ferocity of this unsolicited attack, Ron replied, 'Are you calling me a cunt? And you're supposed to be a journalist?' Tony Wilson had taken things too far this time and his veiled threats would end up costing him dearly. When News Ltd later carried out its own investigation into this incident, Wilson was sacked.

The gloves were well and truly off now and the fallout between the Corbys and their legal team lifted the lid on the deals struck between the family and the media. In an explosive interview with the Nine Network's *Sunday* program Robin Tampoe said, 'I went to the holding cell amongst all the chaos to see Schapelle. I was holding her hand while she was crying. I find out down the track that Mercedes did a live interview—she is making $30,000 with *New Idea* while I'm holding her sister's hand and that, from my point of view, sickens me.'

Ros then hit back at Tampoe's comments. 'We have made some money from media deals, but we still have a long way to go in this case, and that money is being kept for things in the future that we may not even know about yet.' But Tampoe returned fire. 'The only people that I've seen who are profiting from Schapelle Corby being in jail is the Corby family. Vasu and Lily's costs were supposed to be paid by the Australian government in the form of legal aid. Vasu had rendered an account to the Australian government, which was cut in half by the government. When he eventually received the cheque, it had been written out to the wrong person and couldn't be cashed. Ron had given a substantial amount of money to Vasu to bankroll the case.'

By now all the Corbys' outgoings were being met by others—the legal costs, airline flights, accommodation. While they had cleaned up, Bakir had not made one cent. But the Corbys didn't like all this talk about them making money while Schapelle was stuck in jail, so the story was leaked to some friendly media mates that Mick Corby had spent $70,000 from his superannuation fund on his daughter's court case. As Mick told the *Gold Coast Bulletin*, 'I sent it in two amounts of $30,000 and $40,000, and I know what's left is in an account connected to that law firm, and it's not a trust account.' Vasu later said that he'd returned the money to Mercedes, but the Corbys claimed there was still $50,000 missing.

The Australian government certainly invested more money in trying to obtain Schapelle's freedom than the Corbys themselves. In 2009, the Australian government confirmed that it had spent $200,000 on Schapelle Corby's case, plus the costs of getting the prisoner John Ford to testify in Bali. After the verdict, the Corbys made somewhere between $100,000 and $200,000 from media deals and, more importantly, they hadn't had to sell any of their family properties back in Queensland to pay for the court case.

So, to tote it up: In 2000 Mick had bought the home at Tugun for $170,000; in 2010 it was worth at least $500,000.

Despite him initially wanting to sell the house to pay a bribe, the Corbys still own that house today. And, despite all the drama in Bali, Mick also managed to avoid selling his farm, which he bought in 1998 for $100,000. In 2010 it was worth about $500,000. Ros also avoided having to sell her home in Loganlea to raise any funds for the trial. In 2010 her home was worth somewhere between $250,000 and $300,000. All up the Corbys had over a million dollars in real estate, plus from all accounts a profitable seafood takeaway business before they sold it and a couple of hundred thousand from media deals. Given all the money that had been spent on the trial, they weren't doing too badly.

After the verdict, Ros was quick to sell Rox's Seafood Takeaway claiming, 'We need the money to pay for all the court costs.' Suddenly the perpetually unemployed Michael Corby Jnr was without his fish and chip shop gig. When asked by a documentary producer what employment he intended to undertake now that the shop was sold, he was incredulous. 'Work?' he replied. 'I can't work. I have to go back and forth to Bali and look after Schapelle.'

Not many people, particularly a surfie with no regular employment, could afford to be on permanent watch for Schapelle, particularly when his sister and her husband were already in Bali. But by now the whole family was living off Schapelle's fame and media deals. Michael once told the film crew, as he gazed out over the expansive backyard of their Tugun property, 'Schapelle's going to buy me a swimming pool when she gets home.'

Meanwhile, unexpectedly, Schapelle made one final phone call from Kerobokan to 'thank' Ron for all his work. She told Bakir she could only speak for a minute, as she was 'using a guard's phone to call'. She was polite but distant.

SINS OF THE FATHER

'What the hell is your mother going on about?' Bakir asked her.

'She is my mother and she loves me. She doesn't understand a lot of it. She says stuff without thinking,' was Schapelle's reply.

The days of sharing flowery prose with her White Knight were now well and truly over. There were no more poems for Ron from her positive thinking books. Bakir's friends say that he still struggles to understand how it all went so terribly wrong.

But, near the end of this whole trashy saga, support for Bakir came from an unexpected and surprising phone call: 'I just want to say, Ron, that I appreciate everything you have done for our family. I'm sorry about what Mum said. I don't know what's going on. She goes off half-cocked half the time,' the low-profile, flying-under-the-radar Michael Corby Jnr allegedly told Bakir.

The rest of the Corbys had long moved on and the reinvention continued. The old legal team was sacked, except for Indonesian lawyer Erwin Siregar, who encouraged the Corbys to hire a flashy friend—celebrity Jakarta-based lawyer Hotman Paris Hutapea. Famous throughout Indonesia for his diamond bling and his multi-million-dollar homes, his sports cars and his glamorous lovers, Hotman Paris was attracted to the high-profile case and agreed to run Schapelle's appeal case pro bono.

'How can I resist such a beautiful lady?' he said to Schapelle. 'I will get you home.' As they sat discussing the case in Kerobokan, Schapelle put her hand on his lap, leaned her head on his shoulder and flashed him a coquettish smile.

CHAPTER 27

Granny Eastwood Rolls

'Your honour, this matter entails a number of highly unusual features . . . she's a 51-year-old grandmother with no prior convictions . . . finding herself before the court charged with an extremely serious drug-related offence.'

—Judge, Townsville Magistrates Court

For several years, the head of the Townsville end of Malcolm McCauley's South Australian and Queensland drug syndicate, Wayne Williams, had managed to stay one step ahead of the cops. But that was all about to change. As far as bad years go, the Pig Shooter would look back on 2005 as his all-time worst.

On a sunny Saturday morning in May of that year, the same month as Schapelle's verdict in Bali, Williams woke up in a menacing mood. After gathering together seven associates, he led a three car convoy around to the home of a local boxing trainer named Neil Andrew Viney. When Viney saw Williams approaching with a baseball bat, he jumped into his parked vehicle and locked himself inside. It provided little protection—Williams and his posse simply smashed their way through the side door and then using a machete and a garden hoe handle, they stabbed and beat Viney to within an inch of his life. Williams and a 19-year-old accomplice were arrested by police a short time afterwards and three days later they appeared before the Townsville Magistrates Court charged with attempted murder, grievous bodily harm and going armed in public. The cause of the dispute was not revealed. Despite the fact that Viney had spent twelve days in hospital and required stitches to his legs, arms and chest as a result of the assault, Magistrate David Glasgow granted Williams bail that day. Whether police had had a quiet word with the magistrate or not is unclear but one thing is certain—his decision to set Williams free suited them down to the ground. As it happened, the Pig Shooter was already being monitored around the clock due to a separate major incident that had occurred less than three months earlier.

In late 2004, Townsville detectives had launched Operation Tiara with the sole aim of bringing Williams's drug empire down. They knew he was the supplier of enormous amounts of hydroponic marijuana up and down the North Queensland coastline. What they still couldn't work out was how he had consistently managed to source it. They were desperate to unmask his supplier and put the missing pieces of the jigsaw together. Never in a million years did anyone anticipate those answers would finally arrive courtesy of an Adelaide grandmother called Brenda Eastwood.

On the morning of 13 March 2005, Eastwood was pulled over by police on the Flinders Highway between Charters Towers and Townsville. Hired as a drug courier once again by Malcolm McCauley, she had been seconds away from a rendezvous with Williams. In fact he was so close, he had watched with his own eyes as she was intercepted. There was no need to panic, thought Eastwood as she climbed out of the car. She hadn't been drinking. She'd stayed well under the speed limit. There was no reason for the cops to be suspicious. Unbeknown to her, there was every reason.

She had popped up in Williams-related surveillance more than a year earlier, in February 2004. When her vehicle reappeared that fateful day, the police were ready to pounce. They forced Eastwood over to the side of the road and maintained the secrecy of their undercover work by telling her she'd been stopped for a routine breath test. She blew into a tube and, sure enough, returned a negative reading. But, just as she was about to head off, an officer suggested he could smell marijuana in her car. The cops asked rather politely if they could take a peek. Within minutes, they had unearthed 25 one-pound bags of top-quality cannabis.

Later that afternoon, the granny from Gawler caved in and provided a detailed confession at Townsville Police Station. She named Malcolm McCauley as the man who hired her and Jeff Jellese as the owner of the Nissan Patrol station wagon she had used for the journey. She also confessed that Jellese, as the banker behind the business, was paying her between $2200 and $2700 for every five-day round trip, carrying between 15 and 25 one-pound bags of cannabis. She provided a detailed account of her usual modus operandi for Williams in North Queensland, dropping off at Charters Towers and Townsville. When asked about the number of trips completed she stuttered uncomfortably, eventually owning up to 'somewhere between 15 and 20'. Detectives never thought to ask Eastwood about any additional courier work elsewhere because then they didn't really care. They were overjoyed with what information they had. Finally, they were in a position to bust Williams.

They held back, however. Had they arrested him, it would have alerted McCauley and Jellese to the fact that they were next in line. So instead, they left him alone and continued the ruse that Eastwood had come unstuck, by chance, at a random breathalyser check. McCauley recalls: 'Within minutes of Brenda's arrest, Wayne called me. He had followed her into town and saw her get pulled over by the police convoy.' McCauley added: 'He believed it was all random. None of us had any idea she'd spilled the beans. Not straight away, anyhow.'

When Eastwood dobbed in the whole gang that day, it was essential that the confession remain strictly confidential so she was refused bail and kept in jail until her sentence hearing, five months later in August. But, as the old saying goes, sometimes it's not a case of what you know but who you know. Within 48 hours of the ink having dried on her statement, McCauley had inexplicably managed to obtain a copy. McCauley said the syndicate collectively decided to take a couple of months off. 'We did nothing, said nothing and after a while, it all seemed OK,' he remembers. 'Nothing had reared its ugly head, nobody had tapped us on the shoulder, so then we started up again. I was way too relaxed. I'd seen Brenda's confession but I presumed if anything was gonna happen, I'd already have been sent to the slammer.'

Another person who saw Eastwood's statement was Roger Rathjen and, the moment he did so, he warned McCauley to 'pull the pin immediately'. 'I said to him, "Look, mate, they're on to you now. It's written down there in front of you. Quit while you're ahead." But he just wouldn't listen. The truth is, he became greedy.'

Silly McCauley. In the days following Eastwood's arrest,

Townsville detectives had fed a detailed brief through to the Brisbane State Drug Investigation Unit. The Brisbane cops later contacted their counterparts in the South Australian Drug and Organised Crime Investigation Unit. In September 2005, those communications sparked the launch of two major interstate strike forces: Operation Co-Pilot in South Australia and Operation Delta Ape in Queensland.

In the first instance, they initiated a network of phone taps on suspected members of the gang. It resulted in a collection of over 700 intercepted communications on McCauley's home landline and a further 80 on a mobile number belonging to Kathleen. Jeff Jellese was also the subject of more than 500 recorded calls. Thanks to input from Queensland Police, there were also 900 intercepts on a landline number listed in the name of Wayne Williams's wife.

Meanwhile, in Bali, retired syndicate member Mick Corby was spending time with his daughter. Ros had ordered her ex-husband to live near the jail 'until Schapelle comes home'. Mick thought it was a fair enough edict, so Mercedes organised for him to rent a basic room at one of Wayan's relative's hotels in Kuta. Gradually, as the weeks turned to months, newspapers began to pile up in his bedroom—a sure sign he was there for the long haul.

Despite his worsening prostate cancer, he continued to drink and smoke. These were among the few comforts he had left. His bones and jaw were aching and he was constantly in pain. But no one talked to him about the case. Ros and Merc were running the show now, and if he asked too many questions he was told to 'shut up'. No one really bothered to ask his opinion about anything.

As the first anniversary of his daughter's drug bust passed on 8 October 2005, Mick was a defeated man. He confided to the documentary crew that he would sometimes stand alone outside the jail walls that separated his daughter from freedom and calculate the chances of her escaping. After casing the high walls and studying the barbwire and glass shards on top of them, he concluded that it would be impossible for her to 'trampoline out of there'. One option he had considered was to provide a pile of sedatives to Schapelle so that she could drug her cell-mates and the guards and then escape. The detail in which Mick went about explaining such escape plans meant they weren't just mere fantasies. Feelings of desperation made even the most ludicrous plan preferable to the horrendous years in jail that lay ahead for his daughter.

The months spent waiting for the result of the first appeal slipped somewhere between hope and despair for all the Corbys. Mercedes toiled day and night helping the new defence team to find 'evidence' from Australia that could help prove the baggage handler defence. She and lawyer Erwin Siregar trawled over the same ground that the previous legal team had gone through, and unsurprisingly they were hitting a massive brick wall.

Since Schapelle's arrest there had been three internal investigations into the baggage handler conspiracy theory by Qantas, which was assisted by both the Australian Federal Police and Queensland Police. Qantas even went to the extra lengths of replicating the size and weight of the marijuana inside Schapelle's boogie board bag and examined how it could possibly be stashed in a passenger's luggage, and how long it took to move from the oversize check-in counter to the aircraft on the runway. Qantas wanted to determine how much time an airport worker would have had to stash 4.2 kilos of pot inside a passenger's bag.

The first problem for a baggage handler attempting to move a large bag of pot to Bali was finding the right size bag to put it in. The flat vacuum-sealed grass in Schapelle's bag was carefully moulded to fit her boogie board, so the baggage handler would have to be waiting around for a similar-sized bag to appear. But the bulk of passenger luggage is not made up of boogie boards bound for Bali. The second problem was that it was a busy workplace—how could a baggage handler wait around with a whopping four kilo bag of pot while working in a room full of other airport employees? The third problem was finding a bag that was going to the right destination. Qantas's Geoff Askew concluded: 'That always seemed strange to me, the odds of waiting around for the perfect bag going to the right destination. I mean, if several boogie boards come through, are they all going from Brisbane to Bali via Sydney?'

In between her bursts of manic activity looking for a 'smoking gun', Mercedes would often sleep for days on end in a dark room. Her obsession with reading nasty rumours about the family on the internet had left her exhausted, hurt and depressed. There was too much going on, and the ongoing pressure was too much. She was mentally fractured and the grind of being Schapelle's 'lifeline' was crippling. Some days the two sisters would sit in silence beside one another in the jail's grubby visiting area barely exchanging a single word.

Finally, the Bali High Court released the result of the first appeal. Schapelle's sentence would be reduced by five years, from a twenty-year sentence to fifteen years. Thinking that they could further reduce the sentence to ten years, the defence team immediately lodged a second appeal.

When Ros was told the news about the fifteen-year sentence, she let out a primal scream from deep within. 'But they said it was going to go down to ten. You said she would get ten!' she sobbed. 'We can't do nothing! We can't yell, we can't scream, we can't go to fucking Jakarta and say, "Hey, wake up!" We can't sue the customs officer, we can't do fucking nothing. We can't do one thing. We have to be nice all the time!'

Mick Corby had just returned from having a few beers at a nearby pub when the ubiquitous Tony Wilson told him the news. 'She would have got less time if she had murdered that bloody customs officer!' was his dramatic contribution to the general hysteria.

CHAPTER 28

Gotcha!

'I really should have listened to Roger.'

—Malcolm McCauley

By October 2005, the month of Schapelle's first disappointing appeal result, South Australian police had discovered via phone taps that Malcolm McCauley's syndicate was not running smoothly at all. Granny Eastwood's arrest had hit it hard. Despite all the dramas, she had been the best courier McCauley had ever worked with. Now he was desperate for a new driver to fill her shoes.

From a financial perspective, there were no two ways about it—McCauley could not afford to lose Wayne Williams as a client. A year earlier, Schapelle had been arrested in Bali and her father had been forced to permanently shut up shop, cutting McCauley's two regular Queensland runs down to one. If he lost the second, the one to Williams, it would be an absolute disaster. So he needed a reliable replacement for the Gawler Granny.

It wouldn't have meant much to detectives listening in but after two refusals from former drivers, McCauley reluctantly broke a promise he made to himself several years earlier—and re-employed Peter 'Scarface' Dudley as a courier. 'When I began delivering interstate and making new clients, I accompanied Peter on some of the early runs. Seriously, when you are on the road, you don't do anything that draws attention to yourself. Nothing. But Peter thought it was all one big laugh. He was a loose cannon.'

On one of the first-ever runs to Queensland, the pair checked into a motel in Mount Isa 'with a boot full of hooter'. Later, Dudley 'lit up a big fat joint' outside his room door, sending a thick fog across the entire car park and drawing unwanted attention from reception staff. When they checked out the following morning, he also stole a pillow. McCauley recalls losing his nut: 'I mean, Jesus, the motel people had our car rego, our address details, everything. But he just didn't get it.' McCauley also remembers his maiden run to Alice Springs as 'the worst road trip ever'. 'Prior to departure,' he said, 'the contact at the other end asked about the possibility of me bringing up some crabs. So, as a goodwill gesture, I pulled together a large shipment of the best blue swimmers I could lay me hands on. When we got there Dudley grew impatient over the time it was taking to do the deal and threw a major dummy spit. In a moment of complete fucking madness, he lifted the lid off the esky and started hurling these crabs, one by one, straight at me in the hotel room. He then threw the entire box my way. I got clobbered. I went ass over tit and fucked my back up on the floor. What did Dudley do? He left me there stranded, took the keys and drove his car back to Adelaide. Once the deal was done, minus the crabs, I had to fly back on my tod.'

On Thursday 3 November 2005, the cops heard McCauley leave a voicemail message for Wayne Williams: 'Fishing will up your way over the weekend. I'll confirm exact times with you. Catch you later matey. Bye.' The phone lines then fell silent for several days until mid-afternoon on 7 November when Dudley popped up in surveillance expressing growing frustration that he'd already arrived in Queensland—and Williams wouldn't answer the phone.

McCauley rang Williams to see what the fuss was about and his client made it clear: 'I won't do things until dark.'

'Yep, well, do you want to give him [Dudley] a call and just verify that?' asked McCauley.

'Yes, I suppose mate, if you want, yep.'

'Good man,' said McCauley, somewhat relieved. 'It will just get him out of his worries.'

'Righteo mate.'

But four hours later, at 7.41 pm, Dudley was back on the blower, having reached boiling point.

'Hello,' said Jellese.

'Yeah, Jeffrey, I'm sitting here in the fucking dark.'

'Yeah?'

'I can't get on to this fucking wanker 'cause it's dark and he's too scared to answer his phone. I can't get on to Macca either.'

'What . . . has Macca not been in touch with you yet?' asked Jellese.

'No!'

'Well, he's supposed to call you.'

'Yeah? Well, he's a fucking wanker,' yelled Dudley hysterically.

'Calm down. I'm going to give Malcolm a call now and get him to give you a call.'

'Yeah? Well, he's got an hour or I'm heading back with it all.'

'Now, just take it easy . . .'

'He's got an hour or I'm heading back, all right?'

'Yeah, I've got that Peter, take it easy mate.'

'Yeah, well, you're not fucking up here mate.'

'I know that, Peter. Macca will give you a call straight away.'

'Don't give me a call!' screamed Dudley. 'Tell him to phone that fucking idiot [Williams] up!'

The surveillance detectives were getting their money's worth—and it wasn't over yet. In a panic, Jellese rang McCauley: 'Get in touch with Peter and calm him down because the way he's going, he now wants to come back again.'

'Holy shit!' said McCauley, realising the seriousness of it all.

'Yeah, yeah, just calm him down because he's . . .'

'Yeah,' sighed McCauley. 'Trust me,' he added, 'I know from experience exactly what he's like.'

Police listened in eagerly for the next instalment. In no time, it emerged that McCauley had failed to reach his driver in time—Dudley had suffered a major meltdown in front of the Pig Shooter, who was now baying for blood.

At 8.01 pm, McCauley picked up his telephone and had his head bitten off. It was Williams and he was ready to kill. 'Hey, Malcolm, you send him again and he'll go missing.'

'Okay.'

'Right?'

'What happened?'

'You send him again and he'll definitely, definitely go missing.'

Williams was almost hyperventilating as he provided McCauley with a rundown of the chaos Dudley had caused.

'He got out, pulled the thing out, sort of just palmed it off. He never said a word. Then he jumped in the car and spun the wheels off the road like a mongrel dog and carried straight on.' And then there was an ominous threat.

'You send him back up and we'll go pig shooting,' warned Williams, who added: 'It's only you and me that have been running this for a long time. I don't like others coming in.'

McCauley sank back down into his chair and wondered why it had all become so hard. There was one more phone call to make before his next visit to the fridge and it was to Jellese, to confirm the exchange had taken place.

'I'll give you the details in the morning but, yeah, the job's done. The old brother wants to take Peter pig shooting.'

'Ooooh . . . right,' said Jellese.

'Real bad,' confirmed McCauley.

Given the drama that had unfolded that night, one could have been forgiven for thinking that maybe McCauley might need a day off. But business is business and the very next morning, on Tuesday 8 November, he was back working the phones for the next big batch of marijuana to Williams—and a new driver.

He trawled through his phonebook and rang one of his female gardeners, but it was bad news. She had stopped growing because the cops were on to her. 'I'm being watched, someone dobbed us in,' she said. 'They are watching, I guarantee. They've been up the road, down the road and across the paddock for the past two weeks.'

McCauley warned the woman that she still owed both him and Jellese money after borrowing $2500. 'You're two weeks behind and by Friday, that'll make it three weeks. You're supposed to repay Jeffrey at least one and a half,' he said.

'Well, that's not my fault, is it?' she retorted. 'Just like this is not my fault. We have to get out of here. I'm like a bag of fucking shit at the moment. I'm as scared as.'

Four days later, on Saturday 12 November—after some more disappointing phone calls—the search was finally over. He rang Jellese and informed him the driver vacancy had been filled at last.

McCauley didn't elaborate over the phone, but his latest recruit was a man by the name of Dean Patrick Howard. Howard was a cashless, jobless dropout with a chronic dope addiction. When he did have two pennies to scratch together, he would march round to McCauley's place and buy whatever marijuana he could afford. Sure enough, he had pitched up the day before in his usual desperate state, and it was then that McCauley had pounced.

If ever there was a man who looked like a hardened criminal, it was Howard. He was big and he was bulky. He boasted tattoos on both sides of his neck that ran north, right the way up his jawline. His hair, meanwhile, was cropped, rather severely, in a crewcut style.

McCauley says Howard smoked dope morning, noon and night and it had turned his mind to 'mush'. 'I was really scraping the bottom of the barrel when I hired him. He said he could drive, though, that was the main thing.' When McCauley rang Williams to confirm the order, his client still seemed a little prickly following the Dudley debacle. They agreed on a 26-pound shipment, and Williams warned: 'If it doesn't rock up Saturday I'm gonna give it up.'

Jellese later arranged to bring the marijuana to McCauley's house around lunchtime the following day so it could be packed and prepared in time for Howard's departure. It was all the police needed to hear.

By 6.45 am the following morning, a plain-clothes surveillance team from the Investigations Support Branch had surrounded McCauley's address at Degree Road. There were detectives stationed in cars at either end of the street. There were others hidden in houses across the way. Over the next twelve hours, a police log would record McCauley's every move, not to mention everyone else around him.

At 12.43 pm, Detective Senior Constable Scott Copley recorded: 'I observed a dark coloured VY Holden Commodore sedan with a rear spoiler travel into the driveway.' He added: 'At 12.45 pm, I observed an unknown male, referred to in the surveillance log as (M1), sitting in the front yard, talking to McCauley and Jellese.' That person happened to be Roger Rathjen. The retired AFP drug cop had just strolled smack bang into a major South Australian police drug surveillance operation.

McCauley recalls: 'Roger rolled up the driveway in his car and said, "Mate, I reckon you're being watched." I said, "What do you mean?" And he said, "You've got cars down either end of the street. Look like undercovers to me."'

McCauley adds: 'I took a look, but I couldn't see anything. I should have pulled the pin and called it all off. But what did I do? Nothing. I had 26 pound of hooter sitting at the house, waiting to be delivered. I think I said something along the lines of, "Don't worry, Rog, this is the last deal. I'm out of the whole game after today."'

Rathjen, for the record, tells a different story. 'I pulled into the street and noticed there were surveillance cars. They wouldn't have been obvious to anyone else but I realised straight away. When I left Malcolm's house, they were still there.' He adds: 'As far as I can remember, I didn't say anything to Malcolm. I know this may sound naive but, honestly, it didn't twig that they were watching him. I mean, look, I didn't know there was 26 pounds of marijuana in the house at the time.'

Operation Co-Pilot detectives would have conducted a check on Rathjen's car and discovered it was registered in the name of a former high-ranking AFP officer. Exactly when that happened is unclear.

Rathjen remained at the house for the rest of the after-noon, downing beers with two crime bosses who were hours away from sending $80,000 worth of marijuana up the highway to Queensland. The surveillance log shows that at 3.06 pm, Senior Constable Daniel Cresp took over from day shift duties and observed that Rathjen's Holden was still parked in the driveway. Mysteriously, from that point on, Rathjen disappears off the radar completely. There is no further reference to either him or his car.

When asked whether he was ever quizzed about his visit that day, Rathjen responded: 'If I had received a phone call about it I would not have been surprised—but I didn't. In the context of police work,' he added, 'it was too much work to be quizzing everyone who came and went from Malcolm's house. They weren't interested in any sideshow. They were interested in the suitcases going in, the courier setting off for the drive and then later on rounding up the people they had evidence against.'

Did the South Australian police ever interview Rathjen about his involvement with McCauley, in general? 'Never,' he says.

Later that same night, Dean Howard picked up the 26 pounds of marijuana from McCauley's house and at

5.55 am the following morning—24 November 2005—Detective Sergeant Gary Jeffery and Detective Senior Constable Craig Potter were sitting parked in an unmarked police car just off the Barrier Highway at Mount Bryan, approximately 180 kilometres north of Adelaide. Shortly after, they spotted a blue Holden Commodore sedan with Dean Howard behind the wheel. Jeffery had strategically positioned Burra local Police Constable Matthew Hall on that same side of the highway. When Howard cruised past, he gave Hall the all-clear to strike.

Hall flagged Howard down and approached the vehicle. 'G'day, can you turn your vehicle off and step out of the vehicle with your licence.'

Howard climbed out and was immediately surrounded by half a dozen police officers with guns trained on his body. Jeffery then arrived and took control. 'Step to the back of the car and put your hands on it,' he said. 'You're being arrested for taking part in the sale of cannabis, do you understand? Do you understand?'

'Yes,' replied Howard.

Potter activated a video camera. Jeffery, meanwhile, rifled through Howard's pockets and discovered a silver-handled knife in the right-hand pocket of his tracksuit pants. He then located something else—a young boy cowering in the corner of the back seat of the car. It was Howard's 13-year-old son, and he was promptly moved to another police vehicle.

Detective Inspector Trevor Jenkins obtained the keys to the vehicle and opened the boot. Inside were two suitcases containing clothes and a bright orange-coloured beanbag crammed with clear plastic heat-sealed bags of cannabis. Howard had transferred the grass, thinking it was a better disguise than McCauley's suitcases.

'Yep, it's full of it,' confirmed Jenkins as he buried his hands deep inside.

Howard was bundled into the back left-hand side seat of a police vehicle. His frightened son, meanwhile, got to drive first class in the front passenger seat. The car travelled to nearby Port Pirie police station and by the time it had arrived at 8.30 am, there were fireworks exploding everywhere. In clinical, coordinated raids, the whole team was going down within seconds of one another.

At 8.32 am, Detective Sergeant Kenneth Copland knocked on Jeff Jellese's front door at Yatala Vale Road in Surry Downs.

Jellese's wife, Joy, answered. 'He's just finishing work,' she said in a fluster. 'He shouldn't be long because he's got an appointment with the eye specialist at nine o'clock.'

Several uncomfortable minutes later, the family's dog, Ella, suddenly sprang up off the sofa and ran to the window barking. Jellese had just arrived home from a gruelling nightshift. When he opened the door, there were six armed senior detectives there to greet him, along with Ella, who just wanted a pat.

The police later searched the house and found guns as well as marijuana plants and a sizeable hydroponic set-up in the back shed. It was all just icing on the cake—Jellese was going down anyhow.

In Queensland, meanwhile, Operation Delta Ape was drawing to a dramatic close. It was 8.34 am and Wayne Williams was driving the kids to school in his yellow Ford Falcon XR6. The cops knew he would be heading along the Flinders Highway around this time and had set up a command post in preparation. As he approached with his two young girls in the back, he was pulled over and surrounded by a dozen armed police. His daughters were swiftly removed from the equation. Williams, meanwhile, was handcuffed and dragged back to his extensively renovated, lavishly decorated Charters Towers home, where a search warrant was executed.

The police found, amongst other things, $55,340 in cash. More than $42,000 of it would later turn out to be traceable notes that were used by undercover detectives to buy drugs from Williams's agents.

The only member of McCauley's gang who had yet to be ambushed was Peter Dudley. Police had turned up at his Salisbury North address at 8.30 am to find nobody home. He was out walking his dog. The cops sat and waited for more than ninety minutes before he finally showed up.

Williams, Jellese and Dudley were all relatively tight-lipped after being ambushed that morning, but back at Port Pirie police station Dean Howard was singing like a canary. As he filled in the gaps for his interrogators, the biggest firework of the day was about to explode. It was 8.33 am and a group under the command of Detective Senior Constable Daniel Gillan had converged at McCauley's pad in Degree Road, Salisbury North. The modest single-storey home was situated on a corner block and was surrounded by trees and a six-foot olive-green wrought iron fence. There were large iron gates positioned at the front driveway entrance. On this particular morning, those gates were wide open.

It was early, but it was already warm. The street was quiet and the air was still. The officers filed out of the van in stealth mode. Nobody spoke. They didn't want to alert anyone they had arrived until it was time.

After a series of nods, Gillan and Detective Senior Constable James Andrew began to walk several paces ahead of their colleagues towards the entrance of the dwelling. Then, before the pair had even made it to the front gates, an old, thin-looking man suddenly emerged from the property and, without any warning, shuffled out onto the path directly in front of them. There was a moment of complete silence as he stared in their direction.

'How you going, mate. Mr McCauley, is it?' asked Gillan.

'Speaking,' said the man.

'From Drugs and Organised Crime,' Gillan added.

McCauley remembers that particular moment as though it were yesterday. 'I was flicking the top off a cold one when I heard something outside which didn't sound normal, or at least not in the street I lived in.' He added: 'I heard the gentle slam of a vehicle door outside the house. I then heard the same door slam six, seven, maybe eight times. I thought, hang on a minute . . .'

McCauley says there was something else which further raised his suspicions. 'I know the difference in sound between the slamming of an old car door and a new one. This was definitely a new vehicle and, let me tell you, in Salisbury North you don't find too many of those.' He put down his beer, walked out of the front door, through the yard and out into the street. 'And there they were, in all their glory— half a dozen cops, all carrying side-arms. It was quite a sight at that time of the morning. Two of them approached me and the rest of them formed a semicircle around the driveway. That's when I thought to myself, "Malcolm, you're in big trouble."'

Andrew held up a general search warrant and, like a rabbit caught in headlights, McCauley's gaze remained glued to it. He had no idea what it said. Then he was read his rights—he was entitled to one phone call. It was explained to him that it would probably be best spent contacting his wife, but he indicated he might wish to speak to his lawyer.

'Do you wish to phone him now?' asked Andrew.

'Soon as I know what's going on,' he replied.

'We'll be searching here for an investigation in regards to drugs. The matter we're investigating is a serious matter.'

The two detectives ushered McCauley inside. He was asked for a tour of the house and duly obliged.

Gillan surveyed the surroundings, then asked: 'OK, you've indicated to me that you might have some personal smoke, as you put it. Where would that be?'

'In the bedroom,' McCauley replied, and with that he led the way. On the right-hand side of a bed headboard sat a Glad snap-seal bag containing cannabis.

'Is there any other cannabis in this room?' asked Gillan.

McCauley pointed to an inbuilt-wardrobe and a safe which sat inside it, on the floor. After some rummaging for keys, he opened it up and produced a large plastic shopping bag full of cannabis.

Gillan then explained the order in which his team would slowly work their way through the house. 'We'll go from room to room, we'll do a search of that room. If anything's found then this officer here will record what's been found and, at the completion, we'll give you a receipt to say what we've actually taken from here, OK?'

McCauley nodded but his mind was elsewhere.

In his role of exhibits officer, Andrew set up an area in the kitchen and noted everything collected by his colleagues, including the location in which it was found. His log included a cardboard box containing a large quantity of assorted paperwork and bills. There were various phones, maps and scraps of paper with calculations and handwriting on them. There were also diaries, passports and numerous bank statements. As that meticulous process continued, McCauley slowly began to stew in his own fear.

'By this time, I'd been allowed to sit at the table outside and have a smoke. But I'd positioned myself in such a way that I could see almost everything they were doing. And if someone disappeared out of view, then certainly I could still hear them.' He recalls: 'One of the coppers was going through the cupboard. I could see he was getting mighty close to the pot of gold. I thought, "Just keep going, move away from the bloody cupboard, move away" . . . And then, bang, he reached up towards the top shelf and I knew that was that. He stood there for a minute with his back partially turned. Then, out of the corner of my eye, I watched him walk away and out of view. My heart was pumping. I was sweating real bad. The world seemed to stop.'

McCauley says that through the reflection in a wall mirror, he then located the copper once more: 'He was indicating something to the exhibits officer. It was a bunch of photographs.' The same series of photographs taken during his second trip to Bali—when the jailhouse summit was held with Schapelle in the lead up to her verdict.

According to McCauley, the detective was wearing a 'Cheshire smile'. One by one, the cop flashed the photos at his colleague. As he did so, he yelled 'Gotcha!'

CHAPTER 29

The Discovery

'Oh Jesus! Oh Mother Mary! I wish to God those pictures had never been taken, bloody oath! I mean, look at the shit stink they caused. Stupid bloody bastard photos!'

—Malcolm McCauley

Cunning and charming were two words often used to describe McCauley. Unfortunately, neither would claw him out of the hole he now found himself in. The Schapelle Corby story was about to take a dramatic twist and he was at the heart of it. In turn, the painstaking police search had suddenly ground to a halt. Four officers stood, open-mouthed, over his kitchen table.

When Gillan spotted the scene out of the corner of his eye, he ordered a colleague to stand watch beside McCauley outside while he rushed indoors to see what all the fuss was about.

'I had all sorts of things running through my head at that point,' remembers McCauley. 'Shit, they're gonna do a trace back, they'll know I supplied the Bali drugs, it's all gonna fall. I thought to myself, "Malcolm, you better come up with a story, a big coincidence yarn, and you better make it quick."'

McCauley says everything Bali-related appeared to be scattered across the table, but from his position outside it was a struggle to see clearly. 'I wanted to have a stickybeak,' he recalls. 'I asked the copper alongside me if I could have a beer. But, it was a "no". Eventually, I was given permission to make a fresh brew of tea.'

McCauley walked indoors, picked up the empty kettle and filled it with water. As he did so, he turned around and caught 'pretty much everything'. A set of pictures had been pulled out of their packet and were scattered across the table. There were two photographs of Malcolm McCauley dressed in a powdery-blue short-sleeved collared shirt, perched beside a smiling Schapelle Corby in the visiting area of Kerobokan Prison. Another showed Schapelle's mum Ros, her husband Greg, McCauley and Dave McHugh together outside the main entrance to the same jail. Amongst others was a picture of McCauley, McHugh and Ros happily gathered around a table, boozing inside their favourite Balinese bar, the Secret Garden.

The detectives were studying the photos. From an old cardboard box, they were also dragging out Bali brochures, leaflets and various business cards plus, says McCauley, 'all the other general rubbish you bring back and intend to chuck out, but never do'.

Gillan reactivated the audiotape and continued on with the search. 'Have you got your wallet on you?' he asked McCauley.

'Yeah.'

Gillan edged his chair closer to McCauley and then asked him to remove the contents. 'Just leave it on the table here so we can itemise what's there.'

'What, everything?' said McCauley.

Gillan fanned the wallet's contents across the table, like a magician playing with a pack of cards. 'So you've got a 2004 membership card to the RSL . . . membership card for the Salisbury North Football Club 1996. You've got a Centrelink card in the name of Malcolm McCauley of this address. Okay,' he said before now pausing. 'You've got two Australian Federal Police cards for a Mr . . .'

'Roger,' replied McCauley in a flash.

'R. Rathjen,' said Gillan.

'Yeah.'

There was a moment of silence as McCauley's heart skipped a beat. 'There was no reasonable explanation for a drug dealer having a former senior AFP drug cop's card in his wallet,' McCauley said later, 'except to say he was an old mate, which was the truth.'

To McCauley's amazement, however, Gillan let the business cards pass without another word. 'I couldn't work that out,' McCauley remembers.

Gillan continued: 'There's a Department of Defence Edinburgh identity card for a gold club member in your name. And you've got a . . . a business card for the Secret Garden Bar and Café.'

'Mmm,' replied McCauley.

'That in Bali, is it?'

'Yeah.'

Gillan gave McCauley a knowing stare, but once again he chose not to prod, moving on instead to a Commonwealth Bank key card and $170 in cash, which were the only remaining items of note.

'OK, Malcolm, we'll go from here to the Elizabeth Street police station where I intend to interview you. And then you'll be charged.'

Gillan switched off the tape at 11.24 am, but for McCauley the nightmare rolled on. First he was handcuffed, then he was led to a waiting police van parked outside the driveway.

Within thirty minutes, that vehicle had arrived at its destination. McCauley was escorted down some steps and into a small lower-level video recording room. He sat down on a seat next to a desk and steadied himself. There were no windows to stare out of but, as the officers prepared the audio recorder, McCauley studied the floor beside his feet and slowly drifted off, probably to a place that served ice-cold beer.

'The time is 11.54 am on Thursday the 24th of November 2005. The interview is about to be conducted. I am Detective Senior Constable Gillan from Drug and Organised Crime and I now ask all other persons in the room to introduce themselves by name . . .'

And then, for a very long time, they interrogated him methodically and in depth about his role in the drug syndicate, but ultimately they began to ask questions about the Corbys.

'We noticed, when we were searching the different areas of your house, that you'd been to Bali on several occasions.'

'Three,' replied McCauley and then fumbled for dates, adding: 'You'd have to have a look in my passport.'

'And who did you go there with?'

'With the granddaughter, the missus, three or four of us.'

'Do you know any other people that go to Bali?'

'Yeah.'

'Would you care to nominate them?'

'Not if I'm gonna get them in the shit, no.'

'Have you ever heard the name Schapelle Corby?'

'Yeah.'

'Do you know Schapelle Corby?'

'Yeah.'

'How do you know her?'

McCauley paused, then said, 'Without mentioning the name, a mate of mine had a fascination with her and, and he wanted to see her in the court, yeah, and he introduced me to her.'

'So was that the first time you met Schapelle Corby—in the court, when she was over in Bali?'

'Oh, I didn't actually meet her in court. She was outside, in the holding cell.'

'In the holding cell,' repeated one detective, adding: 'Would it be fair to say that the first time you met her was after she had been arrested in Bali?'

'Oh yeah, yeah.'

'Have you ever met anyone else from her family?'

'Yes.'

'Where—in Australia, or over there?'

'Over there.'

'And how did that come about?'

'Um, her mother spoke to us. Said thanks for supporting her. Yeah, Ros.'

'Is Bali the only place you've ever met either Schapelle or any of her family or friends?'

'Mmm.'

'That's yes?'

'Yeah . . . I don't know where this is . . .'

'Because you are aware she comes from Queensland?'

'Yeah.'

'Who was your friend that introduced you to her?

'Not getting him in the shit, am I?'

'You don't have to answer if you don't want to.'

'We've got a big connection here,' McCauley let slip, somewhat rattled, adding, 'Leave him out of it.'

The police were intrigued by the discovery of the Secret Garden card in his wallet, but he explained: 'Well, that was where Schapelle's mother took us to have a beer.'

'Did she now.'

'Yeah, to have a beer.'

'Once?'

'More than once,' confirmed McCauley.

'So you've been to the pub there a couple of times with her?'

'Yeah. Well, wouldn't you at those prices?'

Then suddenly, that was that. The two interrogating detectives ended the interview, and at 1 pm McCauley was formally charged with drug trafficking offences dating between January 2004 and November 2005.

McCauley maintains to this day that, aside from the few questions he dodged on the day of his arrest, South Australian police never again quizzed him about his links to Mick Corby—even though they knew he was delivering to Queensland at the exact same time as Schapelle got arrested. 'It was in their hands and yet for some strange reason, unbeknown to me, they dropped it like a hot potato.' Then he considers all this further. 'Let's face it—I was there for the bloody taking. It seemed to me that elsewhere, maybe higher up the chain, there must have been another agenda. I've had plenty of time to think about all this and, to this day, none of it makes sense. Whether the South Australian Police were told to back off from it by the AFP or not, I do not know. From where I was standing, it certainly seemed that way.'

After McCauley was interviewed and charged that day, he was granted police bail and Kathleen dropped him back at his house. Like his own life, the place was a complete and utter mess. Hours earlier, he had stood helplessly as detectives turned the entire house upside down. Now he was back in the same spot, feeling just as helpless—and very alone. There was no Kathleen any more. Had she been there, she would have told him he had it coming. He could have handled that. He missed her.

More than eighty police had been involved in the two-state operation. While McCauley was charged with serious drug trafficking offences, police could only ever prove he was supplying to Wayne Williams in North Queensland.

Sensibly, Ken Ray had walked away before being caught and Brenda Eastwood had only confessed to a portion of her Queensland runs. It meant that, further down the track, there would be no evidence linking McCauley to Darwin, Alice Springs, Sydney or the Gold Coast.

'They nibbled the crust around the pizza, but they never got the topping,' is his summation today.

CHAPTER 30

The Tooth Fairy

'If you hear a clicking sound that means your phone is tapped . . .'
—Rosleigh Rose

Two weeks after McCauley's arrest, senior police reporter Keith Moor was sitting at his desk at the *Herald Sun* newsroom in Melbourne. The office was humming with the usual buzz of an approaching afternoon deadline and Moor was chewing the fat, as he regularly did, with one of his Victoria-based police contacts. There was nothing much happening in the way of news that day, but then suddenly his source casually dropped an intriguing piece of 'cop gossip' into their phone conservation.

The officer told Moor he'd been chatting with a mate who happened to be a detective based in Adelaide. This South Australian cop had said: 'You'll never believe these photographs that we found here last week. Some of our lads conducted a raid on a major drug figure . . . and in his house were photos . . . of him and Schapelle Corby.'

Moor nearly fell off his chair. 'It seems the South Australian cops involved in Operation Co-Pilot had gone back to the station and told other cops. Those cops then told others,' Moor later explained. 'The Corbys have always held this conspiracy theory that the story was deliberately leaked to me by a powerful police hierarchy who had it in for them. That's simply not true. News of the pictures had spread like wildfire amongst police in Adelaide. It jumped interstate, and ultimately that's how it found its way to me.'

Moor knew he was on to a cracker of a story, but there was major work to be done if it was ever to see the light of day. He spent the next few hours frantically working the phones in a desperate attempt to gather some solid information. In the following days he did everything within his power to get to see the photos, but nobody was prepared to put their career on the line and physically show him. 'I spoke to two people who had seen them,' says Moor. 'One actually had them in his or her hands while they were describing them to me.'

After three days, Moor met with his editor and laid his cards on the table. He knew without a doubt the pictures existed, but he hadn't actually sighted them. He didn't know the identity of the drug dealer sitting alongside Schapelle in the photograph, but reliable sources had confirmed he was a senior figure in a major drug syndicate. Moor could not be sure when the pictures were taken, but those who'd seen them insisted they weren't taken inside a prison. 'I felt I'd gathered enough about the sequence of events to run with a story,' says Moor. 'And so we went with it.'

On 10 December 2005, News Ltd papers across Australia ran Moor's exclusive. In Melbourne the *Herald Sun*'s front-page headline screamed: 'SCHAPELLE TWIST: RAID PHOTOS SEIZED'. The story began: 'Police have seized photographs of Schapelle Corby with a man who has just been charged with marijuana smuggling.' And further down: 'They were found in a raid that police believe helped bust a marijuana smuggling ring operating between SA and Queensland.' The article further asserted: 'The photographs were taken before Corby was charged in October last year with importing 4.2 kg of marijuana into Bali in her bodyboard bag.' Needless to say, it was a story that created shockwaves all around the country.

Over in Indonesia, the Balinese prosecution team could not believe their luck. They were still fuming over the recent appeal judgement by Bali's High Court, shaving five years off Corby's twenty-year sentence. Now, for the first time, there seemed to be hard evidence contradicting the claims that Schapelle had no prior links to drugs. To their delight, the find had coincided with the counter appeal they had just lodged with the courts for her twenty-year jail term to be reinstated. Now demanding a life sentence on counter appeal, Prosecutor Ni Wayan Sinaryati requested immediate access to the pictures, declaring: 'If we can get copies of the photos, we will send them to the Supreme Court. I hope these photos will convince the judges she is guilty.'

Schapelle's defence team, meanwhile, had been left stunned by the latest revelations. Days earlier, they had lodged an appeal against her fifteen-year sentence with Indonesia's Supreme Court in Jakarta. Her new head lawyer, Hotman Paris Hutapea, attempted to hose down the hysteria with a rather bizarre statement. 'You could have your photo taken with prostitutes, drug dealers . . . You never know, until years later someone brings those photos out. It doesn't make you guilty of a crime,' he said.

On Monday 12 December, two days after Moor's story broke, Ros entered the fold, arguing there were so many people now obsessed with her daughter that it was quite possible the photographs were fake. A day later, however, she had dropped that theory and suddenly remembered, with precise detail, that the pictures were taken some six months beforehand inside Bali's Kerobokan Prison, after a request from two strangers holidaying in Bali to meet her daughter. Ros then gave an 'exclusive' interview to her friend, *Gold Coast Bulletin* journalist Tony Wilson.

His article was syndicated to the *Adelaide Advertiser*. Under the headline 'CORBY'S MUM: BLAME ME FOR THE PHOTOGRAPHS', Ros explained: 'I kept thinking that we didn't know anyone in South Australia, but late in the day, after talks with South Australian police, I remembered two men that approached me and my partner, Greg, at the Secret Garden during the trial and, the more I think about it, it had to be them.' She added that, from memory, their names were 'Mal and Don'. The two men had offered to buy her a round of drinks and from there they all 'just got talking'.

Ros told Wilson: 'They seemed like a couple of nice Aussie battlers and this Don guy told us he was a postman, although later he said he lived in a big house, and I remember thinking it was funny that a postman could afford a big house, but I didn't dwell on it because I had a lot on my mind with the trial at the time.'

She explained that the two strangers had asked if they could accompany her to prison and meet Schapelle next time she visited: 'We said it would be OK . . . They were going to get a disposable camera but they didn't in the end, so Greg took the photos on his digital camera and then we got prints for them.'

* * *

SINS OF THE FATHER

On Thursday 15 December, Ros landed in Adelaide on an early morning flight from Brisbane. A day of complete chaos followed. Or so it seemed.

Flanked by a camera crew filming her every move for *The Hidden Truth* documentary, Ros was keen 'to get all this bloody bullshit' on the record. She had apparently been told that the Australian Federal Police were now in possession of the pictures after South Australian police had handed them over. So she dived into a car and headed, first up, to the AFP headquarters. On arrival, she immediately got into a row with a security guard, who wouldn't let the film crew in. She was then sent packing with the news that the pictures had not yet arrived.

With a trail of local media in tow, Ros was piling on the theatrics. She marched straight around to the SA police headquarters and demanded a meeting on the spot with Commissioner Mal Hyde. When Superintendent Neil Smith emerged in his place, she yelled: 'I think it's bloody disgusting what you people are doing and you won't let me see the photos.' Superintendent Smith politely reminded Ros she had already been warned, before leaving Queensland, that a trip to Adelaide would be a futile journey.

Ros had huffed and puffed her way all across the Adelaide CBD. In the process, she had continuously slammed the authorities for not letting her view the photos of her daughter. The media, however, was still far more interested in how the pictures actually came to be taken in the first place. Ros had, after all, paved the way for two supposed strangers to gain exclusive access to Schapelle in jail—at a time when the all-important verdict was just around the corner and her daughter was on the verge of a major meltdown.

It was widely known that, amidst the chaos and hysteria,

Schapelle had been struggling at this time to remain positive and upbeat. She had complained to family members that she couldn't handle the constant crowds and requested that there be no more visitors because, in her own words, she was starting to feel like 'a zoo exhibit'. Yet not only had her mother escorted two slippery-looking men through restricted areas of the prison, one of them grew hydroponic marijuana and the other just happened to be a drug smuggler who was shipping large amounts of grass to Queensland. Still fielding questions about why she allowed them in, she snapped: 'I didn't ask them at the time: "Are you a rapist?" "Are you a woman basher?" "Do you take drugs?"'

As the afternoon drew to a close and the media crews all headed home, it appeared as though Ros had lost her battle. In actual fact, she was hours away from getting her hands on the pictures—and she knew it.

While Ros was in Adelaide, she had asked the documentary crew if they would pick up a new prepaid mobile phone and Sim card for her. Perplexed, but eager to keep the pushy Ros happy, they went and purchased a prepaid mobile with the cash she had given them.

'The whole day was one big stunt,' alleges McCauley. 'It was a smokescreen, a crowd diversion, because she knew, prior to arriving in Adelaide, that they [the police] were not interested in giving her the pictures. They told her that before she left. They explained it wasn't their property to release. End of story.'

McCauley says that throughout the day, both he and Dave McHugh kept in contact with Ros by calling her on a 'brand new number' that she had set up specifically for the trip. 'She had already spoken to Dave numerous times about the second set of photos he had in his possession. It was simply a matter of getting them to her,' he claims. It was then that a plan was hatched so Ros could retrieve the photographs from Dave without the documentary team or anyone else asking questions about how it had come about.

In what McCauley claims was an elaborate and calculated ruse, McHugh agreed to telephone the *Adelaide Advertiser* and announce to a journalist that after hearing the news that Ros was 'looking for the men who had visited Schapelle in jail', he suddenly realised it related to him.

Dave went on to tell the reporter that as luck would have it, he also had copies of the photos. Believing she was part of a major breaking story, the eager journalist immediately rang Ros and informed her of the good news. McCauley claims it then enabled Ros to tell the documentary crew that she had been put in touch with the mystery 'Don' through a third party—after he rang the *Advertiser* and passed on his contact number.

During Ros's subsequent phone calls with 'Don' the camera was rolling as she told him that she was worried the police might be monitoring their phone calls, which is why she had bought a new mobile phone. 'You can tell if they're listening in,' she said, 'there's a clicking sound.' She then suggested to the film crew that the best way forward was for them to go and meet 'Don', because she might be watched. They were instructed by Ros that, when they picked up the photos, they were under no circumstances to film the photo exchange. Ros told them that when they met 'Don' he would introduce himself to them as 'Mr Smoothie'.

Three days later, on 17 December, the *Adelaide Advertiser* published a story revealing that Ros had obtained the shots after being contacted 'on behalf of' one of the men photographed. The article went on to report that the man, known as 'Don', had provided her with his own personal set of the photographs.

Ros said 'Don' had told her that he had met the other man—still only known as 'Mal'—on the plane as they both travelled to Bali. They had then hooked up, met Ros by chance, and visited Schapelle together. 'These are exactly the pictures, all the pictures,' she told the reporter. 'I was so relieved . . . Now I need to get these pictures to Jakarta, to the judges, for Schapelle's appeal—to prove they were taken in Kerobokan and she did not know this person before.'

While the by-now-notorious photos still hadn't seen the light of day publicly, this story ended ongoing speculation about where they were actually taken. In turn, journalist Keith Moor was forced to acknowledge there was one line in his original story that was factually wrong. The photographs of Schapelle and the drug dealer had been described to him as being at a beach-type setting. In his defence, he pointed out that even South Australian Police Commissioner Mal Hyde had told Ros in a fax sent to her that the snaps 'do not appear to have been taken in a prison setting'.

With the pictures now in her hands, Ros was quick to tell Commissioner Hyde exactly what she thought of that. 'I'd like to know what a prison setting is in his [Commissioner Hyde's] book, then,' she said. 'Every magazine that's seen Schapelle knows that's Kerobokan. They [police] just want Schapelle to look bad to keep pressure off corrupt airports.'

Somehow, through it all, McCauley had successfully eluded the spotlight. And then finally, on 13 January 2006, some five weeks after the original story broke, he

SINS OF THE FATHER

finally stepped out of the shadows. And, what's more, the pictures arrived with him. Breaking his silence to the *Adelaide Advertiser*, the mystery man in the photo posing with Schapelle, Malcolm Christopher McCauley, came out publicly and dismissed the whole controversy as one big storm in a teacup. In a page-one story headlined 'CORBY IN THE CLEAR', McCauley repeated the story told first by Ros, and then by McHugh. He explained how he had visited Schapelle on two occasions in Bali the previous year, purely as 'a holidaymaker' offering support during the difficulties of her drugs trial. 'A mate and I were in Bali and we thought we'd go have a look-see in court,' he told reporter Tegan Sluggett, adding: 'She's high profile and she's an Aussie. That's why we were interested in it. Her sister and mother came up to us after and thanked us for being there.'

McCauley explained how Ros had introduced him to her daughter while she was in the holding cell at the court, then later invited him to visit her again in Kerobokan Prison the following day. 'We asked if we could sneak some photos in [while we were there], so we did.'

McCauley later spoke of his 'pride' after Schapelle had penned a letter and autographed a photo for him to give to his granddaughter Kaitlin. The newspaper requested to see the items. After digging them out, McCauley duly obliged. The photo of him and Schapelle sitting side by side in Kerobokan was subsequently published by several newspapers and splashed around the country.

With so much time now having passed between Moor's explosive story and McCauley going public, sceptics could see there had been more than enough time for both parties to get their stories straight. And, looking back, Moor now speaks of his astonishment after seeing his sister News Ltd paper in Adelaide dress the coverage up 'so leniently'. 'They run this page-one headline yelling "Corby in the Clear" but, on reflection, I actually think you could interpret it as being even more damning, knowing those photos are taken in jail. If you are going to think about it logically, then you have to consider the possibility that maybe that drug dealer [McCauley] went in there to say, on the quiet, "Schapelle, keep your mouth shut". I'm not saying that is the case, but it could so easily be the scenario. So we made an initial error and thought the pictures were taken prior to her arrest . . . It doesn't detract from the fact that a major drug figure has somehow gone in there and had some association with Schapelle Corby.'

McCauley and McHugh went one step further in their publicity campaign on behalf of Schapelle. They agreed to be interviewed on camera, sitting side by side, for the documentary *Schapelle Corby: The Hidden Truth*. That interview was conducted at McHugh's brick veneer home in Hallet Cove, Adelaide.

McHugh's sister, Vicky, sat silently watching the interview take place. Again the same story was trotted out about their 'coming together' and it all being just an amazing coincidence. McCauley did most of the talking, with McHugh suffering from a bad case of stage fright. At one point McCauley can't help himself and jibes McHugh on camera, telling him, 'You're a criminal.' Not seeing the funny side of the barb, McHugh hits back: 'I'm not a criminal. Shut up!'

Later McHugh's sister would go to great lengths to contact the producer of the documentary and inform her that, while this interview was taking place, McHugh had a room full of hydro plants growing in the house. 'It made me so angry,' Vicky says. 'He was bullshitting the whole time.'

But, with no criminal record against his name, 'Don'—the Good Samaritan—Mr Smoothie McHugh had somehow managed to come out of the whole episode unscathed. Yet, if journalists had bothered to dig deep enough back then, they would have uncovered a family more than willing to fill in the missing pieces of the jigsaw. McHugh's family were by now so angry about his ongoing drug activities, they had contacted South Australian police and alerted them to the fact that he was growing commercial amounts of marijuana—and making regular trips to Bali. As a result of that complaint, police issued a 'red flag' passenger alert against his name, which remains in place to this day.

Had these details surfaced at the time, then it is safe to say they would have sparked the all-important question: what are the chances of two Adelaide men, both involved in marijuana supply, meeting by chance on a plane to Bali just two weeks after Schapelle Corby's arrest? Then, after returning together during her trial, what are the chances of them also randomly bumping into the Corbys and being fast-tracked into their inner-circle to such a degree that they were given special access to Schapelle in jail just days out from her verdict hearing, when she was feeling at her most vulnerable?

'If you believe in coincidences, then you believe in the tooth fairy,' says McCauley today.

Of course, McCauley and McHugh could have lied about not knowing each other before the first trip to Bali, and could have deliberately engineered the meetings with the Corbys at the Secret Garden without Ros or the rest of the family knowing anything about it. Despite what McCauley implies, you don't have to believe in those coincidences to accept that Ros and her family might have thought two Adelaide holidaymakers were just what they claimed to be.

CHAPTER 31

Sins of the Brother

If the marijuana was mine, like if I did take it, I wouldn't let my sister take the blame.

—James Kisina

After Schapelle's arrest, James Kisina had seemingly fallen off the face of the planet. Ros's instructions to her son could not have been simpler: for your sister's sake, keep out of the limelight and stay out of trouble. But while his mother was away in Bali visiting Schapelle, the moody and unpredictable James committed a crime so selfish and violent that its consequences, in terms of public perception, still reverberate for Schapelle today.

Around 1 am on 17 January 2006, James left Ros's house in Loganlea, climbed into a car and headed towards Rochedale, a neighbourhood located 25 kilometres southeast of Brisbane. Alongside him in the vehicle was his 17-year-old cousin Shane John Tilyard, and 19-year-old Matthew Ratumaitavuki, a New Zealand student who'd only migrated to Australia five weeks previously.

In the stillness of a suburban park, the three men later

watched and waited in darkness for signs of life outside a low-set unit complex across the way. People occasionally came and left, but the three of them weren't waiting for just anyone. Their targets that night were two residents living in the block—a young couple aged in their early twenties. After more than an hour of casing their prey, the trio grew impatient with the lack of movement and decided enough was enough.

At 4 am James gave the nod and, in unison, the men slipped stockings over their heads. Dressed identically in dark blue overalls, and collectively armed with a machete, an iron bar and a baseball bat, they then darted between the shadows of the streetlights over towards the couple's apartment. They tiptoed quietly past a carport at the front of the dwelling and then down a driveway. The unsuspecting couple were fast asleep inside. Unbeknown to them, their worst nightmare was about to come crashing through the back door.

Using his bare hands, Schapelle's half-brother ripped the rear security screen door off its lower hinges so that the bottom half was bent outward at a 90-degree angle. The three men climbed underneath and then inside. By the time the frightened occupants had fumbled for a light switch, the masked intruders were towering over their bed.

James brutally pounded the male across the back with the baseball bat and the two others waded in with several punches to the face. The female, meanwhile, was methodically bound and gagged, using thick industrial-style electrical tape that had been purchased by James at a service station at nearby Meadowbrook en route. Once the couple had been subdued, the three men ransacked the home and made off with marijuana, $900 in cash, a video camera and, bizarrely, a range of cosmetics.

By the time the sun rose, the unit was a crime scene buzzing with cops. The young victims of the violent home invasion, battered and bruised, gave detailed statements to the police. Forensics officers investigated the scene and took fingerprints from the security door. When a positive identity match was later linked to James Kisina, detectives headed straight round to his mother's address at Loganlea armed with a search warrant.

Detective Sergeant Dean Godfrey, from the Slacks Creek Criminal Investigation Branch, was one of the first to arrive at Ros's home that day. 'Immediately upon entry to the downstairs area of the residence, I detected a very obvious and strong odour which I believed to be cannabis, mixed with another odour, which would later be identified as coffee,' he said. Also located was a sum of money ($400), which James admitted was his 'cut of the cash', a video camera under a bed and a green baseball bat lying in the front garden beneath the main external stairs to the house.

Two days later, on 19 January 2006, James fronted Beenleigh Magistrates Court for a brief hearing, charged with nine offences, including two counts of deprivation of liberty and armed robbery in company with actual violence. He was also charged with producing and possessing marijuana, breaking and entering to commit a serious offence and two counts of actual bodily harm. His defence lawyer argued that he had only broken into the home because the couple were allegedly known drug dealers and he believed they might possess information that could help free his sister: 'The situation is the guy is eighteen. He thought that if he approached people who had connections to drugs, he could in some way obtain information which might assist with his sister's case.'

Through thick and thin, the Corbys continued to support each other. Although devastated by James's violent home invasion, Schapelle sprang to his defence in a media interview: 'I'm not angry at him. I'm not at all. He just wanted to help me and he went sussing around everywhere, and he just made a really bad mistake. And yeah, I dunno . . . Maybe he's been watching too many movies and brought it to real life. I mean, come on . . . Bats and, ugh, tying people up and stuff—that's pretty bad, and it's way out of character for him. But that just goes to show how much he's hurting.'

Detective Sergeant Godfrey, however, viewed the matter differently and, in a signed police affidavit tendered to court, said: 'He is suspected of some involvement in the exportation of cannabis, for which his sister has received a twenty-year imprisonment sentence.'

James's lawyer immediately slammed this statement and insisted the claim was in no way supported by evidence. Godfrey, in turn, was hauled in by his superiors and muzzled from speaking out further on the matter. A Queensland police spokesman said Commissioner Bob Atkinson had ordered an investigation to analyse 'the context in which the sergeant made the comments'.

One only needs to look at the finer detail hidden in Godfrey's official police statement to see where he might have been coming from. When the detective sergeant turned up at the house on the afternoon of 17 January he was shocked by what he found. There was marijuana everywhere, including 'several clip-seal plastic bags containing cannabis in jars, plus a further larger clip-seal plastic bag containing a larger amount of cannabis'. There was also 'a clip-seal plastic bag containing cannabis on a shelf of a bookcase'.

The most telling discovery of all, however, was a brand-new-looking set of electronic scales. Godfrey's statement reads: 'James admitted that at least some of the cannabis located was the cannabis stolen from the complainants; that he repackaged some of that cannabis weighing various amounts with the use of a set of scales that he purchased with the stolen money, that he further packaged some of the bags of cannabis inside coffee jars . . . he admitted he did this to disguise the odour.'

The following afternoon, Senior Constable Andrew O'Shea arrived at the property for a closer examination of the marijuana found when James was arrested. As a scenes of crime officer, he had been drafted in to weigh, test and tally the cannabis present. 'I was directed to an area on top of a clothes dresser. At this location was a clip-seal bag of green leaf material (GLM) and two coffee jars. Jar 1 contained coffee and 10 small bags of GLM. Jar 2 contained coffee and another 10 small clip-seal bags containing GLM.'

A police source involved in the case would later say, 'It was like a scene straight out of *Miami Vice*.' In all, there was a total of 23 bags weighing a collective 183 gm. That figure was five times *more* than the amount allegedly stolen during the home invasion—and all sitting in the exact same house from where Schapelle had set off with her boogie board bag on the morning she left for Bali.

Detective Sergeant Godfrey, for the record, never spoke again about his affidavit other than simply stating to the author: 'The facts speak for themselves.' But it was no secret at the time that he was desperate for a chance to cross examine James about his activities, not to mention the hours and days leading up to Schapelle's arrest in October 2004—which, in his eyes, was all totally relevant.

Rosleigh Rose, however, quickly exterminated any chance of that happening. Her son was ordered to plead guilty to all charges and his accomplices were advised to do likewise. Each of the men were sentenced to four years' prison but, taking into account their 'real prospect of rehabilitation', the judge decided to suspend the full terms. But while James only ended up serving ten months in prison, the damage had already been done. It was another nail in the coffin for Schapelle's story of innocence, not to mention the family's all-round credibility. When asked how she felt about having two children in jail at the same time, Rosleigh Rose wasn't fazed: 'At least I know where they are,' was her famously brazen answer.

On the day that James was arrested, the Indonesian Supreme Court rejected Schapelle's second appeal. Even more shocking for the Corbys was the news that the sentence which had been reduced from twenty to fifteen years in the first appeal was now increased back up to the original sentence of twenty years. The Indonesian police prosecutors had appealed against the decision by the High Court in Bali to reduce Schapelle's sentence and won. Not only had the judges in Jakarta reinstated her original sentence, they had also fined her $14,000. And, if her family couldn't pay the fine, then there would be an additional six months to serve on her sentence.

Schapelle's new hotshot lawyer, Hotman Hutapea, was furious about her younger brother's arrest back in Australia and declared, 'This has ruined my case.' The flamboyant lawyer soon resigned from the legal team with the excuse that he wanted to go and earn more money so he could buy another Ferrari.

Inevitably, back in Australia, the spotlight had turned to James and speculation was again rife. Was he the bastard who had set up his sister? Had the beautiful, innocent Schapelle taken the fall for the bad arse kid brother? 'No, I wouldn't take the rap for him,' insisted Schapelle. 'No, I wouldn't. For example, if it was his, he was underage when we came here . . . So, if it was his, why couldn't I just say, "Yeah, it was his. He's underage." No, I'm not taking the rap for anyone. Well, actually I am—but I don't know who.' Schapelle's argument is in fact paper-thin. If the pot in her boogie board had belonged to her brother, it would have been impossible for her defence team to argue that she hadn't known he had put it there—even if he had confessed to the crime. 'A confession from James wouldn't have helped her case at all,' confirms lawyer Erwin Siregar.

But, just when the family thought things couldn't get any worse, it was Mick Corby's turn to be in the firing line. Thirteen days after James's arrest, highly respected journalist Kerry O'Brien introduced a sensational story on ABC-TV's *7.30 Report* with these words: 'The Corby family has always maintained it has no association with anyone linked to the drug trade. Tonight, we explore the relationship between Schapelle Corby's father, Michael Corby, and the friend who was his next-door neighbour over years in two different Queensland locations. This man was arrested and charged with running a sophisticated, commercial marijuana operation just one month before Schapelle Corby's fateful trip to Bali. The relationship between the two men is not in itself evidence that the Corby family has any involvement in the drug trade, but it does raise questions which may warrant further investigation.'

When news of the story filtered back to Mick in Bali he was livid: 'Fucking ABC! I thought it was supposed to be a credible outfit. Fucking prick! . . . There's a bloody vendetta against the family! That's what it is . . . a vendetta!'

Because Tony Lewis was yet to face court for the drug charges that had resulted from the police raid on his property, he wasn't named in the story. But, in the words of the ranting Mick, it was obvious 'to blind Freddy what the pricks are implying'. 'I've got no idea what he [Lewis] was up to. Wouldn't have a clue. I lived next door. Man, is that a crime? Or is that a reason for them to bloody bung on all this shit and innuendo?'

The report featured wide shots of Mick Corby's property, as well as footage of Tony Lewis's front gate. Mick felt violated and threatened all at the same time. Since he had left the farm, it had been looked after by a 'friend'—a large, ominous Kiwi with dreadlocks who was nicknamed the Taxidermist because he had stuffed Lewis's favourite pet pig when it died. The Taxidermist was a formidable figure— the antithesis of your friendly neighbourhood house-sitter. Mick had some heavy mates but, thankfully for him, the *7.30 Report* cameras hadn't filmed the Taxidermist.

After the *7.30 Report* story screened, Lewis was anxious about the impact the program would have on Schapelle and the Corbys: 'The kids haven't really done nothing wrong and they're in all the shit in the world. And if what I've done has contributed to that, I'm very sorry . . . That *7.30 Report* and all that—they tried to link me with Schapelle, and I had nothing to do with anything that they done,' he said, making a mess of trying to make things better.

When the broadcast aired, Mercedes was in Singapore and Ros had returned to Australia to 'sort out James'. Mick had been drinking beer at the pub and was dreading the very idea of having to break more bad news to Schapelle. As he got smashed, Mick's mood increasingly darkened towards himself. He couldn't shake the feelings of guilt that crashed and pounded around in his head. Blaming Kerry O'Brien wasn't making him feel better.

Returning to the hotel trembling and visibly upset, he yelled, 'I feel like I just want to fucking poison myself', leaving Wayan with little doubt that, if there had been any poison available to him on that day, Mick would have welcomed sedation from the relentless remorse he could no longer deny.

Despite the high profile story, few journalists followed the saga of Mick Corby's neighbour closely enough to report on the end result. Tony Lewis and Beth Lavender faced trial in the Rockhampton Supreme Court in May 2006, in a court case that proved to be a disaster for police informer Kim Moore. Kim was an uncertain witness under cross examination and although she had correctly informed police that Lewis had a farm full of cannabis, in court she struggled to prove her allegations that he had trafficked 32 kilos to the nearby town of Sarina in July 2004. And as the local Gladstone police hadn't investigated Lewis or put him under surveillance before they raided his property, her claims were impossible to prove.

Lewis, on the other hand, was a persuasive performer in court, telling the jury about his addiction to pot and the operation he required as a result of clogged arteries due to his excessive smoking of marijuana. He claimed that the 197 plants the police found were for his own use and that he was stockpiling the additional pot for 'a rainy day'.

The jury laughed at Lewis's self-deprecating humour and were sympathetic to a nervous Beth Lavender when she burst into tears midway through her testimony after confessing that she had always been in awe of Kim and had made up stories about Lewis being a drug dealer in order to impress Kim. 'I wanted her to think that I was important in Tony's life and what he did. I remember we had the conversation about Sarina one night when she had called me. I was drunk and she asked me to get her some marijuana. I wanted her to think I had some influence in Tony's life,' Beth sobbed in court.

The prosecutor urged the jury not to be fooled by Beth's crocodile tears or Tony's Aussie bloke persona. 'He may not look like a drug baron, but he is,' argued the prosecutor.

Lewis pleaded guilty to the charges of cultivating and producing marijuana and stealing electricity. He also pleaded guilty to having in his possession utensils to make dangerous drugs. However, he pleaded not guilty to the charge that he had trafficked 32 kilos of pot to Sarina and he was acquitted. Before sentencing, the judge revealed that Lewis had a prior drug possession conviction. He received a light 12 month good behaviour bond and was ordered to undertake rehabilitation for his drug habit.

Beth Lavender pleaded guilty to supplying Kim Moore with 500 grams of 'hydro', but not guilty to running, in collaboration with Lewis, a sophisticated drug trafficking supply network. The judge found her not guilty of all trafficking and cultivating charges and ordered her to serve 40 hours community service.

Throughout the week-long trial, the name Mick Corby was never mentioned. The jury had no inkling that the smooth-talking raconteur in the witness box was best mates with the father of Australia's most infamous drug smuggler. They also had no idea that it was Mick Corby who had driven Tony Lewis to the hospital so he could have his by-pass surgery. Despite Mick's worst fears, once again the Lewis–Corby link had flown under the radar, being well and truly overshadowed by the violent drug home invasion by Schapelle's little brother, James.

CHAPTER 32

Fed to the Wolves

'What do you mean "A to B to C to D?"'
—Sergeant John Moran, police prosecutor

McCauley's life as a free man was drawing to a close, and everything seemed to be slipping away before his very eyes. When he and Kathleen separated, they had divided the proceeds from the house sale. Now South Australian police had frozen all his money under their proceeds of crime legislation and it was just a signature away from being seized. 'That really hurt,' he says. McCauley's pain was compounded by the fact that he thought Mick Corby's family was wallowing in cash: 'They were employing the best lawyers money could buy. I couldn't even afford a packet of smokes.'

Since his arrest he had appeared in court several times for bail hearings, as had the other Adelaide-based members of the drug syndicate. 'Initially I retained the services of my lawyer, Bob Harrop,' says McCauley, 'but after a while, Roger [Rathjen] suggested I didn't need him, and that I was wasting the little money I had left. For some reason, he seemed to think that everything might still turn out all right.

I'm not sure what he was basing this on, but he was under the impression that the South Australian police wouldn't charge me, because the drugs which the police got me for were heading to Queensland.'

When McCauley turned up at Adelaide's Elizabeth Magistrates Court on Friday 7 July 2006, his nerves were jangling. Rathjen and Kathleen were sitting together in the public gallery. Rathjen gave his mate a discreet nod, but Kathleen couldn't bear to make eye contact with her estranged husband and occasionally her eyes welled up with tears. She was heartbroken that it had all come down to this.

At one point that morning Ken Copland, who had arrested Jellese, approached Rathjen for a chat. 'I've known Ken to say hello to for many years and saw him at the court hearing that day,' Rathjen recalled. 'He [Copland] asked me how I knew Malcolm and I said he was a friend from way back. He left it at that. I went on to tell him I hadn't agreed with them seizing the money Malcolm made from the sale of his house because, at the end of the day, he had owned it for thirty years.'

Copland had replied, rather knowingly, 'Don't worry. He got away with it elsewhere.'

McCauley, Jellese, Dudley and Howard stood shoulder to shoulder as Magistrate Ruth Hayes read through the list of charges before she suddenly delivered a bolt from the blue: South Australian police had indeed dropped all charges against the men, just like Rathjen had predicted.

McCauley jumped up and down as if he'd just won a grand final in extra time. He recalls: 'I started celebrating. I actually turned around waving my hands in the air, like I'd kicked a bloody goal. But seconds later, when I stepped out of the court, there they were. The cops from Queensland were standing there, waiting to arrest us. Jeff tried to scarper but there was nowhere to run. They were extraditing us all immediately.'

Queensland Police Detective Superintendent Brian Wilkins fronted a press conference later that day, praising the way regional police had worked together in 'the fight against drugs'. He added: 'The results of this operation illustrate the commitment of the Queensland Police Service and partner law enforcement agencies to disrupt major drug distribution networks, wherever they choose to operate.'

While he was speaking into the microphone, all four Adelaide men were somewhere high above, handcuffed in seats onboard a domestic flight north to Queensland. Queensland Police Detective Sergeant Mark Andrews has since confirmed that on arrival he personally sat McCauley down, and during the course of an interview asked him about his involvement with the Corbys. 'He essentially repeated the same story that had already been wheeled out. He refused to discuss it further and, consequently, my inquiries ended there.'

Two days later, the Adelaide syndicate appeared in Townsville Magistrates Court and another seven months later, on 6 February 2007, their trial dates finally arrived.

On the first morning, Queensland police unveiled their star prosecution witness against the group. Nobody should have been surprised to find it was Brenda Eastwood. She had been released from prison after serving twelve months and had agreed to give evidence against the men.

The court complex at Walker Street was packed well before the scheduled start and tension filled the air when Eastwood arrived. She had agreed to appear as a protected witness and her every move was being shielded by four heavily armed plain-clothes police. In the witness box, under questioning from police prosecutor Sergeant John Moran, Eastwood confirmed everything she had previously outlined in her statement. But during an intense spell of cross examining later in the day, she started to contradict her original story. Suddenly questions were being raised about the number of times she had couriered—and how many locations she had actually supplied to.

'She lost it a couple of times,' says McCauley. 'She started to stray from her statement and at one particular point, she nearly came unstuck. For me, it was a pivotal moment in this whole sorry saga. She was about to blow the whole thing.'

Eastwood knew only too well that if evidence ever emerged of the Gold Coast drug runs, not only would she be staring at more jail time, there would be serious questions raised about the likely recipient. McCauley had already lied his way out of one Corby scandal. If another was to break, people would definitely put two and two together. Schapelle's tale of innocence would be in tatters.

During the morning sitting, Sergeant Moran had asked Eastwood: 'So what was the range that you were paid for these trips? What was the lowest you were paid and maybe what was the highest?'

'$2700 was the highest, $2200 was the lowest,' explained Eastwood.

Later that afternoon, Moran wanted to know exactly when she agreed on a fee for her services as a courier: 'Because I mean, obviously, you wouldn't be agreeing to something like this—illegal and risky as it was—if you didn't know that it was going to be worth some money to you. Putting aside what you were actually paid, what do you say was discussed as far as money goes?'

'The amount that I would be getting?' asked Eastwood.

'Yes,' said Moran. 'Is that the same amount as you got?'

'Yes.'

'Because you told us this morning that it was $2200 to $2700.'

'Yes.'

'Sure it wasn't $2200 to $2500?'

'No, $2200 to $2700.'

'What were you paid the first time?'

'$2700.'

'And what were you paid at the end?'

'$2200.'

'But why did your fee go down?'

'I was asked to do a . . . Oh, how can I put it . . . a . . . a fee of going from A to B to C to D.'

'What do you mean "A to B to C to D"? I thought it was Adelaide, Charters Towers, Townsville, home?'

Eastwood had gaffed her lines. From there, she stumbled: 'It . . . that the . . . that one was yes.'

The courtroom stirred and McCauley's heart was hanging out of his mouth.

'All right. I mean, did you go anywhere else?'

'No.'

'So the only places you visited were Charters Towers and Townsville?'

'Yes, but I was asked to do for several . . . for a couple of other places.'

'Other than Charters Towers and Townsville?'

'Other than them . . . yes.'

'For other people?'

'No.'

'Well, then who for?'

Eastwood paused and then answered: 'For . . . for Malcolm. Malcolm asked me . . . but it never eventuated.'

McCauley says that at that moment he 'nearly died'. 'I looked at Brenda. She looked straight back at me. It was like time had stopped still for several seconds. She gave me an expression as if to say, "I've just fucked up, haven't I?" I gave her one back which read: "Pull yourself together, woman."'

'Where else?' pressed Moran.

'Sydney and . . . Maroochydore.'

'Sydney and Maroochydore. Well, that's a significantly longer drive.'

'Yeah.'

McCauley's first thought was, 'Where's Maroochydore?' His second thought was that he didn't care. 'She had steered us clear of the Gold Coast, that's all that counted,' says McCauley.

But there was trouble ahead. Sergeant Moran still couldn't fathom why her payment had decreased: 'If you were to go Adelaide, Sydney, Maroochydore, Townsville, Charters Towers and back to Adelaide, that's a much longer drive than . . .?'

'Yeah.'

'You wouldn't have done that for less than you were doing?'

'No.'

'Would you?'

'No, that's why I was . . .' And then she paused.

'I'm a little bit lost,' said Sergeant Moran, staring her down. 'How did that end up with you getting paid less for the Charters Towers run than what you were originally being paid?'

It may indeed have been confusing to Sergeant Moran, but the truth was really quite simple. Eastwood had originally been paid a top fee of $2700 to drop off at Mick Corby's and then to Wayne Williams at both Charters Towers and Townsville. A to B to C to D. Her fee fell to $2200 in October 2004, when Mick Corby's Gold Coast run suddenly vanished off the list due to his daughter's arrest.

Eastwood tried to cobble some form of excuse together but it still didn't make sense. 'Well, I don't know, for some reason whether Malcolm took what I gave him as I would do the Charters Towers run for that price. I don't know, but all of a sudden I was . . . started . . . given $2200.'

'You just got bargained down?'

'Eh?' asked Eastwood, before moving up to speed. 'Oh, yeah.'

'You were . . . you were outmanoeuvred?' asked Moran.

'Oh very,' she agreed.

McCauley would later say: 'Can you believe that? He took a bite at the prey and then got bored. She was visibly relieved when he changed the topic.'

On the following day the police wheeled out their second prosecution witness, who was Dean Howard, and from there it was downhill. Ultimately, the syndicate members went on to be sentenced in July that year. Howard was sentenced to two years imprisonment, but was released on immediate parole after it was noted his cooperation with police had involved 'a high level of risk'. Dudley was also somehow treated favourably, on the basis that he 'appeared to be reluctant to become involved in the first place'—he received two years jail but was ordered to be released after three months, the remainder of his sentence to be suspended for three years.

Williams was staring at some serious jail time—he had been a wanted man in Queensland for a long time. He received six years, but it was backdated to include the 455 days he'd been held in custody pre-sentencing. Later that year he was back in court, to face the outstanding attempted murder charge from the machete attack committed in May 2005, before Brenda Eastwood's arrest. That was eventually downgraded to assault occasioning bodily harm while armed in company. He received an additional two years on his sentence and was given a combined parole release date of September 2009.

The biggest loser, by far, was Jellese, who received six years. Crown prosecutor Vivian Keegan described him as the 'supplier and the financier of the venture who received most of the proceeds'. Jellese later claimed that McCauley double-crossed him in statements in order to lessen his own sentence: 'They reckon I made $1.5 million. It's all crap—I might have made $120,000—half was his, half was mine. But what he said to them made me look like the king pin.' As with McCauley police later seized Jellese's assets, including his house, as proceeds of crime.

When it came to his own sentencing, McCauley received three and a half years, to be suspended after fourteen months. By his own admission, he could have done 'a whole lot worse'. 'Let's be fair, I'd already got off light after being arrested for the Wagga run. And also, I never got nailed for any of the other shit. So, as far as jail time goes, I did pretty well when you look back on it.' Far away from the big cities, coverage of McCauley's trial had mainly been confined to the *Townsville Bulletin*. Now he was safely behind bars and remaining silent on his Gold Coast connections. Mick Corby must surely have thought he was home scot-free.

Instead, bitterness and resentment began to grow in

McCauley. 'Roger travelled to see me later in the year, on AFL Grand Final day, but that was about it in terms of visitors,' he says. 'I figured that while I was in there, I'd hear from the people who I thought mattered. I figured wrong. It was as though I'd been fed to the wolves.'

CHAPTER 33

Thirty Pieces of Silver

'We all know that we've been under watch, under scrutiny, everyone's trying to pick pick pick pick . . . anything at our family. Reporters even ring friends, trying to get dirt on me. They're not going to find any.'

—Mercedes Corby

Jodie Power had been friends with Mercedes and the Corby clan for more than fourteen years. Pretty, slim and blonde, she was particularly close to her old boyfriend, Michael Corby Jnr. From the moment Schapelle was arrested in Bali Jodie was a vocal crusader, toeing the Corbys' line that Schapelle was an innocent victim. In 2005, she told the ABC's *7.30 Report*: 'I have never, never seen her smoke marijuana. I have never seen her take drugs, ever in the fourteen years I've known her.'

But as Schapelle's trial progressed, tensions escalated between Mercedes and Jodie. By the time the main trial was over, their relationship had rapidly deteriorated. Word that these two good friends had split soon circulated to Australian newspaper and television networks. In late 2006, the Seven

Network won the television bidding war and paid Jodie Power $100,000 for a 'tell all' interview about the Corby family.

Wired up to a lie detector, over two explosive nights Jodie appeared on Channel 7's current affairs program *Today Tonight* and delivered a series of sensational allegations against both Mercedes and her mother. In particular, she alleged that Mercedes smoked and dealt with marijuana. Mercedes's credibility was now on the line. If she didn't fight *Today Tonight* then most Australians would blame her for Schapelle's twenty-year jail term, so she carefully planned her counter attack. According to Mercedes, Jodie Power was a vindictive liar and motivated by greed. 'I cannot believe she's stooped so low. She's on a vendetta. She's vindictive, manipulative and a liar. She's got mental problems and she'd do anything for money.'

Schapelle also joined the war of words from inside Kerobokan Prison and told a visitor, 'Jodie always used to say she could be vindictive if she wanted to be. Now she's proven it with these disgusting lies about my family. I'm doing twenty years for a crime I didn't commit.'

Predictably, the Corby camp blamed Ron Bakir and Robin Tampoe for the *Today Tonight* stories. A Corby 'insider' said, 'It's got their fingerprints all over it.' Bakir and Tampoe had not been involved with the Corbys for months by now and vehemently denied having anything to do with the stories that were broadcast. In a public slanging match that was getting nastier by the minute, the Corbys then claimed that Jodie Power had turned on Mercedes because Jodie had refused to hand over $5000 from a 'Free Schapelle Fund'. A Corby family friend said, 'Jodie had millions of excuses why she didn't hand it over. In the end it became nasty and the Corby family threatened legal action to get it back.'

Right from the start, the Corby lawyers believed they were on a winner. How could Channel 7 even suggest that Mercedes Corby was an international drug trafficker? As the Seven Network was using 'truth' as its defence, in court Jodie's explosive allegations would need to be backed up by facts and solid evidence. In their frenzy for ratings success, *Today Tonight*'s shoddy and reckless journalism had left Jodie Power vulnerable and exposed.

On 2 April 2007 Mercedes's solicitor, Bill Kalantzis, announced that damages were being sought in relation to allegations that Mercedes was knowingly involved in Schapelle's drug importation to Bali, that she sold drugs, that she was a drug importer and that she had ruined Schapelle's legal defence. In addition, he announced that Rosleigh Rose was also suing the Seven Network for the drug dealing allegations Jodie had made against her.

Mercedes had no criminal record and Ros allegedly only had a conviction for shoplifting as a young woman in Adelaide. The stealing offence was years ago and it had nothing to do with drugs.

In the months leading up to the trial, Channel 7 employed private investigators from a Queensland-based company called Phoenix Global to research and track down potential witnesses for the case. After the *Today Tonight* programs had been broadcast, the Channel 7 website received dozens of emails from people on the Gold Coast who claimed to have information about the Corbys and drugs. The emails were passed on to the private investigators, who started ploughing through them. Many of the emails were bogus, with fake names and telephone numbers, and others were based on second-hand claims or hearsay. The private investigators approached strippers, drug dealers, petty Gold Coast crims, even prisoners in jail. Then there was a second group of people who Channel 7 were trying to subpoena—not junkies or crims, but people who were close to the Corbys.

On the investigators' hit list was Mick Corby's neighbour and best mate Tony Lewis, and his former girlfriend Beth Lavender. The pot-smoking Lewis was eventually ruled out as a candidate for the Seven side, as the lawyers believed he would be a hostile witness to their case. He had in fact already contacted the Corby lawyers and was firmly in their camp. When Seven's investigators approached Beth Lavender, she was no longer going out with Tony Lewis. At first, she panicked and refused to talk. Later, she almost switched sides to align with Seven and agreed to speak, but she wanted money. It was a Catch-22 for the Seven side—as soon as they paid a witness any money, that witness lost all credibility in court. Beth would be labelled a liar by the Corby lawyers, and accused of 'making up stories for money'.

After months of trawling around the Gold Coast, the investigation came to a dead end. They were now doing the real legwork that *Today Tonight*'s journalists should have undertaken before broadcasting their unsubstantiated stories about Mercedes and Rosleigh Rose.

Eventually, however, after months of painstaking digging, one strong lead emerged—it took the investigators to Adelaide, where they tracked down and interviewed a number of McCauley's drug associates. The material they gathered for the trial was intriguing. McCauley's allies— and even his enemies—had all spoken of a relationship that existed with a Gold Coast buyer called 'Corby', which pre- dated Schapelle's arrest in Bali in October 2004.

The advice to Channel 7 was that McCauley would never cooperate in any trial. Even if he did, there were huge legal issues to consider. For starters, he was in jail and it was always going to be a huge issue bringing him in to testify. Later, down the track, he might have ended up tainting other potential witnesses who didn't possess his criminal history.

A case insider said: 'McCauley represented all sorts of potential problems. Kathleen on the other hand was an entirely different proposition. She claimed to have no idea what was going on, but the investigators knew that wasn't true. If they could get her to open up, they felt it might blow the case wide open.' The evidence they could have given, however, would have been limited to McCauley supplying drugs to Mick Corby, who was not on trial, and would not have directly implicated either Mercedes or Ros.

Nevertheless, Kathleen was subpoenaed to appear at the trial and over the coming weeks Seven's lawyer, Richard Keegan, pressed her hard to do so willingly. As she recalls: 'To be honest, I was frightened. I didn't want to incriminate myself. I don't tell everybody what I used to do and what I knew. It was like I had two lives. There was the one life where I was a normal person, doing normal things like going to the bingo and stuff. And then there was another life. As Malcolm's wife, I pretty much saw and heard everything. I didn't want to have to go there [to court] and open up to all that. They expected me to say yes this happened, yes, that happened. I couldn't. He was in jail. I was alone. I was shitting myself.'

As the trial loomed, Channel 7 was left with a huge dilemma about calling Kathleen to the witness stand. The case insider explains: 'At that stage, you have to decide whether or not you're going to risk dragging someone into the box who is likely to be no use to you at all—and make you look like a fool. She was clearly frightened and wouldn't back down. In the end an executive decision was made, by those involved, not to pursue it.'

Another person of interest that Channel 7 was desperate to land was the elusive David McHugh. 'As far as I was concerned back then—and it's still my view to this day—Dave McHugh held the key,' says the insider. 'But again, like Kathleen, he refused to come anywhere near it. While a subpoena is a persuasive tool, there are some people who simply don't care. It was like: "How are you physically going to get me to court? Are you going to arrest me? I don't think so." That was the problem the legal team faced.'

When the trial finally began in the New South Wales Supreme Court in March 2008, Mercedes Corby had undergone a massive transformation. Her long blonde hair was now a mousy brown in colour and she looked like a 'frumpy mum' dropping her kids off to school. The 'in with the in crowd' surfer chick image was gone—for now. The two former friends sat on opposite sides of the courtroom as their lawyers bustled about with trolleys stacked high with paper folders, files and books. It was a small, white, extremely plain-looking courtroom inside the Supreme Court building with an equally small jury of just four men and one woman.

Working on the Corby side was high profile barrister Stuart Littlemore QC. Littlemore has a fearsome reputation and is a lethal opponent when it comes to cross examination. A former ABC current affairs journalist himself (with the groundbreaking *This Day Tonight*), over the years Littlemore had long crusaded against tabloid current affairs programs and he doggedly pursued their unethical journalism practices when he hosted the ABC's *Media Watch* program.

On the first day, Littlemore launched his opening salvo by describing Mercedes as an 'ordinary Australian' who'd been put on trial by the media. He said that Jodie Power was motivated by 'money, hatred and celebrity', and had been paid $100,000 by *Today Tonight* and sent to a ski resort in Canada: 'She lied out of hatred and she lied because she wanted her fifteen minutes of fame.' The court also heard that Jodie was a 'fantasist with a history of a significant drug problem'.

In sometimes heated exchanges, Seven's barrister Tom Hughes QC objected to a number of Littlemore's questions, at one stage accusing him of 'theatrical posing' and asking whether they were designed to 'frighten' the witness. Jodie claimed part of her motivation in revealing that Mercedes had told her she had taken small amounts of marijuana to Bali was to tell the public 'the truth'. When Littlemore asked why she did not go to the police when the revelations were allegedly made to her, Jodie said it did not cross her mind, noting that Mercedes was then her friend. 'You got a lot more than thirty pieces of silver from Channel 7?' he asked. Jodie replied: 'Yes.'

Jodie alleged a series of stories about Mercedes using drugs while travelling overseas. Channel 7 had obtained the letters that Mercedes had written to Jodie in 1993 while she was living in Japan, which included youthful bragging about drug use. Littlemore slammed Channel 7 for somehow trying to make out that Mercedes was a drug dealer: 'This is childhood, youthful exaggeration, trying to gain status— immature, boastful letters written by a kid not much more than a child, with colouring in.'

But what damaged Mercedes most was a photograph of her smoking a penis-shaped pipe and another photograph of her using a mull bowl. After these photos were tendered in court, they were soon splashed prominently in every newspaper across the country. Jodie claimed that Mercedes had been puffing on the pipe and the photograph was proof that Schapelle's big sister used pot. Mercedes said that she hadn't smoked pot since she was a teenager and was just posing for the photo with the pipe. Mercedes was only 19 when the photograph was taken, and now she was in her thirties.

Jodie Power had one more grenade to lob into the Corby camp. The Corbys had always argued that Mercedes's thirtieth birthday party was to be a small affair with about 15 to 20 family and friends attending. However, Jodie said it was going to be a big dance party, more like a rave. She claimed that when she arrived in Bali shortly after Schapelle's arrest, Mercedes was desperately trying to cancel these celebrations. Jodie told the court: 'It was her thirtieth birthday and she said words to the effect that she'd had to cancel a big screen TV that you could watch yourself dance on.'

Jodie's tittle-tattle was damaging, but the only thing she seemed able to prove was that Mercedes had once used pot. The photos could not be denied, but they weren't evidence of any kind of drug dealing and Jodie Power's reputation was about to be destroyed in a very public and humiliating way.

Jodie had two big problems that were overshadowing her credibility. She'd been paid a $100,000 fee by Channel 7 for her interview, and she had a long history of drug use. Littlemore was ready to go in for the kill and he savaged her on the witness stand. She said that she'd spent most of Channel 7's cash on a bitter divorce and custody dispute.

Jodie's ex-husband, Michael Ripley, was about to become the Corbys' secret weapon and he held nothing back when he took the stand, taking the opportunity to tell the court and the media every possible detail of his former wife's drug history. He recalled several occasions when she had taken so much speed that she could not look after her children and Mercedes had had to come over to care for them. Littlemore asked Jodie, 'That is how far off your face you were?' Jodie answered, 'Yes.'

Michael Ripley portrayed Mercedes as a saint-like figure, helping the kids out when their junkie mum lost the plot. He said that Jodie's drug use made her delusional, and she used to see messages coming through the television screen about him cheating on her. On a holiday in Thailand, he said that his former wife had smoked five joints a day and used her childcare allowance to buy the pot. Jodie herself admitted to using marijuana as a schoolgirl, and then moving on to ecstasy, speed, cocaine, LSD and crystal-methamphetamine, otherwise knows as shabu (or ice).

Tony Lewis's informer, Kim Moore, had been flown to Sydney by Channel 7 and put up at a five-star hotel. She had spent her days sending text messages on a fancy new mobile phone. Her fingers trembled as she spoke about her upcoming court appearance. Under fierce cross examination, she became Littlemore's next victim as she stammered to clearly recollect details of Lewis's property. Her former heroin habit came back to haunt her and Littlemore labelled her a 'moll'. Unfortunately the accurate information she had previously supplied to the Queensland police, which had led to a successful drug bust on Lewis's property, was lost in all the courtroom drama.

When Mercedes finally took the stand she started to cry. She said that she was concerned about leaving Schapelle: 'She needs us there for her sanity.' When Littlemore asked her what she would be doing if she was not in court, Mercedes answered: 'Seeing Schapelle, buying food. I do everything.

I wash her clothes. Sometimes I cook, but I also do grocery shopping.'

When asked if she knew anything about the marijuana inside Schapelle's boogie board bag, Mercedes answered, 'No, I've had no knowledge. My sister is innocent.'

When questioned about her drug use, Mercedes didn't deny using marijuana in the past. The photos of the penis pipe and the mull bowl had forced her to admit she had smoked pot, but she denied using other drugs. She denied taking cocaine, ecstasy, speed or ice in the five years prior to 2007. She also said that she'd never smoked marijuana in Bali, and that she'd 'never smoked a full joint in my life. I only had one or two puffs.'

Summing up, Stuart Littlemore said that Mercedes, 'like so many other ordinary, young Australians, occasionally had a joint, dropped the occasional quarter tablet of ecstasy'. Michael Ripley had testified that he lived with Jodie between 2001 and 2006 and that Mercedes had never supplied her with drugs, and that Jodie had obtained her drugs from someone else.

After the claims and counter-claims of this very public show trial, in the end the jury found that Channel 7 was only able to establish, on the balance of probabilities, that Mercedes Corby had possessed and smoked marijuana but not that she had dealt in drugs in any way. She had won this titanic battle, but when the verdict was announced, Jodie yelled at Mercedes, 'Liar!'

Mercedes emerged from the courthouse with Stuart Littlemore on her arm into a sea of cameras. It was her great and only public victory since Schapelle's arrest in October 2004. She declared: 'I can walk out of here and hold my head high, and know I have told the absolute truth and I didn't have to invent any stories about myself.' Littlemore was quoted as saying: 'Mercedes Corby may not be a university graduate, but she's nobody's fool.'

After the trial, Channel 7 announced that it had reached a settlement with both Mercedes and Rosleigh Rose for an undisclosed sum—speculated to be millions. The allegations against Ros were never tested in court.

The Australian media was now concerned about the litigious Corbys and became reluctant to undertake any further investigations into them. As Michael Jnr would often say to people who alleged that he was involved in the marijuana trade on the Gold Coast, 'Prove it, go on, prove it!'

After the verdict Schapelle's biographer, Kathryn Bonella, concluded: 'Channel 7 did an investigation and they didn't come up with anything. Their stories didn't hold up in a court of law. Hopefully that will make people realise the Corbys are not involved in drugs and swing back sympathy for Schapelle.'

But the effect of the dramatic and often tawdry defamation trial was the exact opposite. Certainly Mercedes was cleared of any involvement with the drugs that got her sister into trouble, and of drug dealing and importing and of harming her sister's defence, but one of the most enduring images of the trial was the photo of her holding the penis pipe to her mouth. She may not have inhaled, but an impression had been indelibly left in the public's mind.

CHAPTER 34

The Industry of Innocence

'MEMO Mercedes Corby: put your tits away. Nobody really wants to see them. Your family's foibles are taking on the proportions of a Shakespearean tragicomedy.'

—Tracey Spicer, journalist

60 Minutes producer Kathryn Bonella wasn't a shooting star at the Nine Network, but she was tenacious when in pursuit of a top story. A senior executive producer once described her as 'a good yarn chaser. A bit like Rin Tin Tin—you throw a stick and she will fetch it.' Now, she was about to be thrown a stick by Mercedes Corby.

Before Schapelle's verdict, the Corbys had already made a couple of hundred thousand dollars from various media deals but, from very early on, they realised that the serious money was in a 'tell-all' book on Schapelle's trials and tribulations. Websites, T-shirts, stubby holders, bumper stickers—they were all small stuff. The real money was always going to be in a big book deal. Landing it was the holy grail, but media controller Mercedes needed to unearth an author who could be trusted to believe in Schapelle's innocence. It didn't take Merc long to identify Kathryn Bonella as her Rin Tin Tin.

Throughout Schapelle's trial, Bonella had adroitly negotiated exclusive deals on behalf of the Nine Network with Mercedes, and in the process the two had become close friends. Together they ended up negotiating a lucrative book deal with publishing house Pan Macmillan Australia.

Mercedes saw the book as a win-win situation. It would allow her to clean up the family's image; it would give Schapelle a positive voice; and the timing of publication, just before Christmas 2006, was optimal for sales. An ideal Yuletide gift.

In the beginning, Rosleigh Rose wasn't particularly impressed with the idea and told another current affairs producer: 'Schapelle could write the book herself. Kathryn's just there to check the spelling.' But Bonella had quickly replaced Ron Bakir as Schapelle's new White Knight and she secretly interviewed Kerobokan's most famous inmate over the next few months, while 'book editor' Mercedes kept a steady eye on the subject matter. Certain people and subjects were now off limits, and never to be mentioned in the media again: Clinton, the 'black sheep' of the family; Mick Corby's drug past; Malcolm McCauley, David McHugh and Dad's old next-door neighbour Tony Lewis. These barely rated a couple of paragraphs each, while information on Mick Jnr and half-brother James was conveniently scant too.

Despite the growing list of unmentionables in the Corby circle, Schapelle's book, *My Story,* was an instant bestseller when it was published with a recommended retail price of $35 in November 2006. Within a year, it had sold more than 100,000 copies. The Corbys were right: the book was a goldmine. Pan Macmillan had agreed to pay an advance of $350,000 to Mercedes and Kathryn for writing the book, and the royalties it generated were greater than that.

Inside the front cover of the book is a photograph of Schapelle as a young child dressed as a cute little ballerina. *My Story* is the beguiling tale of an innocent young woman who gets used as an unwilling drug mule. The book blames slack airport security, baggage handlers, customs officers, the Indonesian judicial system, Ron Bakir, Robin Tampoe, Vasu Rasiah, Lily Lubis, Qantas, the Australian Federal Police and the Australian government—everyone gets a serve. On release, Qantas immediately leapt into action and banned any advertising of the book at its airport terminals.

The book ends with a mawkish cry for help: 'I'm innocent, I'm innocent, I'm innocent.' Schapelle writes that she lives in hope that the person who put the drugs in her bag may fess up. 'Maybe someone who knew the truth and just couldn't sleep in bed at night would finally speak out.'

The endless descriptions of Kerobokan Prison as a sub-human jail predictably irritated the prison's then governor, Ilham Djaya. He read the book and requested that Schapelle be moved to another prison. The Corbys then started protesting that Schapelle would not survive in a jail in Jakarta and that she wanted to stay in Bali, so the governor said, 'If she likes it here so much, why would she write that the toilet in the prison is gruesome, that the warden sexually harassed the inmates?' Luckily for Schapelle, the stoush with the governor blew over and she was allowed to stay in Kerobokan.

Kay Danes, from Australia's Foreign Prisoner Support Service, had always been a fervent supporter of Schapelle's plight, but the release of the book filled her with great trepidation for Schapelle's future. Right from the beginning, she had been urging the Corbys to stop doing media deals and found it incredible that the book was published before Schapelle had prepared her case for the Judicial Review— her last legal avenue for a sentence review. Danes believed Schapelle's criticisms of the Indonesian jail and court system would inflame the Jakarta-based judges who were now deciding her fate. Danes, who herself spent almost a year in a Laotian jail on trumped up embezzlement charges in 2000–1, has met dozens of Australians imprisoned in foreign jails and their long-suffering parents. She told the *Courier Mail*: 'I wonder when will people learn that this continued grab at media exposure and exclusives, using Schapelle Corby's plight as their hook, will not help secure her freedom but, rather, may only keep her there longer than necessary.'

Australia's former Foreign Affairs Minister, Alexander Downer, also thinks *My Story* was a big mistake. He says: 'Keep a low profile, don't do media full stop. Don't do media, don't turn your plight into a media circus. Don't think that you can persuade the Indonesians through publicity, just because you have done a deal on *60 Minutes*—tick-tick, tick-tick, "The True Story of Schapelle Corby" and so on. That's not going to convince a judge in Indonesia.'

My Story attacked the Australian Federal Police for not supporting Schapelle's court case, so it was hardly surpris-ing that, in early 2007, the AFP and the Commonwealth director of public prosecutions used the Proceeds of Crime Act to try and seize some of the book's profits. The act had been created to try to stop people from benefiting from their crimes by writing books or cashing in on their notoriety.

Commonwealth prosecutors and the AFP used the Queensland courts to attempt to freeze the authors' receipts from the sale of *My Story* and prevent money going to the Corby family. Pan Macmillan had already remitted $267,000 to a bank account in Indonesia owned by Mercedes's husband Wayan. The publisher was about to send another $68,000 to the Corbys when the court ruled that any royalties from the book sale could be seized by the Commonwealth prosecutors.

A district court in Brisbane later ruled that the money couldn't be frozen, because Schapelle was convicted outside of Australia. For a while the Corbys looked like they were on another winner, but Commonwealth prosecutors appealed the decision and the Queensland court then ruled that the money could be seized because the profits from the book sales were generated in Australia. The Queensland Court of Appeal also froze $15,000 allegedly paid to Mercedes for an exclusive interview in the magazine *New Idea* around the same time.

This legal battle lifted the lid on secret dealings between the book publisher, *New Idea* and the Corby family. Court documents showed that Mercedes was entitled to 85 per cent of both the $350,000 advance and any future royalties. The *Australian Women's Weekly* had paid $110,000 to the Corbys for the right to publish book extracts. The AFP had seized emails from Bonella and the publishing house, and the court heard that Bonella was worried that her payment for writing the book could be seized under the Proceeds of Crime Act. Pan Macmillan non-fiction publisher Tom Gilliatt told Bonella to stop worrying about it: 'My understanding is that you're at no risk since the act is to stop those convicted of a crime profiting from it (and even that's arguable in court).' Gilliatt told Mercedes to invoice Pan Macmillan before the book was published so she could be 'paid before the book becomes public knowledge'.

However, the Corbys ended up having the last laugh. In April 2009, the Queensland Supreme Court ruled that the Commonwealth prosecutors could only seize $128,000 from the book's royalties as proceeds of crime. The Corbys were able to keep $280,000, because the money had been squirrelled away into Wayan's bank account in Indonesia and the Australian authorities could not get access to the funds. Pan Macmillan's Tom Gilliatt said that royalties from the Australian edition of *My Story* were not going to Schapelle: 'No money, directly or indirectly, is going back to Schapelle.'

In 2008, *My Story* was given the new title of *No More Tomorrows* for its publication in international markets. Kathryn Bonella commented: 'It's good it's going to get international exposure. It's a story of a shocking injustice.' It's also good for Kathryn Bonella, of course, who gets her share of the book's international royalties. The FreeSchapelle. com website has an advertisement for the book that says *No More Tomorrows* is now available in six languages— English, Spanish, Dutch, Portuguese, Estonian and Polish.

The enchanting story of Mick Corby's daughter being used as an innocent drug mule has now been spread across the globe. Because royalties from these international editions are probably going into bank accounts held by the Corbys in Indonesia, it's unlikely that Australian authorities will attempt to seize them.

The 'Free Schapelle Corby' website also carries an advertisement for the 'Schapelle Corby Trust Fund', to which readers of *No More Tomorrows* can donate money. The trust fund is a bank account maintained by Ros Corby and the website attempts to reassure the donating public: 'Whilst the family have never asked for public donations, they are sincerely grateful for the assistance many people have offered.'

It's simple. Donors can make ongoing payments by selecting a range of options from $2.50 to $50.00 Australian per month to contribute to the welfare of Schapelle Corby. The trust fund website says, 'The trust accounts are audited each year by an accountant and have no fees except for the PayPal transaction fee and commission, making your contributions fully available.' The Corbys say they need the money to provide practical support for Schapelle. The $280,000 cash injection from the book sale was a sweet victory for the Corbys, and the river of gold has just kept flowing ever since.

The book also incited a range of internet conspiracy theories from around the world. The most popular theory being pushed by Schapelle's supporters is the one about the marijuana found inside her boogie board being imported from South America by the infamous Michael Hurley's cocaine syndicate. But, apart from the endless blaming of other people, the book did something more serious—it painted Schapelle Corby even further into the 'innocence' corner, from which there is seemingly no escape.

PART FOUR

On Release

CHAPTER 35

Truth and Redemption

'Not even as much as a Christmas card.'

—Malcolm McCauley

The early morning sun crept through a tiny gap in the curtains, creating a ray of light that flashed across Kathleen's pillow. Her eyes flickered and, momentarily, she was unsettled by the strangeness of her surroundings. It took several seconds for her mind to register where she was and why. Then the excitement took over and she bounded straight out of bed.

It was 21 May 2008 and Kathleen was lying in a campervan, parked outside a prison. Today was the day her ex-husband Malcolm walked free. He had been locked up for fourteen months and she had missed him more than she cared to admit.

She had flown from Adelaide to Cairns the day before. From there, after hiring the van, she drove south to Townsville, camping overnight beside the Stuart Correctional Centre. There was no way she was going to leave anything to chance.

When McCauley emerged from the gates at 6.30 am, butterflies began to dance in her belly. He loitered for several minutes, saying goodbye to the prison guards. He then spotted Kathleen on the far side of the car park and wandered over.

A little unsure about what to do, she remained in the driver's seat, greeting him with a simple, 'Hello.'

'Never mind "Hello",' muttered McCauley. 'Come here and give me a hug!' Kathleen climbed out and the couple embraced. 'What's the campervan for?'

'Don't ask questions. Just get in,' she said.

McCauley's legs creaked as he clambered aboard. Kathleen then unveiled her next surprise, opening the bar-fridge door to reveal an ice-cold six-pack of McCauley's favourite South Australian brewed beer.

'Express delivery from Adelaide! How's that for service?'

'Aaaah, love, may the stars shine upon your head and peace reign supreme.' McCauley was well and truly touched.

Kathleen had arranged to return the campervan in Adelaide the following week so, over the next five days, the couple cruised back to South Australia on a 2500-kilometre road trip. McCauley got his first taste of freedom in fourteen months, travelling the open road with Kathleen by his side.

'We stayed in caravan parks, except for one night when we pitched up by the side of a road near Cobar, because Malcolm's one wish was to build a campfire,' she recalls. 'It was the noisiest spot you could ever imagine. All night we couldn't hear each other speak because of the sound of semis changing gear to get over the hill. But we built the fire and Malcolm was happy.'

When the McCauleys arrived back at Salisbury, Malcolm was left with no choice but to move back in with Kathleen.

Due to the cops having seized his house and profits, he was now on the bones of his arse.

Kathleen remembers that initially it took time for McCauley to readjust to the outside world: 'He kept doing weird stuff. He'd become so used to asking permission to do everything in prison, he carried on doing the same [at home] without realising. We had to laugh—sometimes he'd stand in front of the patio doors waving his arms about, waiting for them to open automatically.'

While those habits slowly faded, Kathleen and the kids grew concerned because something, as far they could tell, was still not right. McCauley appeared troubled, and they couldn't put their finger on the reason why. Something had slowly eaten away at him while he sat there languishing in jail. Now he was free, he was in a position to rectify it. But the question was: would he?

A month after his release, on 23 June 2008, Channel 9 screened its explosive two-part documentary series, *Schapelle Corby: The Hidden Truth*. Thanks to all the fly-on-the-wall footage obtained in the lead-up to the verdict, the documentary series was able to take viewers into the chaotic world of the Corbys like never before.

In the second instalment, screened the following night, the film introduced McCauley as a man very familiar with the Corby family. There was the footage of Mercedes thanking him for attending her sister's trial. There was also film of Dave McHugh and Schapelle chatting as she stood in the court's holding cell. If that wasn't bad enough, McCauley dropped a major bombshell at the end of the program, claiming to know how the cannabis ended up in her bag. During that interview, which had been taped just as he was to begin serving his sentence, McCauley said: 'I had nothing to do with it, believe me. How it happened is probably for another day.' In dramatic fashion, he then vowed to reveal all after he was released from prison. 'Give me eighteen months and I will tell you. I will be over the courts then. Double jeopardy and everything.' Of Corby's bag, he observed somewhat enigmatically: 'It landed in Denpasar and she got caught and she admitted that it [the bag] was hers. What happened in between is a good story—and the truth.'

Along with two million other viewers around the country, McCauley watched the show that night. He was around at the house of his eldest daughter, Leanne, and she gasped in shock as he delivered his bolt from the blue. She recalls: 'I just looked at him across the sofa and screamed, "Jesus, Dad! Do you know what you've just done?"'

When Leanne arrived at work the following morning, her father was the talk of the office. 'It was a bit strange. I have a different surname, so they had no idea I was his daughter. Everyone was discussing him at their desks, and beside the water cooler. I couldn't escape it. They were like, "Do you reckon he's for real?" I was desperate to put them right. I felt like saying, "Of course he's for bloody real."'

As Leanne dodged the gossip that morning, I was making my way into the *Sun-Herald* office in Sydney with McCauley's words still fresh in my mind. Before I'd even had time to check my emails, I was ushered into editor Simon Dulhunty's office and given my mission for the week: go find Malcolm McCauley.

We had established that in the time since the interview was filmed, McCauley had served his jail sentence and was now out there somewhere. We also knew, only too well, that every other Australian media outlet would be hunting him as well. We talked strategy and decided Adelaide was the only logical place to start. McCauley had lived there his entire life and electoral roll records showed he'd never strayed too far from the Salisbury area of the city. A seat on the next available flight was booked and, by the time I'd touched down in the City of Churches later that afternoon, a local freelance photographer by the name of David Mariuz was on hand to meet me. The chase was on.

There is no tried and tested formula for success on these sorts of assignments. Each one is different, the hurdles never the same. That said, if you're trying to track someone down, it's hardly rocket science. The more doors you knock on, the greater your chances of finding them. The problem, of course, is that people don't always answer doors—especially when reporters are standing on the other side. That's when a carefully crafted handwritten letter occasionally comes into play. I slid one under the front door of a house belonging to McCauley's youngest daughter Kelly. Another was deployed at Kathleen's.

I later knocked at McCauley's last known address in Degree Road and was promptly chased down the street by the present occupants, who had already been hounded by television news crews the night before. I canvassed bar staff and patrons in the Waterloo Station Hotel at Paralowie, and then tried the Salisbury RSL. On each occasion, I was greeted with a series of stares and grunts. I even left my card with two bemused check-out girls in the local supermarket. It was a long shot, but you never can tell.

I later returned to Kathleen's house and was heartened when she answered. She claimed McCauley had headed up into the Adelaide Hills to help a friend with some building work—and wouldn't be back until the following week. I couldn't be sure that was the case, so the following day

David and I conducted a discreet stakeout at the end of the street on the off-chance that McCauley might emerge. Not a sniff.

By the Saturday morning, we'd just about exhausted every possible avenue. With a couple of hours to kill before my scheduled flight back to Sydney, we decided to head back one last time to the Salisbury RSL in the faint hope of finding him at the bar. As was the case two days earlier, we were met with stony silence. But then, later, just as David and I finished our final mouthful of beer and stood up to leave, a man approached our table. He was a chubby, balding fella who had been sitting with a group of men towards the back of the room. He introduced himself as 'Roger'.

'I hear you're looking for Malcolm McCauley,' he said. 'Where you boys from?'

Stunned that someone had finally given us the time of day, David and I launched into our best pitch ever.

Roger listened, but then said: 'He doesn't want to talk. He just wants to be left alone.'

Over the next few minutes, it became apparent that this wasn't entirely true. The bloke known as Roger was toying with us. He confirmed he knew where McCauley was, and then he baited us by saying he could get him on the phone straight away, if required. 'If I'm going to call him, I need to know if there's any money on the table . . . and how much.'

It's a common misconception amongst the Australian public that every media outlet pays for its big stories. The commercial television networks certainly do. Newspapers, however, have varying policies regarding 'chequebook journalism' and the *Sun-Herald*'s stance, certainly throughout my ten years there, has always been the same—there is no chequebook.

Roger laughed when I informed him of this fact. 'Well, then, why would he bother? What else can you offer him?'

'The chance to set the record straight?'

Roger thought that was funny too. For the next half-hour the conversation switched this way and that, without any resolution. Furthermore, I was running out of time.

The *Sun-Herald* is a weekly Sunday newspaper. With our Saturday afternoon deadline fast approaching, it became obvious that no interview was going to eventuate that day. Worse still, with an entire week to wait before our next edition, the chances of me landing the story now looked slim—the chasing pack of other reporters, some armed with money, would surely have caught up with McCauley by then.

As we left the RSL that afternoon, the one glimmer of hope on the horizon was that Roger had at least agreed to pass my contact details on to McCauley. I wasn't going to hold my breath; but then, sure enough, two days later the man himself made contact.

'Malcolm McCauley speaking. I hear you've been looking for me. What do you know? I'm a busy man, so let's make it quick.'

I was in a grocery store with a packet of cereal in my hand. 'You're a hard man to get hold of, Malcolm. I left messages for you everywhere.'

'Yeah, got them all,' he replied. 'Walked into the super-market to buy a loaf of bread yesterday, and even they handed me your bleeding card.'

We struck up a conversation and from there McCauley agreed to meet face to face two days later at the Hahndorf Inn Hotel, a quaint little German pub nestled in the Adelaide Hills, some 25 minutes out of town.

'I'll meet you inside the bar at 7.30 pm,' he said, adding,

'The deal is that I come alone, you come alone.' He went on to warn me: 'If there's anyone else with you, I'll walk. Is that understood?'

'You're on.'

Was it risky? I didn't intend to find out. I packed my bags and flew straight back to Adelaide where David, the photographer, agreed to drive me up into the hills and then sit, discreetly, a few yards down the street.

It was a bitterly cold night, a touch foggy, and I was a little apprehensive. I walked in, ordered a pint of ale and then pulled up a chair in the corner. When McCauley finally strolled in, some thirty minutes late, it became clear he hadn't stuck to the deal either—he had brought Kathleen.

I had no idea how the night was going to unfold and the first twenty minutes were difficult to say the least. I had anticipated one-way traffic, with me doing all the talking. Instead, it was McCauley firing off all the questions, almost as if he was interviewing me for a job. He quizzed me about my family and background. He wanted to know where my career had taken me and, more importantly, why I had gone to so much trouble to find him.

At one point, Kathleen advised him to 'stop with the interrogation'.

'Don't worry, we're going all right,' he said, while winking in my direction. I sensed we were finally beginning to click.

It was less than eighteen months since McCauley had given his interview for the documentary, but on this particular night he looked a decade older than the man who'd appeared on national television the week before. While he had boasted a full head of hair in the documentary, it had now been shaved, rather harshly, down to the skin. He had lost a heap of weight— his face was thin and he looked knackered, almost defeated.

'Why did you say what you said on the documentary?' I asked. 'If you do know the truth, a lot of people are bound to be questioning why you never came forward before.'

He paused, then answered: 'There are two main reasons why. The first is that I was tied up with the whole bloody thing and stood to go down if anyone ever found out. The second reason is that I made a pact with the old man [Mick Corby] and a couple of others. I gave Mick my word I wouldn't talk. His daughter's stuck over there in that hell hole. I wouldn't wish that on anyone.'

I got the impression he was willing to talk, but on his terms. Over the course of the evening and a couple more beers, he loosened up. 'I've just done fourteen months hard time, and do you know what? Not even as much as a Christmas card . . . from any of 'em. No Christmas card saying "We're thinking of you". No Christmas card saying "Happy bloody Christmas—see you when you get out."' McCauley said he would have understood had they chosen not to sign it 'From the Corbys'. 'They could have signed it "From your old mates up this way," or "Everytime we have a Bintang, we're thinking of you" . . . I would have known who it was from.

'You have to understand that, before I went inside, they were ducking and diving for cover. The whole ship was about to sink, and they were all over me like a rash. They needed me then. Then I was locked away and suddenly it's out of sight, out of mind. No need to worry about that cunt any more.

'Shall I tell you something, Eamonn? When things go pear shaped, that's when you find out who your friends are. And I was dropped like a shitty rag.'

McCauley had become engulfed in anger. And he hadn't finished yet: 'I walked out a few weeks ago and, fuck me, the world was a different place, or at least it was as far as they go. They're all rolling in money and you know what the worst thing of all is? That poor girl is still rotting away over there.'

The intensity around the table was inexpressible. We took some time out. Kathleen bought a round, and then we went outside and huddled together in the cold night air for a smoke. When we returned inside, I asked, 'Where do we go from here? What next?' The subject of money was then inevitably raised. 'As I told your friend Roger on Saturday, it's not something I can offer. The paper doesn't pay for stories. If you're after cash, why haven't you made a deal with one of the television networks chasing you?'

'I'm not interested in television,' he said, adding, 'They'll fuck me over. They always catch your ugly side, too.' McCauley went on to explain, somewhat awkwardly, that he wasn't after a fortune. He explained the cops had taken his assets under Proceeds of Crime legislation and that he was now forced to rely on Kathleen, which clearly he was feeling awkward about.

'I can't do it,' I said.

'Then what can you do?'

'I can give you a platform to tell your story and put this whole thing to bed.'

'And how do I know you won't fuck me over? Chop and change—make things up?'

'Because you've just spent the entire evening with me, working me out. If you don't trust me now then, seriously, what can I say?'

I gave McCauley my word that I would let him read and double-check all his quotes before anything went into print. I even offered to get a legal letter drawn up, to confirm the arrangement. I was desperate for an answer on the night, but he insisted he needed time to go away and think about it. We said our farewells outside the pub. I shook McCauley's hand and kissed Kathleen goodbye.

On the way back to Adelaide, I relayed the night's events to my then chief of staff, Chad Watson, and expressed fear that maybe I'd just seen the last of McCauley. It was a natural conclusion, given we had no money to offer. But Chad, ever the optimist, offered words of encouragement and advised me to 'hang in there'. We chatted and decided that, as far as McCauley's credibility was concerned, this was now the ultimate test. He could choose to head elsewhere, grab some quick cash and have his integrity forever questioned for doing so. Or, alternatively, he could do the interview for free with someone he trusted and have the chance to see his story presented fully and fairly, including all its doubts and contradictions, to let readers judge for themselves.

I lay awake the whole night worrying. I needn't have—the following morning, McCauley telephoned to say we were on. We arranged to meet at Kathleen's house late the same afternoon, and he confirmed he was also happy for David to accompany me and take pictures.

When David and I arrived that Friday afternoon, Kathleen opened the front door and led us through to a rear concrete patio area. McCauley was sitting at a table. Also present was the same man who had acted as his agent the week before—Roger.

As we cracked open a beer, it quickly became apparent that all was not well. There was tension in the air. For some unknown reason, this Roger bloke appeared stressed and was in McCauley's ear about pulling the plug on the interview: 'I'm sorry, but I've told Malcolm that, if it were me,

I wouldn't do it. As a friend I've advised him not to. The ball's in his court.'

David and I looked at one another, both stunned. Roger had been more than happy to approach us in a pub to try and broker a quick buck for his mate. Now the serious allegations were about to be made, and here he was hanging around in McCauley's yard like a bad smell, trying to convince him it was a bad idea.

There were moments of unbearable silence as McCauley slowly climbed out of his seat and walked across the garden. He plucked a log from a big pile sitting next to the back fence and then meandered back, throwing it onto a fire that was petering out close to where we sat. The fate of the day now rested on McCauley's next words.

'I've got the fire started now, Rog. I'll probably just sit here a while and have a gasbag with the boy. Don't worry, I haven't promised anything.'

Roger grunted and left. At that particular point, it made no sense whatsoever why Roger had tried to compromise the interview. But back then, of course, Roger was just another bloke.

'What's his story?' I asked McCauley, once Roger had departed.

'Let's not go there,' he replied.

In an afternoon of startling revelations, McCauley went on to name Mick as a Queensland buyer of his marijuana and Bali as its final destination. He spoke of an 'arrangement' involving Mick and corrupt Bali airport officials, who would 'pocket bribe money placed inside the bag' in return for waiving the drugs through: 'I'm tired and I'm exhausted.

I've kept silent all this time about what I know and it's eaten away at me. I've decided I don't want to lie any more. It's time to wipe the slate clean. Tonight I want to sleep with a clear conscience. Once the drugs were delivered to Mick, I had nothing else to do with them whatsoever. But certainly I knew where they were heading, and how.' He admitted lying to police in two states after making 'a pact' with Mick Corby. That promise involved him never revealing their long-standing association. 'I have maintained that agreement until today.'

McCauley explained that, like all his clients, Mick paid $3000 a pound (454 grams) for Adelaide hydro. When the bag of buds later landed in Bali, it was 'divvied up' and distributed across a network of shops and bars, and sold on to local expats and tourists. Sold in ounces, the cannabis was worth up to three times what Mick had paid. When sold to backpackers and tourists in smaller quantities, it was worth even more. 'Surfers, in particular, are hooter connoisseurs and this was no bush weed. This was excellent South Australian hydro and it had an excellent reputation in Bali.'

He said to his knowledge, Mick Corby never encountered problems getting the marijuana through Brisbane Airport and onto a plane. Thanks to crooked security contacts on the ground in Bali, smuggling it through Denpasar Airport was always just as easy. 'I can't say that Mick knew the airport guys personally, but the system was certainly well orchestrated and in place when I started transporting the hooter to him.'

Describing the bribe system as a 'well-oiled machine', McCauley provided details about how Mick Corby's marijuana would sail safely through the airport: 'He would pack it all in a bag and the bribe would go in, too. The arrangement was always US$1000 in cash. No more, no less.'

McCauley said one reason it broke down on the day of Schapelle's arrest was because there was no payment. 'Mick didn't forget it,' he claimed. 'The money was in there, all safe, signed and delivered—almost delivered. It wasn't in there for the simple reason that it had been removed.'

McCauley confirmed for the first time how, sixteen days after Corby's arrest, he made a frantic trip to Bali to assess the 'damage'. He confirmed it was his first-ever overseas trip. 'The purpose of that particular visit was information and to protect my arse,' he said. 'I wanted to know how much detail had been leaked.' He spoke of two additional visits to Bali, including the succession of boozy afternoons with the Corbys at the Secret Garden. There was a period of silence while I attempted to take everything in. McCauley then asked me to consider something: 'You have to remember that, up until the day Schapelle got caught, they were just a bunch of fucking nobodies and Mick Corby was just another buyer and seller of drugs. Then the media got hold of it, and the family . . . Well, they became celebrities. The truth is, she [Schapelle] always knew her dad was a drug dealer. She knew about the trips to Bali, she knew about the system, the bribes. She knew the lot.'

Although McCauley didn't go into great detail, he claimed for the first time that not only did Dave McHugh know more than anyone, he was the mutual friend who had organised the initial introduction. Furthermore, he was still in contact with the Corbys through Ros.

'Do you think Dave would talk to me?'

'I can't see it happening,' he replied. 'Dave's been very loyal. Something major would have to go down for that to ever happen.'

It had certainly been a day of revelations. By the end of

it I was shattered, though not as much as McCauley. As I left him behind in his backyard, I took one last look. He was huddled beside the fire, alone with his thoughts.

On Sunday 13 July 2008, McCauley's revelations appeared on the front page of both the *Sun-Herald* in Sydney and the *Sunday Age* in Melbourne. The story led television news bulletins around the nation later that same night. The coverage, however, had left everyone hanging in suspense. Due to legal constraints, it was not possible to identify the individual McCauley had accused of removing the $1000 bribe from inside the boogie board.

In the days that followed, all the other media outlets were desperately trying to generate their own line. When McCauley refused all interviews, some chose to feed off the scraps being dished out by the Corbys. Within 24 hours, Roseleigh Rose had told the *Herald-Sun* in Melbourne that it was 'absolute rubbish' her ex-husband could ever have been involved in a drug syndicate. And Mick's latest alibi? 'Michael never had the phone on,' she said. 'If he [McCauley] lives in Adelaide and Michael was up here [in Queensland], how did he contact him?'

A week on from the original story, meanwhile, and News Ltd publications tried to discredit McCauley by claiming he'd lied about being in the army. Quoting an unnamed 'long term member of Salisbury RSL', the article said McCauley's application to join the club had stated he was part of Australia's '2/27th' battalion—an army division that finished serving in New Guinea and the Middle East when he was still in nappies. This story, printed in Sydney and Adelaide, has been repeatedly wheeled out on Corby supporter forums ever since. However, official documentation has since been obtained from the Australian Army that shows he served in the (South Australian) 27th Battalion between 1967 and 1969.

'I thought that was pretty harsh,' he said of the story, adding: 'So 15 or 20 years ago, I made an innocent mistake and scribbled two two's instead of one. Did I claim I was a war veteran on the form? Never. Did I attempt to lie about my age? No, I didn't. I was either tipsy or gasbagging to someone at the time. Are we hanging people for making innocent slip-ups on forms now? It would appear so.'

The same article referred to an unnamed police officer who claims to have been involved in the raids on McCauley's home when the Corby photos were originally found. He said the photographs sparked an 'extensive investigation' to determine if there were any links between McCauley's drug syndicate and any of the Corbys. 'We have found no links, nothing at all, no evidence linking the two situations,' he said. 'If he had any further information, it would have been advantageous for him to have told us at the time. There is every likelihood he could have used that as a bargaining chip and that would have been taken into account when he was sentenced. That did not take place and he did not even hint at any connection with the Corby clan.'

I have since approached the South Australian Police for an interview with the detectives who headed the investigation into McCauley. That request was declined.

During a later interview conducted with Malcolm McCauley and Roger Rathjen together, the ex cop said: 'We have in the Australian Federal Police a system that we refer to as "IR"—intelligence reports. Information gets fed into that system. It gathers from various places and it's graded from A1 to F6, according to its reliability. Due to the way Mick Keelty reacted, I have no doubt she was a drug courier, and I have no doubt the Intel reports showed that. I'm sure they would have had information from a variety of places.' He added: 'Unfortunately, because she had a pretty face, people gave her sympathy. Had she been stuck with a face like mine, nobody would have cared.'

Had Rathjen added to that weight of evidence amassed by the Federal Police? Once a cop, always a cop. He openly admits to filing intelligence reports post-retirement. Did he ring and say, 'Further to what you might already have, I'm aware of a bloke who's been supplying marijuana to Mick Corby?'

'I didn't know he was supplying to Mick Corby,' insisted Rathjen.

'Yes you did, Roger,' piped up McCauley.

'Look, what do you want me to say?' Rathjen asked. 'It could be argued that, when I went to the Australian Federal Police 25th anniversary "do" in October 2004 [the same month as Schapelle was caught], I told the drug unit, "This is what's going on." I could have said, "I'm aware of this big drug syndicate and these are the figures involved." Did I? No, I didn't. But . . . would I tell you if I had?

'Never.'

CHAPTER 36

Mr Smoothie Comes to the Table

'I know certain stuff that would make your hairs stand on end.'
—David McHugh

It's the warm smiles and friendly faces of loved ones that greet most folk when they step off planes following holidays abroad. Others are not so lucky. On 3 February 2010, David McHugh had just landed at Adelaide Airport following his latest trip to Bali. He stepped off Virgin Pacific Flight 4194 just after 8.30 am and then headed straight for the luggage carousel to retrieve his bags. The moment he'd grabbed his suitcase, a female customs official appeared alongside him.

'Are you David Trevor McHugh?' she asked.

'Yes,' he replied with that inevitable feeling of what was to follow.

'Would you mind stepping this way, please?'

Here we go again, he thought.

Perhaps it was the previous tip-off from hostile members

of his family, or his links to the Corby family, or an accumulation of other intriguing snippets now resting in his ever-growing police file. Either way, one thing was certain—McHugh's card was marked. In recent times his overseas excursions had all ended the same way—straight-faced customs officials would confront him and haul him to one side. Then, like cats going through a garbage bin, they would proceed to turn his suitcase upside down and inside out.

Such baggage checks usually took place in the cordoned-off area inside Adelaide Airport he'd become familiar with; he didn't mind so much because other passengers were usually nearby, enduring the same painstaking procedure. Occasionally, he liked to zone out by viewing the many weird, wonderful and at times embarrassing items being dragged out of other people's cases. On this particular day, however, there would be no such opportunity to pry.

The female officer escorted McHugh down a long straight corridor and then ushered him into a private interview room. He was in unfamiliar territory and it made him feel nervous. His suitcase was slapped on a table. Moments later a second woman strolled in and there was a loud bang as the door slammed shut behind her. McHugh later recounted to me the morning's events from that moment on.

'We have brought you in here today, Mr McHugh, because we have reason to believe you may be carrying something you shouldn't be.'

'Well, I ain't,' he replied.

'Are you carrying any narcotics, any substances or products that are prohibited under Australian law?' she asked.

'Definitely not.'

'Well, we'll just go through your bag then if you don't mind,' said the customs officer.

McHugh's suitcase was unzipped and the two officers began rummaging in silence. There was nowhere for McHugh to look except at the search unfolding in front of him. It seemed to last for an eternity, but he reassured himself that they wouldn't find anything—because there was nothing to find.

Once the search had been completed, the same female customs officer said: 'Okay, once again—we have reason to believe you may have returned from Indonesia with narcotics or substances that are forbidden under Australia law. Is there anything you'd like to tell us?'

'I told you before, I've got nothing.'

'Are you carrying anything on your body that you haven't disclosed to us, Mr McHugh?'

'Why would I want to do that?' he replied, somewhat flustered.

The two women whispered something to one another and then announced to McHugh that they were sending for a sniffer dog. One officer left the room and the other, who had been doing all the talking, asked McHugh to pull up a chair next to the table. She glanced down at paperwork containing some rather messy handwritten notes.

McHugh squinted from across the desk, trying to decipher what they said. Without his glasses, it was always going to be a struggle. He realised this particular search was a major step up from the usual routine. In a weak plea of desperation, he asked the officer: 'What's all this about?'

'Can I ask why you keep returning to Bali?' she inquired.

'Because I like it.'

'According to our records, you'd never travelled anywhere until 1999, and then all of a sudden you start moving back-wards and forwards between Australia and Bali. Sometimes for visits that are so short, one might argue they're hardly worth taking.'

'I own greyhounds,' he replied. 'It's hard for me to get anyone to look after them.'

'What do you do for work these days, Mr McHugh?' she asked.

'What?'

'What's your occupation?'

'I don't have a job,' he said. 'I used to be a postman, but I'm not any more. I'm on a disability pension. I've got arthritis.'

'Well, then, can you explain to me, please, how you source the necessary funds, the disposable income, that enables you to travel to Indonesia as often as you do?'

'I'm pretty tight with cash,' he responded.

It soon became clear that the customs officer knew more about McHugh than he initially realised. She recounted the fact that in 2008 he had transferred a sum of money into an Indonesian bank account belonging to a female Balinese citizen. 'You used your Western Union account to transfer that money, did you not?'

'What?' asked McHugh, trying to take in what he'd just heard. 'How'd you know that?' he added rather sheepishly.

'Because I've viewed the transaction,' the woman replied. She quoted the recipient's full name and the exact amount of money involved. She then asked McHugh to explain their relationship.

'You threw me initially, because you gave me her Balinese name,' said McHugh, beads of sweat dripping from his forehead.

'Her name's Cindy, um, her friends call her Cindy. She's an old girlfriend.'

'Well, where did that money come from? You certainly seem to be finding extra finances from somewhere. Can you help me to understand how that happens?'

'What's your point?' he asked.

'Are you involved in the distribution and sale of marijuana, Mr McHugh?'

'No, never.'

There was a brief moment of silence. The officer then drew attention to the fact that McHugh had been linked, via the media and photographs, with Schapelle Corby.

'Explain what happened there,' she said.

'Um, I met Schapelle's mother in Bali and I sort of got to know them all. We went back and I, um, visited Schapelle in prison with a mate.'

'Hmm. And do you think she's guilty?' the woman asked.

'I don't know anything.'

'I didn't ask whether you knew anything, Mr McHugh, I asked you what you thought.'

'Um, I'm not sure.'

The customs officer had certainly been doing her homework because she then threw another bombshell McHugh's way. 'Mr McHugh, it's been brought to my attention that next week you're due to appear in Adelaide Magistrates Court charged with growing an illegal quantity of hydroponic marijuana. What can you tell me about that?'

The room suddenly felt five times smaller to McHugh, who had no idea how to respond.

'A picture is beginning to build here, wouldn't you agree?' asked the woman.

'Look . . . it ain't like that at all.'

'Well, then, what *is* it like?'

Suddenly the tension in the airport interview room shot

up another notch as the door swung open and the second female customs officer reappeared with a male colleague holding a black Labrador retriever on a leash. The canine appeared frantic and excited, darting this way and that. Stage two of the interrogation was about to commence.

'Mr McHugh, stand up for me please and step away from the table,' instructed his main interrogator.

McHugh climbed out of his chair and shuffled over to where she was pointing. The dog and the handler then moved in behind him. He began complaining about his treatment and was adamant he had nothing to hide. The dog, however, had just sat down beside the tattooed tiger on his right leg, suggesting otherwise.

'Are you sure you don't have anything on you?' asked his interrogator.

'Look . . . I swear . . . I don't.'

'Well, the dog seems to be indicating something. Have you been in a room where there were drugs perhaps? Someone smoking a joint or something?'

'No.'

'Do you object to us searching your body for anything that may have been brought in illegally?'

'What . . . like a pat-down?'

'Yes,' said the officer.

'Do what you have to do,' he replied.

McHugh was asked to empty his pockets. He placed his wallet and mobile phone on the table. He was then told to extend his arms out straight and the second female officer began frisking him from head to toe. Again they found nothing.

'Can I go now?' he snapped.

McHugh's question went unanswered. Instead, the second

female officer grabbed McHugh's phone and took it out of the room while the dog handler trailed behind. It was now just McHugh and the main officer.

'Take a seat again, please,' she said. 'I have to inform you that the next step in this process is for us to have you transported to hospital . . . for a forensic examination.'

McHugh then blew up. 'This is fucking outrageous,' he said. 'Okay, do it,' he added. 'I told you at the start I have nothing to hide. This has all been a waste of your time and my time. Take me to hospital. I don't fucking care . . . Come on, let's go. And where's my phone? Where's she gone with my bloody phone?'

The woman sat in silence as McHugh continued to ramble. 'Every time I come back from Bali, you guys go through my bags. Why?'

'Why do you think, Mr McHugh?'

'Beats me. Why do you want to take me to hospital? Why are you so convinced I'm carrying something?' he bleated.

'I'm not at liberty to discuss that,' the customs officer replied.

When the second female officer returned several minutes later, she poked her head around the door and asked her colleague to step outside briefly. McHugh was left alone to stew in his own juices. When they both arrived back, his phone was returned to him and he was told he was free to leave.

The ordeal had lasted over an hour and McHugh's mind was racing as he finally headed home. He was naturally relieved he'd escaped a hospital probe, but at the same time he was livid about what had just unfolded. They had clearly spent time researching his shadowy past. He wasn't sure what bothered him most. Was it the fact they knew about his drug charges? That they had gone through his bank account with a fine toothcomb, or was it the insinuation that they knew about the Schapelle Corby connection?

McHugh had somehow managed to keep his nose clean for years, but on 2 April 2009 he had inevitably become the latest member of the syndicate to fall when South Australian police executed a search warrant at his home and discovered not one, but two hydroponic set-ups—one in a back shed, the other in a spare bedroom. Detectives confiscated nine adult cannabis plants and a heap of equipment capable of harvesting much, much more.

Since that day, McHugh had tried his best to keep news of the raid and of the charges that had arisen from it secret from everyone. Six weeks after the raid, however, on 15 May 2009, the *Sun-Herald* in Sydney found out about the incident. Realising the significance of the bust in terms of the overall picture, journalist Matthew Benns got straight on the phone to Rosleigh Rose for a comment.

They exchanged pleasantries and then Benns cut straight to the chase. 'Have you spoken to David McHugh lately?' he asked.

Clearly caught off-guard, she answered: 'Er, I spoke to him the other day. He rung me up and said Schapelle had been in the *Adelaide Advertiser*.'

'Did he mention that he had been arrested for growing drugs?'

There was a brief moment of silence and then she replied: 'Why would he? I am not really his friend or anything. He just said Schapelle was in the *Advertiser*.'

Benns had rattled Ros's cage several times in the past while writing Corby-related articles and he was about to do it all over again. He continued: 'After all the drama those two blokes caused you . . . why would you still be speaking to David McHugh, if he's not your friend?'

'Look, what's this got to do with Schapelle or us? How would I know what he is bloody doing?' retorted Ros angrily.

Benns then pointed out to Ros that the two Adelaide men who gained access to Schapelle just before her verdict had both now been shown to have links in the marijuana trade. 'Is it another coincidence?' he asked rather cheekily.

Ros responded in an aggressive tone: 'I met him [McHugh] at the Secret Garden a few years ago with that bloody liar rotten thing from Adelaide [McCauley]. I don't really know them at all, and I have never met that McCauley fellow except at the Secret Garden.'

'But then, why are you still in regular touch with . . .?'

It was too late. She'd already hung up.

Once upon a time, prior to his drug charges and the airport interrogation, it had seemed altogether unlikely that McHugh would ever break ranks, let alone speak to a journalist investigating Mick and Schapelle. It had become blatantly obvious, during the research for this book, that an association had existed between McCauley and McHugh long before the alleged chance meeting on a plane. Marijuana was clearly the connection. But the question was: how had it all started, and when did McCauley and McHugh actually first meet?

McCauley had been happy to cooperate in most areas, but when it came to talking about McHugh there was a line he didn't feel comfortable crossing. They were friends and former business aquaintances, after all. 'I've told you enough already,' he would say. 'If you want the missing pieces of the jigsaw, work them out yourself or find a way of speaking to Dave.'

I continually doubted whether that would ever happen but, in late 2009, McCauley tipped me off about some 'major developments'. It seemed resentment had been building within McHugh about the manner in which he'd apparently been recently cast aside by Ros. Here was a man who had played the game, toed the line and publicly lied through his teeth to keep Schapelle's tale of innocence intact. The series of random meetings surrounding McHugh's story had always seemed far-fetched but, so long as he continued to remain loyal and play silent, nobody could prove otherwise. Now, not only had McHugh been caught with cannabis, he'd been banished.

McHugh was renowned for being volatile at the best of times. Rather than turn up at his door unannounced, I decided it would be safer to approach him at his next court hearing, which was scheduled for 2 December. Arriving at Adelaide Magistrates Court that morning shortly before 11 am, I spied McHugh at the top of the stairs inside the building. He was pacing the floor repeatedly, but then unexpectedly plonked himself down on a chair several metres away from where I was sitting. It was an opportune moment.

Introducing myself as someone writing a book about Schapelle Corby, I promptly added that I'd flown down from Sydney on the off-chance he might give me a minute of his time. I had anticipated the cold shoulder but, surprisingly, he was open to having a coffee immediately after his hearing.

McHugh's case ended up being held over, so afterwards he and I strolled across Victoria Square, along Gouger Street and then through the hustle and bustle of Adelaide Central Market to a nearby coffee shop. I had no preconceived plan of what to say, so I started to explain that, during the course of researching the book, I had uncovered numerous friends, associates and sources all now naming Mick Corby as a man deeply entrenched in the marijuana trade. I also explained that I'd uncovered a host of new material, which I preferred not to go into.

'But the Corbys will keep denying,' he reasoned.

'They can deny it all they like,' I said. 'Mick Corby was smuggling pot to Bali.'

We sat in silence for several moments, and then I hit McHugh with the nitty-gritty.

'I know you lied, Dave.'

'Ha, is that right?'

'I know you know more than you've let on.'

'And what are you going to do if I tell you what I know?'

'Fill in the last few gaps. Set the matter straight.'

McHugh went on to confirm there had been a connection for far longer than had previously been claimed. Swigging back the remainder of his coffee, he seemed on the verge of saying more than he wanted to at this particular stage. He asked for an assurance that I wouldn't write anything about his court case until after it had finished. 'I've got an old relative who's sick,' he said. 'They don't need to know about all this right now.'

As we stood to leave, McHugh's parting note was an enticing one. 'You come back in February, when I'm done in court, and, if you don't write anything in the meantime, I'll give you what you need.'

Christmas 2009 passed with minimal contact between McHugh and me. Then, in January 2010, he flew out on Virgin Blue Flight 4195 for his holiday to Bali. When he arrived home eight days before his sentencing, the interrogation at Adelaide Airport occurred—and for several days our agreement was suddenly in doubt. In a paranoid state, he exploded over the phone and accused me of having tipped off the authorities.

After realising that would have served no purpose whatsoever, he later said: 'I've got enough on my plate without having to worry about the repercussions of talking to you. And anyway, I don't know what's going to happen in court. I'm expecting just a fine, but what if I go down? I won't be around to talk to you anyhow.'

'Well, my flight to Adelaide is booked now so I might as well come anyway,' was my response.

So on 11 February 2010, I hooked up with McHugh once again at Adelaide Magistrates Court for his date with destiny. He held a brief private meeting with his lawyer, and then at 11.30 am we walked into Courtroom Four.

The court heard from police prosecutor Jackie Young that when Strikeforce Mantle raided McHugh's home: 'They located a shed at the rear of the property and uncovered six mature cannabis plants being grown under hydroponic conditions. A further search inside the premises located a spare bedroom where a further three mature cannabis plants were being grown.' Detectives had ultimately confiscated a total of 13 electrical transformers, 13 custom-designed umbrella light shades and 13 globes, as well as four containers of fertiliser and two timers being used for each of the operations.

In response, McHugh's lawyer argued that his property had been kitted out in such a way for his own personal and medicinal use, adding, 'He wasn't aware it was illegal' to cultivate in such a manner. She said the plants had all been grown to 'specifically assist with a number of medical issues, including arthritis in his hands and knees'. Her client was remorseful and now understood that he had to 'utilise legal means to address his pain and discomfort'.

'Your Honour, he does travel overseas every couple of years and only recently returned from a short trip to Bali. He was in fact questioned by customs in relation to this matter, even though it wasn't finalised, which almost resulted in him having to attend hospital for an intimate search . . . so it's already caused him some difficulties in terms of overseas travel.' She added that if he were to receive a criminal conviction, it would hamper future travel plans. 'I ask Your Honour to consider a large fine, as opposed to a conviction being recorded.'

When asked if there was anything additional she might like to add in response to that argument, police prosecutor Jackie Young replied: 'Your Honour, my only submission would be that nine plants would make Mr McHugh an extremely heavy user.'

Magistrate Maria Panagiotidis paused to think, and then gave him the benefit of the doubt. In the end, with court costs included, Dave McHugh's sentence amounted to a $1200 fine. After walking out of court, he threw a wide grin in my direction and remarked that he'd almost soiled himself when a mention of prison had arisen. 'I did notice that,' I replied.

And so it was barely half an hour after McHugh had wiggled his way out of a criminal conviction that we sat down for the first in a series of meetings in which he would finally fill in the missing pieces of the Corby jigsaw. McHugh started from the beginning and confirmed that, like McCauley, he had gone through most of his life without getting involved in the drug game, but that 'fifteen years ago, that all changed'.

'I saw an opportunity with a mate of mine that was doing it. He was eating out every night, dining in fancy Thai restaurants, and I said, "Where are you getting hold of all this money from?" So he took me to one of his houses one day and, when we walked inside, he said, "Take a look at these. These are money trees."'

'I've been involved ever since,' McHugh added. 'I learned off him for twelve months, and then I did it myself.'

McHugh then revealed how the Gold Coast run originally came about. 'I was in the Marion Hotel one day. It's my local in Adelaide—everybody knows me there—and a friend of mine, we'll just call him Peter, he wanted me to find 20 pound. I said, "Who's it for?"' It was for Corby.

McHugh said that, after sourcing the initial 20 pounds, he took the run over from Peter. In a later interview, Peter confirmed this: 'I was sending 10 to 15 pounds every week to ten days for several years. The majority of that grass was moved to Queensland on domestic flights and a small amount by road. I gave it [the business] away to Dave back then, because it was a lot of work and my missus had just given birth to our daughter. I didn't want to throw everything away. I realised it was the right time to get out.'

McHugh reflected back on that period. 'If I hadn't been in a certain place at a certain time around 1999 [the Marion]—I'd never have met any of them. Once that first lot got there safely, I was always doing it. I'd receive a phone call and the next week, it was supposed to be there.'

McHugh explained how easy it had once been to courier the marijuana using domestic flights. 'I'd go to the old Adelaide airport which was nothing like the new one today. I'd just turn up at the counter, with my suitcase, and order a stand-by ticket to the Gold Coast. You could give any name you wanted back then because nobody ever asked for identification. Like clockwork, they would then come and say, "you're on the next flight" and that was that.'

McHugh said that on arrival, he would then head to the same self-contained apartments situated close to Jupiter's Casino. He claims that once he was booked in, the same person nearly always met him. He has identified the individual who cannot be named for legal reasons.

When asked how many people from Adelaide had been involved in the Gold Coast arrangement, McHugh confirmed: 'First, Peter, and after that me, and then Mal.'

McHugh explained, finally, how he and McCauley first met. 'It was around 1995. Mal had a boat, and he would charter it when he could. I met him on his boat. I used to fish a lot back then and one day four of us hired Mal's boat. That's how it all started, me and him.'

In the years that followed, the two of them got sucked into the drug game and began working as a team. 'Mal had his own business sending it [the marijuana] everywhere, including places like Charters Towers. With Corby, we would both pull it together and away it went. He used to cover the north side [of Adelaide] and I used to do the south. Mal's couriers took it to Queensland from there.'

I had pieced together by this time, through sources, that McHugh might also have been the mystery figure who had angrily confronted Virgin Airlines staff after a suitcase full of marijuana went missing in 2004. 'Yeah, it was me,' he said. 'But it wasn't 70 grand's worth. There was about 15 pounds in there . . . which back then was worth $45,000.' He added: 'Someone took the gear out of the case. It had me beat [how they found it] because it was double packed. Maybe they were going through every case. Maybe there was a puncture or something. In the end there was nothing I could do. There was nothing anyone could do. It just got nicked.'

When McHugh and McCauley are around one another, it is clear they share a love-hate relationship in which sparks sometimes fly. McHugh said of McCauley: 'He's got a big mouth—especially when he's on the drink. I got a bit worried in Bali that first time we were over there. We were walking down the street one day [after Schapelle had been caught] and he was pissed. Don't know if you've ever been to Bali but if you know where to look, you can see people selling it [marijuana] on the streets. We walked past this one bloke and Mal yells, "Dave, that's probably our gear! I bet that's our stuff." I thought "You fucking idiot." That's typical him. He doesn't think.'

Backing McCauley's version of events, McHugh explained that Mick Corby had been 'paying people in customs for years'. 'You know what the wages are like in Bali. You can do anything if you've got cash.'

McHugh still reflects on the pivotal moment that dragged him and McCauley into the spotlight. 'When you think back,' he pondered, 'if those photos hadn't been found by the cops in Mal's house, none of this would ever have happened. Me and Mal would never have got caught up in any of this. Nobody would have known who we were.'

After that, McHugh said it was 'one lie after another'. 'After them photos were leaked, it would all have been over if it hadn't been for me and Mal. We went through everything time and time again. All the possible fall-out . . . we discussed. All the shit that could happen, we talked about it. And the reason we went along with everything was because we didn't want to get dragged into it any more than we already had. You have to understand I had never been arrested or caught for anything back then so I had everything to lose. I was happy to say I met Mal on a plane. I was happy to say anything just to make it all go away.' McHugh—and McCauley—have made additional allegations which cannot be published due to legal reasons.

McHugh said he had watched on with interest, eighteen months beforehand, when McCauley had walked from prison and then broke ranks by telling the truth. 'That was his choice. I just continued to keep my head down. I've been smart enough to live under a rock and not be part of it.' But like McCauley, he said he now felt completely betrayed. 'I was used to protect a bullshit story. And then I got spat out. It happened to others. It happened with Mal, and now it's happened to me.

'All the time, they keep telling Schapelle, "You're coming home, you're coming home." And while they're doing that, they keep raking in money.'

PART FIVE

Taking the Rap

CHAPTER 37

In the Name of
the Father

'If she were my sister, I would be telling her that it's clear you're not going home with your innocence intact. Get on your knees and start begging.'

—Kay Danes, Foreign Prisoners Support Group

In August 2009, *New Idea* appeared on the news stands with a photograph of Schapelle on the front cover posing behind bars with a forlorn look, accompanied by the blazing headline, 'Special report from Bali jail: Top Aussie psychiatrist warns bring Schapelle home—or she'll die.' This appeared to be the start of a new strategy by her family to secure her early release.

The story inside stated that Schapelle was on the verge of insanity and that she believed 'her family lives underground coming up for air', 'other people control her thoughts by means of microchips planted in her teeth', 'birds outside her cell speak to her in code', 'numbers and letters have eyes and noses', 'her tears have the power to cause the death of others' and 'she has been drugged with ant poison'. *New Idea* also reported that Schapelle had climbed the water tower in Kerobokan Prison in an apparent suicide attempt.

The magazine failed to mention that it had paid for the psychiatrist, Associate Professor Jonathan Phillips, to fly to Bali and assess Schapelle's mental health, obviously with the Corbys' blessing and an upfront media deal in place for the front cover. Dr Phillips is a former president of the Royal Australian and New Zealand College of Psychiatrists and has plenty of credibility. There is no suggestion that being paid by *New Idea* would have influenced his opinion. He concluded that Schapelle needed to be brought back to Australia to be treated properly or, at a minimum, moved to a mental hospital in Bali. He predicted that if she was not moved out of the jail she would probably die.

The prison's Indonesian doctor told the *Sydney Morning Herald* that Dr Phillips had spent no more than an hour with Schapelle, and that the claims she was receiving medication from other prisoners and had attempted suicide on two occasions were untrue.

Technically, Schapelle can appeal to the Indonesian president on humanitarian grounds without admitting her guilt. But most prisoners don't do this, because it looks disingenuous—they would not look sincerely sorry or remorseful. Kay Danes from the Foreign Prisoners Support Group, who campaigns relentlessly for the rights of Australian prisoners in overseas jails, explains that 'contrition is a key part of any presidential pardon anywhere in the world'. But she adds: 'One way around a confession is to be declared insane. By getting a psychiatrist to produce a report that says the prisoner has gone mad and has no responsibility for their actions, a face-saving deal can be struck, where the prisoner has a reason for not admitting their guilt.' Behind the scenes, Danes had been actively supporting the Corby case and constantly urging Mercedes to produce a report about Schapelle's mental health, and then go through diplomatic channels to lobby Australian and Indonesian officials.

A month before the story about 'insane Schapelle' appeared in *New Idea*, Kay Danes sent an email to the Schapelle Corby Support Group warning it was important to use an independent psychiatrist to assess Schapelle so the resulting report did not appear to be 'paid for' or 'fake'. She strongly suggested that the Corbys work with local Indonesian psychologists and base a report on Schapelle's mental state being caused by depression experienced while nursing her terminally ill father and exacerbated by the intense media coverage during her trial. She argued that this approach was smarter, because it wouldn't cause a loss of face and embarrassment to the Indonesian authorities about the conditions inside their own prisons.

When Mercedes went down the path of getting *New Idea* to pay for a psychiatrist, Kay Danes was appalled and wrote a letter to the magazine: 'I think it isn't any wonder that poor girl is where she is today when you consider that such complex situations are best dealt with diplomatically away from the media.'

In early 2009, media outlets were informed that publicity agent Stephen Moriarty was now representing the Corby family. He then struck a deal with *New Idea*, rumoured to be around $100,000, for an exclusive series of front-cover stories that would run throughout 2009. This was to be part of a new campaign to 'Bring the Girl Home'. It succeeded in getting large-scale media attention in Australia, but predictably had little impact in Canberra or Jakarta.

With the Corby family so focused on media deals and stunts, the unconditional support and advice given over many years by the Foreign Prisoners Support Group had obviously been discarded. In a stinging email to Mercedes, Kay Danes wrote:

Did you ever stop to wonder why you don't ever get replies from the Australian Government? Did you ever stop and think that perhaps you are not the best person to steer your sister's case to a better conclusion? No one could ever doubt your loyalty or dedication to Schapelle but if you were my client, I would have made you a cup of tea long ago and asked you to sit quietly in the corner. Your unwillingness to accept that some things are beyond your capability is detrimental to your sister's ongoing situation and that is the cold hard fact of the matter. I feel so sorry for you and your family to be suffering so unnecessarily for so long, and more so for Schapelle and her supporters. I do believe that she may unwittingly succumb to a terrible demise through frustration and bad advice.

No doubt this brings us to the final conclusion of a very weary relationship to which I have gained no satisfaction at all, in watching you and your family blunder along without ever heeding any logical advice given by myself and others of experience in such matters. No doubt this email will be somewhat upsetting but not any more upsetting than for me enduring your manipulations over these past five years. I no longer have any desire to subject myself to this charade and since my help is not required, then there's no point pursuing any of this any more. Still, I wish you well in your endeavours and hope that Schapelle does come home.

* * *

'Schapelle is one of the best actresses there could possibly be, or she is telling the truth.' That was criminologist Paul Wilson's assessment after he flew to Bali in 2005 in the lead-up to Schapelle's trial, in a bid to prove she didn't fit the profile of a typical drug courier.

Schapelle is a good actress, with an act born of desperation and media hype. Her story of innocence captivated Australia and convinced many amongst us that the Indonesian justice system had conducted a sham trial and unfairly convicted 'our Schapelle', the Aussie girl-next-door. But when we look behind the scenes, the circumstances surrounding this most famous of drug busts tell a very different story.

In 2004, Schapelle Corby was in a bad way. She was depressed, working part-time in her family's fish and chip shop and had dropped out of a part-time beauty course at TAFE. She was 27 and floundering.

Drug traffickers are rarely at the top of the food chain. Most people caught smuggling drugs are desperate, poor, struggling with addictions or under pressure to do someone a favour. It's unlikely that Schapelle organised the logistics of the Bali operation, sourcing and packaging the marijuana. But, when you're depressed and at a loose end in Tugun, carrying a bag on and off a plane for a stack of cash doesn't seem such a crazy idea.

Schapelle's Bali nightmare began when she checked in her boogie board bag at Brisbane Airport with 4.2 kilos of pot meticulously packed inside. The flight attendants witnessed her meltdown as the plane got closer to Bali. They were forced to cut off her drink supply after she became agitated and abusive. There was clearly something wrong with the young woman from the Gold Coast, and when they later saw her on the TV news surrounded by Indonesian police officers it all made perfect sense.

Schapelle was not the innocent, squeaky-clean beauty student portrayed in her pre-trial media blitz, but then neither was she a professional drug runner. She'd been to Bali before and seen the signs at the airport promising the death penalty for anyone caught trafficking. As she stepped off the plane, her nerves were starting to get the better of her; she knew she could be stepping on an escalator to hell, but now there was no way off.

When Schapelle was arrested inside Bali's Ngurah Rai International Airport, the marijuana packed in her boogie board bag was the largest amount ever found on a western tourist arriving in Bali. Compressed into two vacuum-sealed bags to make sure it didn't smell or tear, it would have taken hours to get ready, pointing to the fact that it was meticulously prepared to be shaped to the same size as the boogie board before its arrival at the airport. What's more, it was packed by someone who knew what they were doing. This is an important fact that has been overlooked on more than the odd occasion, most recently in June 2011 when Channel Nine news unveiled an unidentified woman called 'Sue' who claimed she dated a Brisbane Airport baggage handler for a short time who had a colleague who in October 2004 went to work with 'a large bag of marijuana'.

With her face heavily pixilated, she alleged: 'When the supervisor was coming the guy panicked, and the first thing he did was look for somewhere to hide it. And he grabbed one of the bags that was behind him and hid it there.' Nevermind the fact that the story was essentially hearsay of hearsay by someone speaking anonymously, what were the chances of Sue's boyfriend arriving at the airport with a huge bag of marijuana shaped and curved identically to Schapelle's boogie board bag—which was laying directly behind him when his boss suddenly appeared?

There was plenty of debate after Schapelle's arrest about why she might be innocent—after all, who takes pot to Bali? But it is now clear, the payoff was there. The high-quality Aussie Gold was worth an easy $60,000 to $80,000 in Bali, a lot of money in anyone's book.

Of all the children in the Corby family, Schapelle was always Mick's favourite. As a child it must have been a relief for her to escape with her father on holidays away from the chaotic family home at Loganlea, with Ros repeatedly blowing up as the household heaved with the strain of new stepkids and their different fathers coming and going. When Dad whisked her away on school holidays, he was cashed up—with a beachside retreat at Sarina on the outskirts of Mackay and later a farm near Gladstone.

There was something magic about Mick's life—he always had money to buy property and treat the kids. The magic was marijuana. It was easy dough and it offered a life that was much more fun than lining up at Centrelink or flipping burgers in a takeaway shop. And, after all, pot wasn't heroin—it wasn't a big deal. Plenty of people even said it should be legalised—so why not make money from it?

It's hard to believe that Mick Corby would allow his beloved daughter to try and make it through the customs area by sheer luck and thus roll the dice on a 20-year jail term. Given that he flew to Bali just two weeks before Schapelle arrived, evidence now suggests he was there to lay the foundations for the trip—a meet and greet with people in on the scam, including contacts working at the airport to help get the bag through. With this in mind, Schapelle's arrest displays all the hallmarks of a major stuff-up—a customs man who didn't turn up for work, a bribe gone wrong or, more likely, an airport worker who became scared once I Gusti Winata spotted something strange on the x-ray machine and wanted to take a closer look. If Mick had lined up an Indonesian airport worker, the hired help would have bailed out of the operation once Winata had honed in on the bag. It was all over—goodbye, and good luck. While it may never be revealed exactly what went wrong, let's not forget that many of the central cast members in this drama all share one thing in common—marijuana.

Even before she set off, Schapelle's trip was consistent with a courier run. Traffickers often book their tickets as late as possible, to avoid tipping off authorities about their flight plans. Then there was the flight to Bali via Sydney. Why fly all the way from Brisbane to Sydney and then back to Bali? Schapelle claimed the direct flights from Brisbane to Bali were booked out, but she and her friends had been planning their Bali holiday for months. By travelling via Sydney Schapelle was able to check in her boogie board at a domestic check-in at Brisbane Airport and then fly to Sydney, where the bag was automatically transferred onto an international flight. She avoided an international check-in.

Back in 2004, there was no x-ray screening of bags on domestic flights. Bags going onto the Australian Airlines international flight were only screened in Sydney by a large mobile x-ray machine. Mick would have learned that the domestic check-in at Brisbane Airport was subject to far less rigorous security screening than an international check-in at either Sydney or Brisbane. Unfortunately for Schapelle, the bag made it all the way to Bali. She would have been far better off if she'd been arrested in Australia.

By chance on the very day Schapelle flew to Bali via Sydney, security resources at Sydney Airport were focused on an AFP operation targeting Michael Hurley, a major organised crime figure. The cops had been trying to bust Hurley for years and they knew he had people bringing in cocaine on 8 October. Schapelle's bag of pot passed unnoticed while the police and cameras were trained on Hurley's syndicate. The drug-trafficking minnow snuck through while the AFP zoomed in on the big fish. Apart from flying to Bali via Sydney, there are other signs that Schapelle and Mick were trying to reduce the risk of getting caught. Her boogie board bag was left unlocked—just in case she was busted, so she could make the claim that someone else put the drugs in her bag.

But the fact remains that even without Schapelle's involvement, Mick Corby was always likely to come up a cropper one day. He was identified by police informant Kim Moore as a person suspected of taking drugs to Bali just one month before Schapelle's arrest. While it is claimed that that tip-off was never acted upon, Tony Lewis's arrest was a clear sign that fortunes were starting to turn. The Bali run was a high-risk operation, and while it may have been running for years as a 'well-oiled machine', every machine breaks down sooner or later.

In many ways the story of Mick Corby and his daughter isn't unique. There are thousands of Australians like Malcolm McCauley and Dave McHugh living in towns and cities dealing in hydroponic marijuana for a living. What is unusual about Mick and Schapelle Corby is that they took the business overseas. Once Schapelle was busted she was in dire straits, because she couldn't roll over and cut a deal with the Indonesian police. Giving up Mick and other people involved in the syndicate back in Australia might have reduced her prison sentence, but she would still have to serve time and would suffer guilt for implicating her sick father. Schapelle took the rap for her father and his mates. Mick Corby always believed his daughter would never break. Loyalty to the family had been ingrained in her from an early age. 'She knows she's innocent and she's not gonna say she's guilty. She'd need a guarantee that she'd be out of there. That's the only way she would do it. Well, where's the guarantee?' Mick told the documentary team.

Given that all the circumstantial evidence points towards Schapelle's guilt, how could she have saved herself from enduring such a heavy sentence? Was there any other option available to her apart from claiming to be innocent? Prosecutor Ida Bagus Wiswantanu, the man who recommended to the panel of Indonesian judges that Schapelle should receive a life sentence for her crime, now reveals for the first time that he would have reduced his sentence recommendation if she had confessed. Wiswantanu said it was obvious to the Indonesians that Schapelle was guilty and holding back information about other people involved in the drug run was not a good move. 'Corby might get a shorter prison sentence if only she cooperated with the police, admitting her guilt and identify the people she was taking the marijuana to. According to Indonesian law, by cooperating with the law enforcement, Corby shows a deep regret and thereof the court will see her as a criminal trying to improve her life and will not repeat the same mistake in the future. This kind of person would absolutely have no difficulties to assimilate with the normal life.'

Wiswantanu was not sure about how much time

Schapelle's sentence could have been reduced by if she'd been willing to give up other people, but her refusal to say anything about where the marijuana had come from and where it was going had a major impact on her sentence. He said, 'I can't really say how many years in the prison she would get if she cooperated with the police, but one thing for sure, this cooperation would reduce the sentence significantly.'

So poor Schapelle has paid a hefty price for her increasingly intricate web of lies and deceit. The Australian public, meanwhile, has grown weary of the continual theatrics of her family. None of the Corbys could have foreseen that her arrest would create media deals worth over two million dollars—but they were quick to sign up to them. Time and time again, they have opted for big money exclusives. Whether these were in Schapelle's best interests was not always clear. When she is finally freed from jail she'll also make hundreds of thousands of dollars in media deals; but she will never admit to the crime and will go to her grave claiming that someone else stashed the marijuana inside her bag. Why? Because there is far too much at stake. Her furiously proclaimed innocence has painted her, and everyone surrounding her, into a corner.

The Corbys have always claimed that if it was ever possible, Ros or Mick would have been willing to trade places with their daughter. 'Of course we've all thought about it, but the government won't give immunity,' said Mercedes. 'It makes no difference to us. An innocent person is in there anyway, so it would be like swapping her with another innocent person,' she carefully explained.

In the final years before his death, Mick Corby would spend countless frustrating hours weighing up the consequences a confession from him or Schapelle might bring.

Mick had always been able to solve the most difficult of cryptic crosswords, but in his heart he knew he and Schapelle were dammed even if he 'confessed' and offered to swap places with her. As he told Janine Hosking's documentary team: 'Yeah, I could say I put it in the bag. What have I got to lose? The doctors won't tell me how long I've got to go. You should have seen all the scenarios I've had in my head, about how I could have put it [the marijuana] in the bag. But how could I have done it without her knowing? What was I gonna say about what was supposed to happen? You can't just say, I put it in and let her go on her merry way to be caught at the other end. All that would do would have had us both bloody locked up!'

As the prostate cancer painfully consumed his body, Mick Corby hoped he would live long enough to see Schapelle's freedom. It never happened. His battle ended on 18 January 2008. In a statement to the *Daily Telegraph Online*, Mercedes announced her father's death:

Schapelle has been told the news about our dad's death and is very distraught. She is devastated that she's been unable to see dad for more than 18 months. She'd been desperately hoping he'd get to make one last visit, but he was too sick to travel. Our dad was a beautiful hearted man, generous and loving father who lived for us three kids— Michael, Schapelle and me. He devoted his life to us and his three grandchildren. Before he got too sick he spent months in Bali to be with Schapelle and me.

He struggled with prostate for four years and during the past three has also had to endure humiliating rumours and lies about himself and his family in the press, which hurt him a lot. He was a very intelligent, hardworking, caring and honest man. All his friends and family will miss him greatly. We hope he is now at peace.

Back in 2004, when Mick Corby's cousin Alan Trembath first saw Schapelle on the TV news after she had been busted in Bali, he had only one thought, 'Mick, what have you got your daughter into now?' Alan summed it all up like this: 'Honestly, I don't think Schapelle would have known any different, you know—because she would have been around drugs all her life.'

While the Corby clan has a steady 'cash for stories' income stream to share, Schapelle is paying the ultimate price. No amount of money will make all those years in an Indonesian jail worth it. Money will no longer be a problem—the problem will be the life lost, the years wasted and the knowledge that her father allowed her to risk so much.

Epilogue

MALCOLM McCAULEY spends his days drinking beer, reading books and watching the back lawn grow in Salisbury Downs, South Australia. Has reconnected with his family. Never happier than when the grandkids are giving him grief or his mates pop over unannounced with a case of West End Draught.

KATHLEEN McCAULEY has a full-time job raising her granddaughter Kaitlin. Was recently taken on an all-expenses-paid cruise around Asia, courtesy of her daughter Leanne. She is keen to see more of the world when her lottery numbers come up.

DAVID McHUGH: At one stage, the ever-temperamental McHugh threatened to withdraw his participation in this book to pursue an exclusive television deal instead. Initial negotiations fell through after he rowed with a television producer. In recent months he has shed several kilos and is looking trim. He has a new girlfriend whom he really likes.

EPILOGUE

PETER DUDLEY: Still spinning tales of bravery, still smoking dope and trying his best to stay out of McCauley's way in Adelaide.

JEFF JELLESE: Was finally released from prison at the beginning of 2010. He returned to Adelaide. While he was serving time for his part in the syndicate, his wife passed away.

WAYNE WILLIAMS: Returned to his wife and children in Charters Towers. Another member of the syndicate now living the quiet life, although sources confirm he still likes to let off steam by heading out into the bush for a good old-fashioned pig hunt.

BRENDA 'GRANNY' EASTWOOD: The drug granny went to ground after she gave evidence in court against the syndicate. Channel 7 lawyers did everything they possibly could to locate her prior to the court cases with Mercedes and Ros, as did the author of this book. Word is she left Adelaide and moved to Queensland. Destination unknown.

ROGER RATHJEN: Loves to recount stories from his days in the AFP. Malcolm is one of the few people who doesn't mind hearing the same tales over and over again.

TONY LEWIS: Survived all the controversy and continues to avoid the headlines and any Corby-related dramas.

BETH LAVENDER: Broke up with Tony Lewis and has never spoken to the media about the Schapelle Corby case.

KIM MOORE: The police informer lives in fear and claims she has received death threats.

TONY WILSON: The *Gold Coast Bulletin* reporter was sacked by News Limited as a result of his unethical and threatening phone call to Ron Bakir. Wilson realised his dream to publish a gushing book about Schapelle and his relationship with the family. It bombed.

KATHRYN BONELLA: Schapelle's biographer has written a second book, titled *Hotel Kerobokan*. The book's revelations about the jail have been condemned by both prison authorities and prisoners as 'sensational lies'. She was more recently slammed on ABC's *Media Watch* for failing to check the source of a fake document which alleged Schapelle was being uprooted to another prison in East Java. This exclusive, for which she was paid, appeared under her name in a women's magazine. Bonella's lucrative magazine handouts continue to drop in editors' laps—usually when the Corby campaign is in danger of going quiet.

ROBIN TAMPOE: Revealed to the Australian public that he had made up the baggage handler defence in the Channel 9 documentary *Schapelle Corby: The Hidden Truth*. Shortly afterwards he was struck off by the Queensland Law Society. Tampoe's baggage handler defence contributed to the federal government's multi-million-dollar Wheeler Report, an independent review of airport security and policing procedures at Australian airports, resulting in a multi-million-dollar overhaul of Australia airports and security. It comes as little consolation. The Corby case cost him his legal career. He remains 'shattered' by the episode.

EPILOGUE

RON BAKIR: Now a successful property developer, he is no longer interested in talking about the Corby case.

WAYAN WIDYARTHA: Wayan is back on the surfing circuit. He recently starred in a YouTube clip featuring Rosleigh Rose yelling at him and threatening to tell Mercedes to divorce him. No one knows why.

MICHAEL CORBY JUNIOR: Still keeps a low profile and lives between the Gold Coast and Bali. Was last seen surfing.

CLINTON 'BADGER' ROSE: The Badger has gone 'straight' and no other convictions have so far been added to his lengthy rap sheet.

JAMES KISINA: Narrowly avoided more jail time in January 2010 after breaching the rules of his suspended sentence. He was charged with a public nuisance offence following a brawl with five men at a Brisbane taxi rank after a night out. When he appeared in court, James's heavily pregnant girlfriend was there to support him. His lawyer said in court that his client was now training to become a full-time fitness instructor and was doing his best to live a clean life. The judge saw James was about to become a dad and warned him to stay out of trouble, adding: 'Your child needs you.' He is now father to a baby boy named Semisi Kisina.

ROSLEIGH ROSE: Shortly after the death of Mick Corby, her partner Greg Martin died from cancer in April 2008. After receiving an undisclosed defamation payment from Channel 7, she has stepped back into the shadows and remains at the Loganlea home that Mick gave her. The Queensland-based lawyer Kerry Smith-Douglas (who works on a pro-bono basis for Schapelle) seems to do most of Ros's talking nowadays.

MERCEDES CORBY: Throughout her defamation trial, Mercedes was a demure brunette. But after her triumphant victory, the blonde hair was back and Mercedes Corby made the front cover of *Ralph* magazine wearing a low-cut white swimsuit with the headline 'Mercedes Corby reveals all!' The eight-page *Ralph* spread displayed Mercedes wearing a range of bikinis, showcasing images seemingly airbrushed to within an inch of her life and with what appeared to be surgically enhanced breasts. Sydney newspapers reported that she was paid $50,000 for the 'Bare All, Tell All' shoot.

MICK CORBY (SENIOR): Finally succumbed to prostate cancer on 18 January 2008. He was farewelled to the Rolling Stones's raunchy classic *Little Red Rooster*. There was no death-bed confession.

SCHAPELLE CORBY had five months shaved from her sentence in August 2011 as part of the traditional holiday remissions that mark Indonesia's Independence Day. This brings her current release date forward to 12 April 2024. However, prison sources have suggested that from 2011 she could be eligible to have eight months cut from her sentence each year. With additional remissions offered for good behaviour and religious holidays, it is rumoured Schapelle could be released as early as 2014.

The Corbys are hoping to secure her freedom before then, having lodged a plea for clemency with Indonesian President Susilo Bambang Yudhoyono, which hinges on the argument that Schapelle is suffering psychosis and has become clinically insane. Kerobokan governor, Siswanto, claims she is not mentally ill. A decision could take years.

The Australian government is locked in continued negotiations with Indonesia about a prisoner exchange program. In the meantime, the world remains fascinated by Schapelle and her story. According to a *Sun-Herald*/Nielsen poll conducted in August 2010, a third of Australians feel she has served enough time in jail—but only one in 10 now believe she is innocent.

Acknowledgements

There are a number of very important people without whom this book would not have been published. The two most significant don't need to be named but they know who they are—thank you.

I'd like to thank Allen & Unwin and its excellent consulting publisher Richard Walsh, whose vision, direction and encouragement made it all happen. A huge round of applause also to my wonderful editorial director Rebecca Kaiser—whose professionalism, support and calmness under pressure was much appreciated throughout.

I would like to acknowledge my dear family, particularly my dad Eddie, my sister Tara, my uncle Eamonn and my two young 'brothers' Martin and Edward—I know you are always alongside me in spirit, supporting me wherever I roam. Thank you from the bottom of my heart.

I must also thank my friends for their ongoing backing, patience and tolerance, first and foremost Paul, Christina and Milla for putting a roof over my head and keeping a smile on my face during all those trips to Adelaide. Then there's Rod Allen, Maurizio Lombardo and his wonderful family,

ACKNOWLEDGEMENTS

Simon Gaudry, Andrew Webster, Emily Forder-White, Laura O'Donnell, Daniel and Kathy Clark, Charlie Wyett, Rose and Steve Jacobs, Sal Rizzo and Ben Davies, Richard and Anya Spicer, Natalie Peters, Amanda Cole, Laila Dwyer and the wonderfully witty Katherine Danks—you all chipped in with your own special brand of friendship and support when I needed it most. Thanks guys.

At Fairfax Media, I must thank Chad Watson, Simon Dulhunty and Liz Hannan for allowing me the time to complete this project, and my colleagues past and present Matthew Benns, Rachel Browne, Alicia Wood, Andrew West, Kate Cox, Lee Besford, Anthony Johnson, Adam Hollingworth, Jim O'Rourke, Caroline Marcus, Melissa Singer, Sarah Whyte, Janie Barrett, Heath Aston, Mags King, Tim Barlass and the late Les Kennedy for their continual guidance and advice.

Last but certainly not least, an enormous thank you to Malcolm McCauley and his wife Kathleen for their time, trust and hospitality.